PUBLISHED BY BAISDEN PUBLISHING

OTHER BOOKS BY MICHAEL BAISDEN

Do Men Know What They Want?

Men Cry in the Dark

God's Gift to Women

• • •

Love, Lust & Lies (DVD)

Do Women Know What They Want? (DVD)

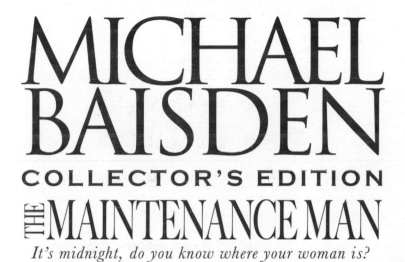

MICHAEL BAISDEN

COLLECTOR'S EDITION

THE MAINTENANCE MAN

It's midnight, do you know where your woman is?

PUBLISHED BY BAISDEN PUBLISHING

LEARN MORE BY VISITING WWW.BAISDENLIVE.COM
Follow Michael on Facebook at BaisdenLive and on Twitter @BaisdenLive

DEDICATION

To my energetic and passionate aunt, Dorothy Wilson,
who passed away on October 31, 1997.
I'll never forget you, Sweet D.

COLLECTOR'S EDITION
THE MAINTENANCE MAN

It's midnight, do you know where your woman is?

PROLOGUE

CONFESSION (2008)

CHICAGO SEPTEMBER 2008

Just as the casket was being lowered into the ground, the clouds darkened and the rain began to fall. It seemed so appropriate. Malcolm's mother grabbed his hand tightly and began to cry.

"I can't believe he's gone; I just can't believe it!"

"It's gonna be all right, Mama."

After the minister said a few last words, Malcolm exchanged hugs with friends and family, then escorted his mother over to where his best friend, Simon, was standing.

"Are you okay, Malcolm?" Simon asked.

"I'll be fine. I just need a minute alone. Can you take Mama to the limo and wait for me?"

"No problem, partner."

Malcolm handed over his umbrella to Simon and told his mother to go with him to the car. She smiled and gave him a gentle kiss on the cheek. "I understand, son. Take all the time you need."

3

MICHAEL BAISDEN

It began to rain more heavily as Malcolm knelt at the edge of the grave. He turned his head toward the stormy sky and reached out his hands as if to confirm the rain was real. He wanted to break down and cry, but he fought it. This was as close as he was ever going to be to his father, and he wanted to spend those last moments talking the way they used to. Malcolm had unresolved issues and needed to release. Deep down in his heart, he knew his father could hear him.

"Dad, I've always admired you for being a strong man and for providing for our family. I never wanted for anything, not money, not attention, and definitely not love. But despite how great you were as a father, I hoped and prayed I would never be like you. As far back as I can remember, you cheated on Mama, not with one or two women, but with five and sometimes six at a time. I hated you because I saw the pain in her eyes that you never did, or maybe you just ignored it. I kept my resentment toward you buried deep inside, which is why I always neglected to call you on Father's Day.

"Ever since I was seven years old, I've been listening to you lie, cheat, and break women down. There was a vent in the basement that led directly to my bedroom. I remember a conversation you had with a woman named Rachel. I was thirteen then. You were arguing because she suspected you of sleeping with her sister. You were cold busted, but instead of confessing, you took the offensive. Ten minutes later, you had everything turned around and she was apologizing to you. It was sad to see how women with low self-esteem allowed men to treat them."

Malcolm paused to regain his composure. His voice choked and the tears began to well up in his eyes. He quickly leaned his head back and allowed the rain to wash them away. He took a deep breath and continued.

"I'm making this confession because my prayers went

unanswered. Not only did I become you, I've become worse than you. I'm a gigolo. Now, don't start with your preaching. I'm not some cheap prostitute hanging out on street corners. My job is escorting rich women out to business functions and social events. I've already earned two hundred thousand dollars and I travel all over the world. Not bad for a twenty-five-year-old rookie. I lied to you and Mama because I didn't want you to know that I dropped out of music school. I thought about calling home for help with tuition, but my pride wouldn't allow it.

"So, I decided to make it the best way I knew how, and that meant using women. Everything I needed to know I learned from watching you: how to walk, talk, dress, and how to use sex to control women. By the time I was seventeen, I was charging my classmates fifty dollars each to escort them to prom."

Malcolm paused again, this time only for a second, then he burst out laughing.

"It's great to be able to joke around with you like this. Too bad we didn't have a chance to do it more often while you were alive. But isn't that the way life always seems to work out. People don't appreciate how precious something is until it's been taken away."

The tears began to well up in Malcom's eyes again; this time he allowed them to flow.

"Before I go, I want you to know that I love you…and I forgive you. And I hope you will forgive me, too. I know that I can pull my life together and make something out of myself. I want you and Mama to be proud of me."

Malcolm stood up and brushed the mud off his pants. Then he pulled a neatly folded piece of paper out of his suit pocket. On it was a song he had written especially for his father entitled "When Players Pray." He kissed it and threw it on top of the casket.

5

"I was hoping to play this song for you when I came home for Christmas," he said. "I've been practicing it every day on that Steinway piano you gave me on my eighteenth birthday. I've gotten pretty good, too. Who knows, maybe I'll get a chance to play it for you at Carnegie Hall. Rest in peace, you old player."

As Malcolm walked toward the car, he was filled with guilt because of the lie he had told his friends and family. In the obituary it said a burglar shot his father. But the truth was he was killed while cheating with the married woman who lived next door. Her husband came home early from work and shot them both—his wife twice in the back and leg, and Malcolm's father once in the head. The wife survived. When she was asked why they didn't go to a motel, she said Malcolm's father was too cheap to pay for a room.

PART I

MIAMI HEAT (2011)

CHAPTER 1

THE MAINTENANCE MAN

It was nine-thirty when Malcolm's flight arrived into Miami International Airport, right on schedule. He grabbed his garment bag from the overhead compartment and rushed to meet his limo. His appointment with Helen was at midnight and Tina was waiting at the Ritz Carlton Hotel on South Beach. He was determined to kill two birds with one stone.

When Malcolm arrived at baggage claim, he didn't see his driver. He flung his bag over his shoulder and stepped through the automatic doors into the brutal Miami heat. June was always humid in southern Florida, even at night. He looked around for his usual car service, but the only limo driver he saw was a tall, distinguished-looking black man. He was smoking a cigarette and talking to a young Latino woman who didn't appear to Malcolm to be more than 25 years old; she was wearing blue-jean shorts and a tight top that was tied up to show off her slender waist. As he walked closer, Malcolm recognized the limo as his usual car and there was a cardboard sign in the window with his name on it. He tapped the man on the shoulder to get his attention.

"Excuse me, buddy!"

"Hey, man, don't you see I'm busy?" he snapped at Malcolm without bothering to look back at him, and then he went back to his conversation.

Malcolm set his garment bag down and tapped him on the shoulder again, with more force.

"You must be outta your damn mind!" he said as he spun around with his fist balled. "I will bust a—!" he stopped mid-sentence. "Mr. Tremell, I apologize, I was just—"

"Save it, let's get going, I'm running late."

"Yes, sir!" he said while picking the bag off the ground. "Allow me to get that."

He opened the limo door and Malcolm slid inside. After putting his bag in the trunk, he hurried into the limo and sped off.

"So, who are you anyway?" Malcolm asked.

"My name is Allen, but everybody calls me Big Al!"

"Ok, Big Al, so what happened to my regular driver, Jimmy?"

"Well, ah, he had to quit the night shift. He said the hours were...ah, affecting his health."

"Yeah, right!" Malcolm said with a sly grin. "You can cut the bullshit and tell me what really happened."

"Jimmy was right about you...you get straight to the point."

He reached inside his suit jacket and pulled out a photo and handed it to Malcolm.

"Jimmy asked me to give you this."

Malcolm turned on the interior light and held the picture up to it. When he recognized it, he laughed.

"Well, I'll be damned!"

It was a photo of Malcolm and Jimmy standing outside of The Miami Velvet Night Club surrounded by a dozen beautiful women. They were both holding a drink in one hand and a woman's butt cheek in the other. On the back of the photo was a message that read: *Thanks for the best time of my life! Jimmy!*

"I guess the wife must have found a copy of the photo and that was all she wrote."

"Well, he lasted six months; that was a record," Malcolm said while clicking the light off. "Let's just hope you're not whipped, too. It's getting harder to find good drivers."

"You don't have to worry about me, Mr. Tremell. I'm the king of my castle!"

"Big Al, let me give you some professional advice; don't try to impress me by bragging about how you're running shit at home. I saw the ring on your finger. There's nothing wrong with being accountable to a woman, especially a good one."

"Yeah, after twenty years we're still going strong!" he said while twirling the wedding band on his finger. "But you know how it is, you get bored. Sometimes you need something strange, you know…something new!"

"Well, Big Al, everything that looks good ain't good for you, like that pretty young thang you were talking to at the airport. Young women are nothing but trouble. They're not emotionally developed and they have nothing to lose. That's a recipe for disaster."

"I never thought about it that way."

"That's because you're thinking with your dick. Now step on it, I'm already late!"

• • •

The drive to South Beach took twenty-five minutes. Malcolm gave Big Al instructions to pick him up at eleven-thirty, then rushed into the hotel. Tina checked into Room 1001, like always. Malcolm hopped aboard the elevator hoping she was ready.

As Malcolm approached the room, he could smell the familiar aroma of jasmine incense burning. He knocked on the door and put his hand over the peephole.

"Who is it?" Tina asked apprehensively.

"It's the plumber, ma'am," Malcolm said, trying to disguise his voice. "We received a call that the sink was backed up."

"There's nothing wrong with my sink. Are you sure you have the right room?"

"I'm looking right at the job order, ma'am. It says Room 1001. Guest needs drain unstopped."

When he burst out laughing, she was on to him. Tina opened the door buck-naked and popped Malcolm upside the head.

"Malcolm, you scared the hell out of me!"

"I'm sorry, baby. Let me make it up to you."

Malcolm backed her into the candlelit room and dropped his garment bag. Then he lifted her by the cheeks and carried her over to the bed.

"I love a man who knows how to take control," she said.

"And I love a woman who knows how to let a man be *The Man*." He gently laid her down on the bed and began taking off her clothes.

"Hurry up, Malcolm," she said while pulling at the buttons on his silk shirt. "I'm horny as hell."

"Slow down, baby. These clothes aren't cheap," Malcolm said while backing away. "Let me do this."

"Why are you worried about your damn shirt?" She sounded upset. "I can afford a thousand shirts."

What she really meant was her husband could afford a thousand shirts. Tina was going through an ugly divorce with a former NBA star. Every dime she had came out of his bank account.

Malcolm didn't want to ruin the mood so he poured two

glasses of the Dom Pérignon champagne she had chilling, then he proposed a toast.

"Here's to six months of good conversation, good company, and great sex."

"I'll drink to that!" she said.

While he sipped on his drink, he casually looked at the clock on the nightstand; it read 10:15. He excused himself to the bathroom and immediately went into action. He hung his clothes neatly over the shower rod, brushed his teeth, shaved, and took a quick shower. Within ten minutes he was ready.

"It's about time," Tina said with an attitude.

"I promise you, it will be worth the wait."

Malcolm pulled a Trojan condom out of his pants pocket and grabbed the metal flask of coconut oil that was sitting on the nightstand. "Turn over on your stomach, baby," he told her.

He poured the warm oil on her back and massaged it into her shoulders. Once she relaxed, he slowly ran his tongue from her lower back to the base of her neck.

"*Ssss,* do that again, baby," she begged.

"Say please," he insisted.

"Please, please, please, with sugar on top."

Malcolm used his tongue like a wet probe, boldly going where no man had gone before. Twenty minutes into the foreplay, Tina couldn't take it anymore. "Stop teasing, baby," she said, sighing. "Give it to me." He pushed her legs back toward the headboard as far as they would go, then dove in. The candlelight cast an erotic shadow onto the hotel room wall. It was like looking into a smoked mirror. He tried to concentrate but he kept staring at the silhouette of her body. With every flick of his tongue, she winced and quivered.

In a slow circular motion he ascended from her pierced belly button to her supple nipples. She inhaled, then turned her head to the side and let out a soft moan. "Oh, Malcolm, you feel so good. Don't stop. Please don't stop."

He moved his hand slowly down her long smooth leg until he felt the warmth from within. He paused briefly to massage her, then he put on his condom and slid inside. Her head sprang up in one quick motion.

"Wha—wha–what are you doing?" she stuttered.

"I'm doing my job," I replied confidently. "Now, lie down!"

She flopped back down onto the pillow and began to shake violently. Seconds later she let out a loud scream. "Oh, shit, that's the spot, baby, right there!" Her legs tensed as she grasped the sheets into her fists. "I'm cumming! I'm cumming!" Tina bit down on her lip and frantically tossed her head from side to side. If there were an Academy Award for best orgasm, she would have won, hands down. When it was over, she rolled onto her side, clutched the pillow between her legs, and dozed off.

"Perfect timing!" Malcolm said with a sly grin. "Mission accomplished."

The clock read 11:09 P.M. Her time was up. He tiptoed into the bathroom and closed the door. As he ran the shower, he checked his cell phone to confirm his appointment. It read: Helen—Melvin's Jazz Club—midnight. "So much for a long, hot bath!" he said in disgust.

He turned the shower lever to hot and quickly jumped in. While he washed in the hot drizzle, he tried to relax. The ten-hour flight from Paris had worn him out. He thought about canceling his appointment but Helen was a priority customer. According to the article he had read in *Fortune* magazine, she was worth ten million dollars. He wasn't about to disappoint his golden goose, especially for a basket case like Tina. She had more drama in her life than a soap opera: death in the family, relatives in jail, and a pending divorce. He couldn't help feeling sorry for her. So, he penciled her in as a courtesy fuck.

After ten minutes of standing in the steam-filled shower, he was rejuvenated. He stepped out of the bathroom and slipped on his clothes. He expected Tina to still be asleep, but she was standing outside on the terrace naked, smoking a cigarette. The moonlight accentuated her tanned skin and long silky hair that extended to the middle of her back. He paused to admire her one last time. As he was about to announce he was leaving, she muttered something.

"Did you say something, Tina?" he asked while walking toward her.

"You heard what I said; men are no damn good! All they do is tell lies, get you pregnant, and then move on to the next young piccc."

"I don't know what kind of drug you're on, but I don't have time for another one of your tantrums, not tonight. Now, if you don't mind, I'd like to collect my money and leave."

She turned suddenly, her eyes filled with tears. "Fuck you, Malcolm!" she shouted. "I knew you didn't give a damn about me. All I am to you is another trick."

She tossed her cigarette over the balcony, then stormed past him looking for her purse.

"Here, is this what you want?" Tina pulled ten crisp hundred-dollar bills out of her wallet and threw them in his face. "Take them!"

Malcolm looked at her like she was out of her mind. Then he calmly took his black book out of his pants pocket and began writing.

"What are you doing?" she asked, sounding concerned.

"I'm scratching your name out of my book."

"But I want to see you next month." Tina quickly composed herself, clearing her throat and wiping phony tears from her eyes.

"Next month? I'm scratching your crazy ass out for good," he said. "I'm sick and tired of these dramatic episodes. This is the third time in six months I've had to deal with this shit. Enough is enough!" He put his book inside his pocket and headed for the door.

"Where do you think you're going?" She tried to block his way with her naked one-hundred-and-twenty-five-pound frame. "I paid you for your time, plus a hundred-dollar tip."

"You think you can throw money at me like I'm some kind of cheap prostitute? I couldn't buy a decent suit with that chump change."

"I'm sorry, Malcolm. Don't go, please don't go!" Tina gathered the bills off the floor and handed them to him. "You know this divorce has me under a lot of pressure."

"I can't believe you're still trippin' over this bullshit," he said. "Let it go and get on with your life."

"I gave that bastard the best years of my life. I'm not about to let him walk away scott-free."

"Scott-free? He offered to settle out of court for three million dollars, the house, the Range Rover, and five thousand dollars a month in child support. What more do you want?"

"I want to break that son-of-a-bitch, that's what! If it weren't for me he would never have gotten that twenty-five-million-dollar contract with Nike. I'm not going anywhere until I get paid!"

Malcolm lifted her by the waist and tossed her onto the bed. "You're nothing but a gold-digging tramp."

"You'll be back, Malcolm," she said seductively while caressing her breasts. "I'll give you a call when I get my first million. We'll spread it on top of the bed and fuck on it."

"You're pathetic," he said. Then he rushed out the door.

While he waited on the elevator, he searched through his

pocket for the small pack of aspirin he always carried with him. The stress of playing the role of lover and psychiatrist was getting the best of him. His reflection in the corridor mirror spoke volumes. His eyes were red and his hair was graying in places. As he stepped onto the elevator, he popped two Tylenol and laughed, "I'm getting too old for this shit!"

CHAPTER 2

THE MAINTENANCE MAN

I t was 11:50 when Malcolm arrived at Melvin's Jazz Club. The line was a block long and the valet parking was full.

"Blow the horn and flash the headlights three times," Malcolm told Big Al.

The valet quickly stepped aside and the bright orange partitions parted like the Red Sea.

"You must be a regular," Big Al said.

"Let's just say it's a popular place for people in my line of work," he replied with a sly grin.

Every city has its professional hangouts. In Miami the hangout for musicians, celebrities, and gigolos was Melvin's.

"Good evening, Mr. Tremell," the valet said as he opened the door. "I can see you remembered the signal."

"Sometimes it comes in handy, Roscoe," Malcolm said while slipping him a twenty. "Thanks for taking care of me."

19

Big Al was standing on the driver's side of the limo with his mouth wide open. The women standing in line were attractive and dressed provocatively, most of them wearing high heels and short dresses that barely covered their asses.

"Hey, Big Man!" Malcolm shouted to break his concentration. "You wanna join me for a drink?"

"Am I off the clock?" he asked.

"As far as I'm concerned."

"In that case, let's do this!"

He loosened his tie, ran a comb through his hair, and popped a Tic Tac in his mouth. After handing over his keys to the valet, he escorted Malcolm through the rowdy crowd. Big Al stood six-five and weighed at least 250 pounds. His wide body made for a perfect wedge. Malcolm never saw people move out of the way so fast.

When they entered the club, Malcolm could see Melvin standing at the bar wearing a black pinstriped suit and white brim. He was chewing down on his trademark Cuban cigar flirting with a group of young women. Malcolm stood a few feet away until they made eye contact.

"Hey, Cool Breeze!" Melvin shouted in his deep, raspy voice. Then he rushed over and threw his arms around him. "When did you get back?"

"I just flew in from Paris a couple of hours ago! How's business?"

"Look around!" he said while gesturing with his arm, "not an empty seat in the house!"

"Looks like another hot night, Old Man!"

"So, Cool Breeze, what's up with the big fellah?" Melvin looked at Big Al from head to toe. "Don't tell me you've hired a bodyguard to keep the women off you."

"This is my driver, Big Al. Big Al, this is the infamous

Melvin Butler."

"It's an honor to meet you, Mr. Butler," Big Al said nervously while extending his hand.

"Thank you, young man," Melvin replied "But, please call me Melvin. Any friend of my son's is a friend of mine."

"I didn't know Melvin was your father?"

"He's more like a surrogate father, that's why I call him Pops." Malcolm said while hugging Melvin around the neck. When I left Chicago to move here to Miami, he took me under his wings and taught me about the club and music business...and about life."

"If you don't mind me asking, how did he come up with the name Cool Breeze?"

"Because this, my friend, is one of the baddest Jazz pianists in the world," Melvin said proudly. "He strokes those keys so smoothly it will send chills down your spine!

"You play the piano, Mr. Tremell?" Big Al asked.

"He does more than just play the piano, son, he makes love to it," Melvin boasted. "Speaking of which, are you sitting in with the band tonight, I got her tuned just the way you like?"

"I'll have to take a rain check, old man. I'm here on business tonight."

Melvin knew what he meant and didn't press the issue. He chewed down on his cigar and gave Malcolm an inconspicuous nod.

"Let me get you a table in the VIP section." Melvin signaled the host. "I'll be over to check on you later. Meanwhile, enjoy yourselves. Drinks are on the house."

As they walked through the dimly lit room, Malcolm felt right at home. The rhythm of the music, the aged brick walls, and the chatter of the crowd created a cool ambience. There's no place on earth like a jazz club, especially one with a history like Melvin's. You could practically feel the ghosts of the immortals like Miles Davis, Ella Fitzgerald, and Billie Holiday.

The VIP section was situated across from the stage and consisted of six tables and two booths. People perceived it as a place of status. For Malcolm it was a comfortable seat away from the unwelcome attention and annoying conversations.

Melvin's was a hot spot for celebrity watchers and wannabes who wanted to be seen with the in-crowd. He got a kick out of watching people wearing sunglasses inside of a dark room and chatting on their cell phones as if they had important business.

"They should call this place Perpetrators R Us," he laughed.

"You can say that again. This place is a circus," Big Al said as he glanced across the room, "and we're sitting in the center ring."

Beautiful women from all sides of the room smiled flirtatiously trying to get his attention. He caught the eye of a blonde who dipped her finger in a wine glass, pulled it out, and sucked on it. There was another woman, who was with a date, gestured for him to meet her at the bar. She thought it was cute, but to Malcolm it was disrespectful.

"Do you always attract this much attention?" Big Al asked.

"In my line of work, attracting attention is considered free advertising. You'd be surprised how far an expensive suit and the scent of a good cologne can get you."

"I hope this isn't too personal a question, but what is it that you do exactly?"

As a rule, Malcolm never discussed his business; the only exceptions were Melvin and his best friend, Simon. Even his mother didn't know what he did for a living. She thought he was selling real estate. But he felt comfortable with Big Al. Call it intuition.

"I own an escort service," he told him.

"Escort service, huh? Is that a fancy way of saying you get paid to have sex with women?"

His ignorance made Malcolm laugh.

"Any bum off the street can stick his penis inside of a woman," he said. "Being a professional is about having class and intellect. And most importantly, boosting your client's self-esteem!"

"Are you telling me these horny women are spending big bucks for deep conversation and compliments?"

"Sometimes it's that simple."

"Get the hell outta here! Women today are no different than men. They just want to get their freak on."

"Take my word for it, this business is not about sex. Most of my clients are married women who just want a little companionship and an occasional date for a social event."

"But why hire you if they're married?"

"Because their rich husbands are too damn lazy or too busy fucking their secretaries, that's why!"

"So, basically, you're an expensive arm piece?"

"I see myself more as a therapist. Nothing gives me more pleasure than sending my patients home to their sorry-ass husbands feeling beautiful and desirable."

"Sounds to me like you're a high-priced maintenance man."

"Exactly!"

A waitress interrupted their conversation by setting two glasses down on the table in front of Malcolm, a glass of water and a vodka and cranberry.

"Thanks for the water, but I didn't order a drink," Malcolm said.

"The drink is from an admirer." She pointed in the direction of the bar.

When he leaned over, there was a tall, beautiful black woman wearing a red-sequined dress looking him dead in the eyes. She smiled and lifted her glass in the air. Malcolm did the same to show his appreciation. He was hoping she wouldn't perceive his gesture as an invitation to get better acquainted. Unfortunately, she did. A few seconds later, she gestured to the woman next to her to watch her purse, then started toward him.

"Well, Mr. Maintenance Man, I hope you've got your toolbox handy," Big Al said as he stood up from the table.

"Very funny, Chris Rock. Now, if you don't mind."

"No problem, boss," he said jokingly as he stepped aside to allow the woman in red to sit. "I'll be at the bar when you're ready to go."

Her timing could not have been worse. It was 12:30 A.M. and Malcolm was expecting Helen to arrive at any moment. Even if she didn't show, he was in no mood for casual conversation. His mind was focused on one thing: getting paid.

"Hello, I'm Stephanie," she said while extending her hand. "What's your name, handsome?"

"Malcolm."

"So, where are you from, Malcolm?"

"Chicago."

"Chicago? I love Chicago!" she said enthusiastically. "In fact, I'm going next week to visit my girlfriend."

"That's nice," he said while conspicuously looking down at his Rolex.

"Are you expecting company?"

"As a matter of fact, I am." He was intentionally being short, hoping she would get the hint. But she was persistent.

"Girlfriend, wife, or just a friend."

"That's personal, don't you think?"

"I thought this was a personal conversation," she said while sliding her phone number over to him on a napkin.

He was becoming irritated by her awkwardness. Helen was a half hour late and he was tired from his flight.

"Look, Stephanie, let's not waste each other's time with all the small talk," he said in a soft but stern voice. "I don't engage in small talk for free. If you want to continue this conversation it's going to cost you a thousand dollars an hour, plus expenses. And you've already taken up two minutes of my time. Now, if you can afford that then leave me your business card and I'll call you to set up an appointment. If not, please stop annoying me with your boring conversation."

Her cheerful smile quickly changed to a look of embarrassment. She covered her face with her hands. One look into her big brown eyes and he knew he had made a terrible mistake.

"I don't have a damned business card," she said with contempt. "I'm a cashier at Wal-Mart!"

"I'm sorry, I didn't mean to come off so harsh."

"You don't have to apologize to me, Mr. Ladies' Man. I'm nobody special," she said trying to compose herself. "I don't have any money. I don't drive an expensive car. Hell, I can't even afford this damn dress I'm wearing. I have to take it back to Saks tomorrow for a refund." Her hands were on her hips. "But I'll tell you what I do have, Malcolm, I have a good heart. That probably doesn't mean much to a coldhearted son-of-a-bitch like you."

She picked up his drink off the table and threw it in his face. "By the way, you're welcome for the drink." Then she stormed off.

Malcolm felt like a complete heel. His face was soaked with Grey Goose and his shirt was stained. Some of the people in the club saw what had happened and were gossiping and snickering. Big Al rushed over with a stack of paper towels and handed them to him. Malcolm could tell by his expression that he had been laughing, too.

"What happened?" he asked trying to keep from smiling.

"I got what I had coming," Malcolm replied, wiping himself off.

"I think I'm going to change your name from Maintenance Man to Rain Man."

They both burst out laughing as they walked out of the VIP section headed for the door. On the way out Malcolm said goodbye to Melvin.

"You leaving already, Cool Breeze?"

"Yeah, old man, I've had all the drama I can take for one night," he gave Melvin a fatherly hug. "I'll call you after I get some rest."

"Stay out of trouble, son."

People were still lining up outside the club waiting impatiently to get inside. The valets were running around like maniacs trying to park all the expensive cars. Bentleys, Aston Martins, and Ferraris lined the streets. Big Al grabbed the keys from the valet box and went to get the limo himself. While Malcolm waited, he pulled the napkin out of his pocket that Stephanie had written her number on and contemplated going back inside to apologize. He wrote a note on the back of the napkin and was about to turn to go back inside when suddenly a white stretch limousine pulled up. Helen emerged from the back door before the driver could get out of the car. She had on a black Armani mini dress with black Christian Louboutin shoes.

For a woman in her early fifties, she had one hell of a figure, 36-26-38. While the men all gawked, Malcolm stepped up to greet her.

"Sorry I'm late, darling," she said nonchalantly. "But you know what they say, business before pleasure."

He looked down at his watch, it read 1:15 A.M., then he pulled out his appointment book.

"Well, I have a saying of my own," he replied while scratching out her name, "Phone first!"

"Excuse me?"

"You heard what I said. The next time you expect to be late, have the common courtesy to call in advance."

"I know you can't be serious, Malcolm," she said while stroking his face with her hand. "What if I pay you another two thousand? Will you forgive me?"

"I wouldn't give a damn if you paid me ten thousand, I don't tolerate inconsiderate clients," he told her while moving her hand off his face. "Now, if you will excuse me."

He turned and started walking back towards the door. At that moment Stephanie and her girlfriend walked right past him. He followed her down the street calling out her name; when she wouldn't stop, he grabbed her by the arm.

"Hey, slow down for a second! I want to talk to you."

"I don't think I can afford your time," she said sarcastically and pulled away.

"I just wanted to tell you how sorry I am for being such an asshole. What I said to you was totally uncalled for."

"Apology accepted, now good night," she said abruptly. Then she began to walk away.

"Hold up," he said as he blocked her way. "Don't act like that."

"How do you expect me to act? You hurt my feelings. I've seen you in the club a few times and you seemed like a gentleman but you're no different from the rest of these creeps in Miami."

"You're wrong about me, Stephanie! But I can't change your mind, not in one night," I said. "I just need to know that you sincerely accept my apology so I can sleep with a clear conscience."

"I already told you, I accept."

"Can we at least shake hands or hug or something?"

"If I give you a hug, will you leave me alone?"

"I promise, cross my heart and hope to die." He made an X over his chest.

"Okay, but don't try anything fresh."

When she put her arms around his neck, he squeezed tight and carefully slipped something into her purse. She was involved for a moment then pulled back. "That's enough," she said while straightening out her dress. "Now leave me alone like you promised." He stepped aside and allowed her to go on her way.

Once she was safely in her car, he headed back towards the club. Big Al saw him coming and made a U-turn and headed toward him.

"Need a taxi, sir?" he joked as he pulled up to the curb.

Malcolm took off his jacket and jumped in.

"So, where do we go from here?" Big Al asked.

"Home! I've had enough excitement for one night."

Just as they were pulling off, there was a knock at the back window. It was Stephanie. Malcolm cracked his window just enough to hear her.

"Malcolm, I can't accept this."

"What are you talking about?"

"I'm talking about the three-hundred dollars you slipped in my purse."

"Stephanie, put that money in your purse and get your ass back in the car!" her girlfriend screamed from the car behind us.

"Why don't you take her advice?" he said to her.

"Malcolm, let this window down so I can give you this back."

"The window is broken."

"Well, open the door."

"The door is broken, too."

"If you don't take this back, I'm going to leave it here on the street."

"That's your prerogative," he told her. "I would rather you use it to purchase that dress you're wearing. You look like a queen in that dress. I want you to have it. Consider it a gift."

28

Malcolm signaled Big Al to pull off and they sped off down the street. As they merged onto the expressway, he took a deep breath and turned the volume up on the radio. A song by Fleetwood Mac, called "Dreams" was on.

Oh, thunder only happens when it's raining

Players only love you when they're playing

"Hey, Al, remember this old cut?"

"Of course, I remember. Back in those days I used to throw rent parties in my basement."

"My father used to throw those parties, too. Back then you could hear Steely Dan, Madonna, and George Clinton all on the same station," he laughed. "Yeah, those were the good old days."

"Where is your father now?"

"He died a long time ago."

"I'm sorry to hear that. What did he die of? Cancer, heart attack, stroke?"

"No, he died of an overdose of women," Malcolm said in a regretful tone. "I just hope I get out of this business before I O.D., too."

CHAPTER 3

The next morning Malcolm was abruptly awakened by the loud noise of a blender. He reached over to the digital clock on his nightstand and turned it around to check the time, it read 8:15 A.M. "Damn, Damn, Damn!" he yelled, then he rolled out of bed and put on his drawers to see what all the commotion was about. When he opened the kitchen door, his maid, Ms. Ruby, had the counter covered with fruit and was cutting it up to make a smoothie.

"Good morning!" she yelled over the loud motor.

"Ms. Ruby, what are you doing here?" he asked while rubbing the sleep out of his eyes.

"What?" she yelled.

Malcolm walked over to the blender and turned it off.

"I said, what are you doing here? I thought I gave you the day off."

"Yes, sir, but today is a special day, so I decided to come over to make you breakfast." She winked.

31

"The only thing special about today is that I can't get any sleep," he said, then he walked into the living room and pushed the remote to close the blinds. "Why are you torturing me? You know I can't stand sunlight."

"Are you sure you don't have a coffin in your bedroom?" she laughed.

"As a matter of fact, I do. And if you don't let me go back to sleep I'm going to bite you on the neck."

"Vampires aren't supposed to age," she said as she winked again.

"Ms. Ruby, is there something wrong with your eye?"

"Malcolm, you are a pitiful soul. You can't even take a hint?" She pulled out a white envelope and shoved it at him. "Here, take it!"

"What is this, a letter bomb?"

"I wish it were, you party pooper. It's a birthday card."

"Today is my birthday?" I asked. "I thought it was tomorrow."

He went over to check the calendar on the refrigerator to confirm the date. Sure enough, it was Thursday, June 29. Suddenly, he had a burst of energy. He ran over to Ms. Ruby, grabbed her around the waist, and twirled her around in circles.

"Let me go, boy!" she shouted.

"I'll never let you go, you domestic goddess. I can't live without you or your collard greens."

"Malcolm, you are so crazy. Let me go before you make me drop this knife."

"Well, drop it and show me what you're working with, old lady."

She stopped smiling and put her hands on her hips. "Who you callin' old?"

"Did I say old?" he said sarcastically. "I meant... experienced."

"That's what I thought you meant. Besides, if anybody is old around here, it's you." She walked back into the kitchen and poured the smoothie into a glass and handed it to him. "One day that young pistol of yours is going to run out of bullets. Here drink this, I added protein powder."

"Well, I can always reload with Viagra."

She snatched the damp towel off the refrigerator door and chased him around the apartment. For a 65-year-old woman she was quick on her feet. Just as he thought he had gotten away, she popped him right on his ass.

"Ouch!"

"You deserved that, you little heathen!" she shouted. "Maybe next time you'll have more respect for your elders."

Just then, the phone rang!

"Tremell residence," Ms. Ruby answered. "Hello, Mrs. Tremell, how are you? Yes, he's right here!"

She handed Malcolm the phone and popped him on the behind one last time.

"Hello, Mother!"

"Happy birthday, son!"

"How did you know I would be up this early?"

"Who do you think told Ms. Ruby to wake you up and feed you?" she asked. "Ever since you stopped eating red meat you've gotten skinny."

"Who you callin' skinny? I'm as solid as a rock!"

"I swear, ever since Oprah did that show on the beef industry, people have lost their minds," she complained. "A slab of ribs and chitlins never hurt anybody."

"Mama, I'm eating just fine. Ms. Ruby is taking good care of me."

"Son, what you need is a wife," she went on. "Somebody to take care of you and give me some grandbabies!"

"There you go again, trying to marry me off. You're starting to make me feel like an old maid."

At that moment, his other line rang.

"Perfect timing," he whispered. "Mama, my other line is ringing, I've got to go, tell everybody I said, hello. Love you... bye!"

He checked the caller I.D. and clicked over to the other line. "Wassup, fool?"

"You're wassup," Simon said. "Happy birthday, Bro!"

"Thanks, partner, I guess Mom put you up to calling me, too!"

"Man, your mother is like a Twitter and Facebook Ninja. She Skyped me last night to remind me to call you," he laughed. "I had to stop working to talk to her and the club was jam packed. But you know I'll do anything for her!"

"Speaking of the club, how's business?"

"Busy as ever, man. I even got on the turntable last night and did a little mixing. Remember back in high school when I used to try to mix while you played the piano? We sounded horrible."

"You mean you sounded horrible, I was jammin'!" Malcolm joked.

"So how's business with you? You sound whipped."

"Man, you have no idea. I've been to New York, London, and Paris all in the same week; I need some down time to reboot."

"Why don't you take a break and fly into Atlanta this weekend. You can sit in with the band in the new jazz room."

"The last time I sat in with the band at your club, it damn near burned down, along with the piano my dad gave me for my eighteenth birthday, remember?"

"How was I supposed to know my bartender was smoking crack in the storage room? And by the way, I did reimburse you after I got the insurance money."

"No amount of money could replace that piano," he told

him. "But I'll try to get down there anyway. Just let me check my schedule and I'll get back with you."

"Don't give me that crap about your schedule." He sounded annoyed "I'm not one of your clients you pencil in your little black book. I'm your friend."

"Okay, I'll come. Damn, you're worse than my mother. Besides, I've got to check out your new place. What did you decide to call it?"

"Club Obsession. And it's taking off like a rocket. We even added male strippers on Thursday nights. Cynthia came up with the idea."

"Cynthia!" Malcolm said with disgust. "When did you start seeing her again?"

The phone suddenly went silent. "I was saving that surprise for when you got here," he said. "We've been back together for about a month."

"Simon, don't you think it's a strange coincidence that she came back a week before the club opened?"

"What are you trying to say?"

"What I'm saying is Cynthia just wants to shine in your spotlight," he explained to him. "I guess being a local news reporter wasn't enough for her."

"Don't start preaching to me, Malcolm. I know what I'm doing."

"Open your eyes, Simon. That woman is nothing but a no-good—"

"Stop!" he interrupted. "I love Cynthia and no matter what you say, we're getting married. Why can't you accept that and just be happy for me?"

Malcolm wanted to blow up, but he bit his tongue.

"Okay, partner, I got your back. Just don't make me regret this. I don't want to have to say I told you so!"

"Thanks Bro," he said. "I'm going to let you go. I'll see you at the club Saturday night. Enjoy your birthday." Then he hung up.

Malcolm looked at his tired reflection in the mirror and shook his head. "Damn you, Simon, when will you ever learn?"

CHAPTER 4

S imon arrived at Club Obsession just before five o'clock, two hours before the doors were scheduled to open. He parked his red Ferrari in the back lot and took his nine-millimeter pistol out of the glove compartment. Growing up on the Southside of Chicago had taught him never to get too comfortable with his surroundings. Although the club was in the affluent Buckhead section of Atlanta, he knew he could get jacked at any time.

After deactivating the club's alarm system, he unlocked the two dead-bolt locks and went inside. Simon was there to set a trap. For the last three weekends the cash at the door had come up short. He had a hunch the club manager, Darren, was skimming off the top but he needed proof. So he drilled a hole inside a light fixture behind the cashier's window and mounted a tiny camera, like the ones they used in Vegas to watch the blackjack tables and slot machines. He ran a thin black wire along the ceiling and into his office where he connected it to a monitor. "Now, let's see what kind of fish we catch," he said to himself.

After putting away his tools, he mixed himself a gin and tonic and put on his favorite song, "Mind Blowing Decisions" by Heatwave. He grabbed a broom handle and pretended like he was steppin' at the Fifty Yard Line in Chicago. Those were the good old days, he was thinking as he danced around the freshly waxed floor. Just as he was getting into a nice groove, there was a loud knock at the front door. Bam, bam, bam! He turned off the music and walked slowly toward the door with his pistol drawn. "Who is it?" he shouted as he peeped out of the window.

"Mr. Harris, my name is Ariel Daniels. Can I talk to you for a moment?"

"How did you know I was here?"

"I was having dinner across the street and I saw you drive up," she told him. "I was waiting for the club to open so I could talk to you about a job."

Simon put away his pistol and let her in. He was impressed with her poise and beauty. Ariel stood erect at five-nine and spoke with perfect diction. Her cinnamon-brown skin was flawless, and her hair was cut short and natural. She tried without success to cover her firm breasts under the light-blue jacket she wore. Simon tried not to stare as he escorted her into his office.

"Have a seat," he told her. "So, what can I do for you?"

"Mr. Harris, I've been an admirer of yours ever since you opened your first club in Marietta back in ninety-three. I always wanted to work for someone with your vision."

"I appreciate your admiration for my hard work, but what are you qualified to do?"

"I'm currently working as a marketing manager at Coca-Cola. But I've been in the nightclub industry ever since I was in college. I worked as a waitress, bartender, and as a manager," she said. "Here's my résumé."

She pulled a folder out of a black leather briefcase, and

handed it to him. While he looked it over, she glanced around the room at the pictures on the walls.

"You mind if I look around?" Ariel asked.

"Be my guest."

She walked over to the poster of Cynthia and stared at it like she was trying to make a connection. "Isn't she a reporter on Channel Five?"

"Yes, she's my fiancée."

"Congratulations! I'm glad to finally meet a man who isn't afraid of commitment."

"I take it that you're single?"

"I'm probably the most single woman in Atlanta." She laughed nervously. "I haven't been on a date in months."

"That's hard to believe. I mean, you're very beautiful. And judging by your résumé, you've got brains, too."

"A home in Stone Mountain, a Mercedes, and a master's degree don't make you an ideal mate. Most men are intimidated by strong, independent women."

"So I've heard."

"Look, Mr. Harris. I want to work for you," she said passionately. "I know I can help make Club Obsession an even bigger success. Just give me a chance."

"I would love to hire you, Ariel, but there aren't any positions open for anyone with your qualifications," Simon explained. "But if that changes, you'll be the first person I call."

"Thank you for taking time out to see me, Mr. Harris," she said as she reached out to shake his hand.

"Please call me Simon," he insisted. "'Mr.' makes me feel old."

Simon escorted her out to her car, and cordially opened her door.

"Before I go, I want to tell you how much I appreciate your professionalism," she said as she let the top down on her convertible. "You don't know how difficult it is for an attractive woman to be taken seriously."

"Well, that's the difference between me and most men, I don't allow my smaller head to make business decisions," he said. "Besides, I love Cynthia too much to do anything to jeopardize our relationship. It's just not worth it."

"Now, there's something you don't see every day," Ariel said as she put her car in drive.

"What's that?"

"A gentleman."

CHAPTER 5

A t 9:00 P.M. hundreds of women stood in line outside Club Obsession to see the strip show. It was Ladies' Night and the first 100 women would get in free. When the doors opened, they rushed inside to get the best seats near the stage. But the strippers hadn't shown up or even called. The manager, Darren, was sweating bullets. This was the second time in four weeks he had failed to secure the entertainment on time.

"We've only got an hour before show time," Simon said. "Where the hell are they?"

"I've been trying to contact them all day," Darren explained. "Maybe they're on the way."

Simon knew they weren't coming. Darren had put him in another tight spot. He wanted to fire him right then but he needed him, at least until he found a replacement.

"I'm going to make some calls to see if I can find someone on short notice," Simon said as he walked toward his office.

"What do you want me to do?" Darren asked.

"Stay here and try to keep these women from tearing down my place."

Simon frantically scrolled through his Rolodex and called every talent agent and strip-club owner in Atlanta. Thirty minutes passed before he finally contacted a group out of Decatur. They called themselves Hot Chocolate. The manager, Theodore Simmons, was very arrogant and shrewd. He insisted on a fee of two thousand dollars, almost twice the amount of the original group. Simon was in no position to argue, so he agreed.

When he came out of his office to tell Darren the news, the number of women in the club had doubled. Some of them were drinking heavily and getting loud.

"This could get ugly," he said to Darren. "Call downtown and tell them we need extra cops."

"I already did," he said.

"And?"

"They didn't have any available."

"I'll be damned," Simon said with his hand on his hip. "I sure hope those guys show up in time."

"If they don't, then what?" Darren asked.

"If they don't, you're going out there to explain why the show was canceled."

"Why me?"

"Because you're the dumb son-of-a-bitch who got me into this mess in the first place."

• • •

By 9:55 P.M., the crowd was getting restless. Some of the women began to demand their money back. Simon stood on the second floor where he could get a view of the front entrance.

Every time a car pulled up, he cringed. "Where are they?" he asked, while looking down at his watch every two minutes.

At 10:05 P.M. he gave up hope and went downstairs to tell Darren to make the announcement. But Darren was nowhere to be found. He checked Darren's office, the kitchen, and the rest room, but there was no sign of him anywhere.

"Never ask a boy to do a man's job," Simon said as he walked toward the stage. The overzealous crowd suddenly got quiet. Simon grabbed the microphone out of the stand and cleared his throat to deliver the bad news.

"I want to apologize for the show not starting on time," he said. "It's just been brought to my attention that—"

Before he could finish his sentence, the deejay signaled the group had arrived and was ready to go on. Simon played it off brilliantly and made the announcement seem like a part of the act.

"As I was saying, it's just been brought to my attention that the show is about to begin! Ladies, please put your hands together for the men of Hot Chocolate!"

The lights dimmed and the deejay played the song "Pony" by Ginuwine. The crowd erupted. Red, green, and orange lights flashed in rhythm with the music. When the smoke cleared, four muscular men stood onstage wearing cutoff T-shirts and thongs. Women were screaming at the top of their lungs, "Take it off!"

It was a scene right out of an X-rated comedy. Well-dressed women in business suits were knocking over chairs and one another trying to get to the stage to put money in the strippers' crotches. The deejay turned up the music and began remixing the lyrics, I'm just a bachelor, looking for a partner.

The strippers worked their way through the impassioned crowd, bumping and grinding while women stuffed their thongs with dollar bills and phone numbers. Midway through the song, the men tore off their shirts and jumped on top of tables, flexing their muscles and pushing their pelvises in women's faces. Some of them got carried away and pulled their penises out from under their thongs. It was a wild scene.

When the song ended, the strippers ran back onto the stage and took a bow. The women applauded apprehensively hoping the show wasn't over. Three of the dancers went backstage to get chairs while the other grabbed the microphone.

"I have a special treat for you tonight, ladies!" he announced. "Do you want it?"

"Yeah!" they yelled.

"Are you sure you can handle it?"

"Yeah!" they yelled again.

"I can handle it, baby!" shouted an intoxicated woman in the front row.

"Before I give it to you, I want the women who are celebrating birthdays to come up here to the stage."

Several women rushed the stage claiming their birthdays were in June. It took a few minutes to sort out the pretenders. Once they were sorted out, three women sat onstage looking nervous as hell.

"What's your name, sweetheart," he asked the woman sitting nearest to him.

"Crystal," she said shyly.

"That's a pretty name," he told her. "Let me ask you a question, Crystal. Do you keep stuffed animals on your bed?"

"Yes," she giggled.

"Do you have a teddy bear?"

"No, I don't."

"Well, I'm going to give you a teddy bear for your birthday," he said in a sensual tone.

The lights dimmed again, and white smoke blasted from the floor as the song "Pony" by Ginuwine echoed through the huge speakers. The beat was hypnotic.

"Ladies, it's my pleasure to bring you the man of the hour. Put your hands together for Teddy Bear!"

When the lights came on, a bald man stood in the center of the stage sporting a long white fur coat, a matching brim, and a black cane. He slowly peeled off his coat revealing his naked and oiled black body. The women onstage fell backward in their seats and the crowd went wild.

"Come to Mama," one woman yelled as she reached out with a twenty-dollar bill.

"Damn girl, look at the body on that man!" another woman screamed.

At six-five, 240 pounds, Teddy Bear was an awesome sight. He had a washboard stomach and muscular thighs. Most of the attention was focused on his midsection. Simon damn near choked on his drink when he saw how long it was. "Make damn sure he doesn't get an invitation to the company pool party." He slapped five with one of the bartenders.

Women in high heels and business suits rushed the stage to get a closer look and to touch. Security guards stood in front of the stage to keep them from killing one another. Five minutes later the situation was totally out of control.

Simon had to end the show and clear out the club. "That's it!" he yelled. "Party's over!"

The bouncers moved in and directed the frustrated crowd toward the exit. Simon told the bartenders and waitresses to cash out and go home.

"Where in the hell is Darren?" he asked one of the bouncers.

"He was at the cashier's window a minute ago," he answered. "You want me to get him?"

"Get everybody out of here first. Then find him and tell him to meet me in my office."

"Yes, sir."

Simon rushed back to his office to check on the camera he had set up behind the cashier. He pushed the reverse button on the monitor and rewound the tape until Darren came into the picture.

"Well, well, well, what have we here?" he said as he watched Darren take a stack of twenties out of the register. It was obvious the cashier was in on it, too. She kept looking around very suspiciously, like she was watching his back. When Darren was finished, he gave her a kiss on the cheek and walked out of the booth wearing a sly grin. "Smile you dirty bastard, you're on Candid Camera," Simon said as he paused the tape.

Just as he was about to go looking for Darren, there was a knock at the door.

"Who is it?

"It's Darren. You lookin' for me?"

"Hold on a minute."

Simon covered the front of the monitor with a briefcase he found on the floor and he used his suit jacket to camouflage the top.

When he opened the door, Darren was wearing the same silly grin he had on camera.

"Have a seat."

"I'm sorry I wasn't there to make that announcement," he explained. "There was a situation at the front door I had to deal with."

"Don't worry about that," Simon said as he blocked the door. "I've got another job for you."

"What's that?" he asked nervously.

"I want you to go to your office and clean out all of your shit."

"Huh? What are you talking about?"

"Don't play me like a chump, you crooked son-of-a-bitch!

If I have to repeat myself, I'll throw your ass out." Simon had his fists balled. "Now what's it going to be?"

Simon was only five-eight but he was stocky. He was just looking for a reason to wipe the floor with Darren's narrow ass. He didn't weigh more than a hundred-forty soaking wet.

"Okay, I'll go. But first I want my check for this month."

"I'll give you something to take with you." Simon grabbed him by the collar and punched him in the nose, followed by a stiff uppercut to the jaw. Darren fell to the floor like a bag of cement.

While he was lying there bleeding, Simon reached inside Darren's pocket and took back the money from the cash register. Then he picked him up off the floor and threw him out of the door. "Now get out of my sight!" Simon yelled. "And don't forget to tell that thieving bitch she's fired, too."

Theodore was sitting at the bar sipping on a glass of milk watching the drama unfold. He knew it was none of his business, but he couldn't help making light of the situation.

"I hope that wasn't the accountant," Theodore said.

"Don't worry. I've got your money." Simon walked over and handed him an envelope. "You must be Theodore."

"You must be Mr. Harris."

"In the flesh," he said as they shook hands. "So, where are your friends?"

"Those are my employees, not my friends," he said smugly. "I try not to mix business and friendship."

"Well, I have a business proposition for you. How about performing here on a regular basis?"

"Give me a call and we'll talk about it," Theodore said as he walked toward the door. "Right now I've got to make it to another gig. A man's work is never done in Hotlanta," he said, laughing.

Simon locked the doors behind him and took a deep breath.

"What a night," he said, sighing. He walked over to the bar and mixed another gin and tonic. Then he put his Heatwave CD inside the stereo, advanced it to track six, and turned up the volume.

"Mind blowin' decisions causes head-on collisions," he sang along.

The smooth beat of the music was relaxing and therapeutic. He grabbed the broom handle from behind the bar and began dancing with his make-believe partner. He dipped, turned, and shuffled, just like it was the real thing. Then suddenly, bam, bam, bam! There was a loud knock at the door. Simon turned off the music and reached behind the bar for his gun.

"Who is it?" he asked as he walked slowly toward the door.

"It's me, Ariel."

"Ariel? What in the world are you doing here?" He unlocked the door and let her in.

"I'm sorry to bother you, Mr. Harris, but I left my briefcase," she explained. "I would have waited until tomorrow but my driver's license is in there."

Simon went to his office to see if he could find it. And there it was sitting on his desk. It was the briefcase he had used to hide the monitor from Darren.

"Here you go," he said. "It came in handy."

"I'm really sorry for interrupting your little party," Ariel said, trying not to laugh.

"You saw me steppin'?" he asked, looking uncomfortable. "I'm so embarrassed."

"Don't be," she told him. "You're pretty smooth for an old guy."

"Who you callin' old?" Simon stepped back and looked her up and down. "How old are you?"

"Now, you should know better than to ask a woman her age," she said with her hand on her hip.

"I'm going to find out eventually."

"And how is that?"

"When you fill out your application for the manager's position."

"You mean, I got the job?"

"Not so fast," he said. "First you've got to do something for me."

"I hope you're not talking about giving up the booty," she said jokingly.

"Of course not, silly. You have to learn to step."

"You're on!" Ariel set her briefcase down and took off her jacket. "Are you sure your fiancée won't mind?"

"All we're doing is dancing," Simon said as he turned up the music. "And besides, she left today for the Essence Music Festival in New Orleans."

"In that case, lead on!"

CHAPTER 6

E ven with his dark sunglasses on, Malcolm was squinting from the bright sun that pierced through the tinted windows of his limousine. Traffic was backed up on Interstate 195 from Alton Road to the Star Island entrance.

"How in the hell do people function this early in the morning?" he said to Big Al. "And where are they all going?"

"Some of us actually work for a living, sir."

"Are we going to make it to the airport on time?"

"Well, it's 8:15 now" he said, glancing at the digital clock on the console, "and your flight is at 9, so it's gonna be tight!"

"You know me, I like it tight!" he laughed. "Just do your best to get me there, my buddy's gonna be pissed if I miss this flight!"

Just then, Malcolm's cell phone rang. He pulled it out of the sleeve and checked the caller ID. It was Helen.

51

"Hello, Helen, I thought I made myself clear the other night."

"Malcolm, please don't be cruel to me; I called to apologize for showing up late at Melvin's. You were right, there was no excuse for not calling. I promise you it won't happen again," she said with remorse. "If we can put that behind us, I have a business proposition for you."

"I'm listening."

"I need an escort for a benefit at the Fox Theatre tonight in Atlanta. I'm willing to pay five thousand cash...plus expenses, if you can fit me into your schedule."

"I'm on my way to Atlanta now; I'll call your assistant when I land to let you know if I can make it. Fair enough?"

"Fair enough. And again, I'm sorry for what happened. I hope you'll give me a chance to make it up to you," she said seductively. Then she hung up.

"Sounds like your personal trip just turned into work."

"Business is business, Big Al. Now stop eavesdropping in on my calls and put that big-ass foot on that accelerator; my time just turned into money!"

CHAPTER 7

THE MAINTENANCE MAN

The marquee of the Fox Theatre read: FUND-RAISER TONIGHT—
UNITED NEGRO COLLEGE FUND. Hundreds of rowdy fans lined
Peachtree Street to get a peek at their favorite celebrities. One by
one, freshly waxed limousines arrived carrying famous athletes,
actors, and politicians. Flashbulbs exploded and TV camera
lights blared as reporters scrambled to get sound bites for the 11
o'clock news. Not being the shy type, Malcolm was anxious for
his five minutes of fame and free publicity.

When the valet opened the door of his black Cadillac Escalade,
Malcolm stepped out in his black Armani tux and posed for the
cameras like a seasoned veteran.

"I loved you in your last movie!" a woman shouted, mistaking him for Denzel.

"Can I please have your autograph?" another woman shouted while reaching over the ropes with her notepad.

Malcolm stopped for a moment to sign it, gave her a hug, and then proceeded toward the entrance while waving and blowing kisses. "I'm such a ham," he laughed.

The lobby was colorfully decorated with red, black, and green ribbons. African-American art was on display along with photographs of prominent black leaders like Dr. King, Malcolm X, Sojourner Truth, and W.E.B. Dubois. A huge banner was draped over the concession area bearing the slogan: a mind is a terrible thing to waste.

"Excuse me," he said to the usher while showing him his ticket. "Can you tell me where this seat is located?"

"Right down the center aisle, row A. That's the first row from the stage." He handed Malcolm a program. "You might want to hurry, the show is about to start."

He decided to stop at the restroom before going to his seat. He didn't want to get up in the middle of a program, especially sitting in the front row.

The second Malcolm walked into the restroom he could feel the arrogance in the air. Men were standing around in little cliques smoking cigars and bragging about their business deals, exotic cars, and stock options. Malcolm smiled as he stepped up to the urinal; these were the same kinds of men whose wives he was fucking in Punta Cana and the Virgin Islands every weekend. The two men standing next to the bathroom attendant were the most obnoxious. One was a short, chubby white man wearing a bad toupee, the other a tall, light-skinned black man.

"How are those stocks doing, Bob?" the black man asked loudly enough for everybody to hear. He spoke properly with a

54

high-pitched tone.

"They're doing pretty well, Eric," he told him. "Thanks for putting me up on it."

"It was the least I could do after you invited us to stay at your condo in Hilton Head," Eric replied while combing his hair in the mirror. "My fiancée really enjoyed the sauna and golf course."

While Malcolm was peeing, he made eye contact with the guy in the urinal next to him. They both had that expression on their faces that said, "What jerks!" After relieving himself, he walked over to the sink to wash his hands. Eric was still admiring himself in the mirror and was blocking the sink.

"Excuse me," Malcolm said politely.

"Be my guest," he answered as he stepped back slightly, giving Malcolm just enough room to squeeze in.

"You're going to have to move back farther than that, my man," he said in a tone that made it clear he was irritated. "I'm too big to fit into this tight space."

Eric took another small step back and looked over at Bob with a smirk on his face, as if to say, "Who in the hell does he think he is?" Eric went back to admiring himself in the mirror. Malcolm stood as erect as he could and looked Eric straight in the eyes through his reflection in the mirror. Although they were about the same height and weight, Eric was noticeably out of shape. One punch to that weak-ass stomach and he would fold like a cheap lawn chair, Malcolm was thinking.

After spraying himself with cologne, Eric tipped the bathroom attendant five dollars and walked toward the door with Bob trailing closely behind, all the while staring at Malcolm in the mirror. Once Eric was gone, he rinsed his face with cold water to compose himself.

"That fool was five seconds away from an old-fashioned Chicago ass-whipping," Malcolm said to the bathroom attendant.

"Don't pay no attention to that asshole," he said while handing him a paper towel. "He'll get what's coming to him, sooner or later."

"I just hope I'm there when it happens." Malcolm put twenty dollars in his basket and headed for the door. "Have a good night."

"You do the same, young blood," he said. "And by the way, I had your back if you would've jumped on that prick. I may be old, but I could've taken the chubby white guy with no problem."

"That's good to know; maybe next time, old man," he laughed and threw a playful punch at his chin.

The host of the event was presenting an award for community service as Malcolm made his way down the main aisle. The audience stood up and applauded, which gave him the perfect cover to make a mad dash to his seat. Helen was looking out for him and waved as he came strolling down the aisle.

"I'm glad you could make it." She gave him a firm hug and a kiss on the cheek. "I thought I was going to need a bodyguard to keep these dirty old men off me."

When Malcolm stepped back to get a better look at her outfit, he understood her point. Helen was wearing a black Versace halter dress. The soft silk fabric hugged her small waist perfectly, accentuating her large breasts. Her hair, streaked with brown highlights, was pinned up neatly, just the way he like it.

"I don't know if I can make it through the rest of the show," he said while taking his seat. "How long before it's over?"

"At least two hours."

"Two hours? We'll be lucky to make it through intermission," he whispered in her ear.

"You know I love it when you talk dirty to me, Malcolm," she said while inconspicuously rubbing his inner thigh.

The lights dimmed in the theater as the next act was introduced. He checked the program to see who was performing.

It read: Inzinga Dance Company—solo by Ms. Antoinette Grayson. When the long curtain rose, four black women in raggedy clothes stood still in separate spotlights. The backdrop was an urban alley scene, complete with old trash cans and street lamps, set in the late 1950s. It was a captivating sight. The theater was so quiet you could hear a pin drop. He held his breath in anticipation.

Suddenly, a funky drumbeat broke the silence and the women began to move to the rhythm. As the tempo quickened, so did their gestures. A piano and a saxophone joined in creating a smooth jazzy groove. Their movements were strong and fluid. It was a dance that told the story of four women looking for a way out of the ghetto. As the story went on, four con men came dancing into the alley with promises of fine jewelry and fancy clothes. Three of the women went away with the men, leaving only one woman behind. She fell down onto her knees in sorrow and the lights dimmed on the set.

The audience began to applaud, but the show wasn't over.

A few seconds later, the spotlight came on center stage and she stood with poise, wearing a white leotard and white satin ballet shoes. Her brown skin, light brown eyes, and long, slender frame made her appear even more elegant. "That must be Antoinette Grayson," Malcolm whispered to Helen. But she didn't respond. It was obvious she didn't appreciate his enthusiasm. As Antoinette began to pirouette, the song "Cherish the Day" by Sade played softly in the distance. The passionate beat and poetic lyrics perfectly accentuated the mood.

> *You're ruling the way that I move*
> *and I breathe your air*
> *You only can rescue me*
> *this is my prayer.*

Malcolm could feel the intensity of her every move. Antoinette swayed from one side of the stage to the other, then leaped high into the air landing squarely on her toes. Her facial expression was serious and intense. The more he watched her, the more he became engrossed by her beauty and grace. She was flexible, strong, and precise. For the finale, she made a series of turns, which positioned her in the center of the stage, directly in front of Malcolm. As she took her bow, their eyes met. She paused for a split second, and then smiled. Malcolm smiled back. The audience gave her a standing ovation as the other dancers joined her onstage. He stood and applauded, too, while Helen sat there with an attitude.

Malcolm was determined to meet this fascinating woman. He wasn't interested in selling his services or getting her number. He wanted to tell her how much he enjoyed the show and that he admired her talent. Somehow, he had to figure out a way to get away from Helen long enough to make her acquaintance.

• • •

When the show was over, hundreds of people gathered in the lobby to congratulate the performers and get autographs. Helen had her arm wrapped around his arm like a python, making sure he didn't get out of her sight.

"Let's go to the hotel and get in bed," she said. "I'm horny as hell."

"What's the hurry?" he answered. "Let's get a glass of wine and mingle."

"Okay, but just for a little while. It's been a long day and I'm getting tired." She gave him one of those phony yawns.

They walked over to the concession area to order drinks.

While they waited for the bartender, Helen recognized one of her girlfriends on the other side of the bar. She frantically waved to get her attention. For a woman who was supposedly tired, she seemed awfully eager to show him off.

"Helen, darling, how are you?" the woman said as they exchanged hugs.

"I'm absolutely wonderful, Gloria."

"I can see that," she said while looking Malcolm up and down like a piece of meat. "Aren't you going to introduce us?"

"Gloria Randall, this is my friend Malcolm Tremell."

"It's a pleasure to finally meet you, Mr. Tremell. Helen has told me some great things about you." She extended her hand.

"The pleasure is all mine," he said as he kissed it.

Gloria was a sassy woman who bore an incredible resemblance to Lena Horne, bright smile and all. She had to be at least 55 but she was looking damn good for her age.

"He's even more handsome than you described, and muscular, too." She was still holding his hand.

"Okay, that's enough," Helen said as she stepped between them. "He's already taken."

"Calm down, sweetheart, I was just admiring the merchandise. Besides, I brought my own toy to play with. You want to meet him?"

"Sure, why not? Are you coming, Malcolm?" Helen asked.

"I'll be right over after the bartender brings our drinks."

"Okay, baby, don't be long."

The second they walked away, Malcolm quickly disappeared into the crowd, heading in the direction of the autograph area. The lines were long and rowdy fans were pushing and shoving trying to take pictures. His height made it easy to see over everyone's heads. Most of the singers and three of the dancers were sitting down at the draped tables signing autographs, but Antoinette was nowhere to be found. I guess it wasn't meant to be, he was thinking.

As he turned to walk away, he noticed a woman walking back inside the empty theater. It was hard to make her out. She was wearing a sheer hood, which partially covered her face. But when she briefly turned, he saw those beautiful brown eyes. It was Antoinette.

Malcolm fought his way through the crowd, determined not to miss her. "Excuse me," he yelled. "Pardon me." Before he went inside, he stopped at the flower vendor's booth and purchased a dozen red roses.

"I've only got eleven," the vendor told me.

"You gotta be kidding me!" he said.

"I'm sorry, sir, this is the last bunch I have for sale. Take it or leave it."

"I'll take it!"

Malcolm handed him a fifty-dollar bill and grabbed the poorly wrapped flowers out of his hand. When he opened the door to the theater, Antoinette was standing on the stage with her back to him.

"I hope I'm not late for the finale," he said.

"Oh, my goodness!" she said sounding startled.

"Sorry, I didn't mean to frighten you," he said. Then he walked up to her and handed her the flowers. "I just wanted to give you these."

"You're the gentleman from the front row."

"That would be me."

"Thank you," she said, looking apprehensive. "But what are these for?"

"For your performance tonight. You were great!"

"I appreciate the compliment, Mr.—?"

"My name is Malcolm, Malcolm Tremell."

"Pleased to meet you, Malcolm." She bent down to shake his hand. "My name is Antoinette Grayson, but everybody calls me Toni."

"Well, Toni, I just wanted to let you know how much I admired your dancing," he said. "I wish you continued success. Have a good evening."

"Wait a minute," she said. "That's it?"

"I'm not going to bug you to death trying to get your phone number. That's not my style. Besides, a beautiful woman like you probably already has a man. Am I right?"

"As a matter of fact, I'm engaged. But—"

"You see what I mean?" he interrupted.

"Would you let me finish?" she said, cutting in. "I don't see anything wrong with being friends. I just moved here from New York and I don't know a single, solitary soul."

"The Big Apple, huh? I used to go to school there."

"Which school was that?"

"Juilliard. I studied jazz piano."

"Yeah, right," she said. "You look more like a model than a musician."

"I'll take that as a compliment," I told her. "But if you don't believe me, why don't you come hear me play tomorrow night?"

"I don't know," she said.

"Don't be such a party pooper. The least you could do is stop by for one song."

"Okay, okay, I'll think about it. But I'm not making any promises." She reached inside her purse and pulled out a pen and piece of paper. "So, where is this place?"

"It's in Buckhead on Peachtree Street, two blocks down from The Cheesecake Factory. It's called Club Obsession. Just give the guy at the door your name, I'll make sure you're on the VIP list."

"You've got it like that, huh?"

"I'm not trying to impress you. My best friend owns the place."

"So are you from Atlanta?"

"No, Chicago, but I live in Miami."

"You sure do get around," she said. "Are you in the military or something?"

"That's a long story." I told her. "I'll explain it to you when I see you tomorrow."

"Listen to you, sounding all confident."

"All I want to do is have intelligent conversation over a glass of wine," he said sounding sincere. "I promise I'll be the perfect gentleman."

Malcolm politely shook her hand and turned to walk away. Right as he was about to go out of the door, she yelled. "Hey, Malcolm, I'll come on one condition!"

"And what's that?" he yelled back.

"That you have the other red rose to make up this dozen."

"You've got yourself a deal!"

He left out of the theater feeling like he had just hit the lottery. "Yes!" he said pumping his fist downward. His heart was racing like a schoolboy with a crush on his third-grade teacher. For the first time in years, sex and money were not factors. Toni's presence would be all the stimulation he needed.

When he finally caught up with Helen, she was outside standing next to the limo. She was furious. Malcolm didn't even bother to lie about where he was. She already knew. Before he could open his mouth to apologize, she slapped him across the cheek. Smack!

"Here's half your money for doing a half-ass job." She handed him a brown envelope. "Don't expect to hear from me again."

"I'm sorry, Helen."

"I'm sorry, too, Malcolm," she said as she stepped inside the limo. "I hope she was worth it."

THE MAINTENANCE MAN

"She was," he told her. Then he gave her the envclope back. "You can keep your money, what I got tonight was priceless!"

PART II

THE SITUATION

CHAPTER 8

The headboard of the bed slammed against the wall knocking down Cheryl's wedding pictures. "Whose pussy is it?" Teddy Bear asked.

"It's yours!" Cheryl screamed.

"Say it louder!"

"I said it's yours, Daddy! It's all yours!"

"You're damn right it's mine! Now, turn over and spread your legs!"

Teddy flipped her onto her stomach in a doggy-style position and stroked her as hard as he could.

"Take it easy, baby. You're hurting me!"

"It's supposed to hurt!" he told her. "I'm gonna make sure your old man can't get any of this for at least a week."

Cheryl screamed so loud she woke up her six-month-old daughter who was sleeping in the room next door. "Teddy, stop! I have to go check on the baby."

"She's not going anywhere," he said. "Let me get my nut first."

Cheryl used her hand as a brace to keep her head from banging against the headboard. Her long braids swung violently back and forth as Teddy thrust his 240-pound frame against her. She begged him to stop, but that only turned him on more.

"Stop whining! You know you love it, don't you?"

"Yes, baby, but you're getting too rough!"

"Don't move. I'm cumming! I'm cumming!"

Cheryl buried her face in the pillow and screamed as Teddy jerked and shivered. When he was finished, she quickly put on her robe and rushed to check on the baby.

Teddy lay back on the king-size bed sipping on a glass of orange juice. Suddenly, his cell phone went off. He checked the name on the caller ID. It was his girlfriend, Karen. "What in the hell does she want?" He took a deep breath and pressed the talk button.

"Hello? This better be an emergency!"

"It's an emergency alright, I just found a pair of yellow Victoria's Secret panties in my drawer!" she said angrily.

"Congratulations," he said sarcastically. "What's that got to do with me?"

"They're not mine, that's what!"

"And how would you know that? Do you get your panties monogrammed?"

"Don't play me like a fool, Teddy! I know what my body smells like!" she shouted. "What I want to know is how did this heifer's drawers get in my house?"

"How should I know? Maybe they belong to one of your girlfriends."

"You better get your black ass over here right now before I start throwing your shit out the window. I mean it!" she said and then hung up.

He sat up on the bed and laid his face into his hands. He

knew the panties belonged to one of his women. He just couldn't remember which one.

It was the third time in six months that Karen had found evidence of his cheating. The phone numbers in his pocket and lipstick on his collar were easy to justify. But physical evidence was not going to be easy to explain away.

Teddy reacted with his usual arrogance. He took a long hot shower, put lotion on his body, and calmly slipped into his clothes. When Cheryl came back into the room, he was slipping on his shoes.

"Where are you goin'?" she asked.

"I've got some business to take care of."

"Can't it wait until later? I was ready for another round," she said while unsnapping his pants.

"Sorry, baby, duty calls."

"You are such a tease, Teddy," she said. "Every time you leave here I feel like I'm going through sex withdrawal."

"Maybe you wouldn't be so horny if your old man wasn't traveling around the country five days a week. He must be crazy leaving a fine young thang like you home alone."

"You leave David out of this. He's a good man," she said defensively. "And good men are hard to find."

"Yeah, but a hard man is good to find, wouldn't you agree?" He collected his things and headed for the door. "By the way, can you loan me fifty bucks? I left my wallet at home."

"I swear, Teddy, you're the most conceited and manipulative son-of-a-bitch I've ever met," she walked over to her purse and pulled out a fifty-dollar bill. "You think you're God's gift to women."

"Does that mean we're still on for next week at 11?"

"Make it 10," she said while stuffing the money in the front of his jeans. "My husband should be long gone by then!"

Teddy pulled into the circular driveway and parked his Navigator behind Karen's Mercedes. He reached inside the glove compartment and grabbed the recycled Tiffany's jewelry box and shoved it into his pants pocket. He sat there for a minute to make sure he had his lies straight, then he took a deep breath and got out of the car. "Oh, well, here we go again," he said to himself.

When he walked into the house, Karen was waiting in the living room sipping a glass of wine. The yellow panties were spread out on the cocktail table like evidence in a court case.

"Okay, I'm here. What's up?"

"You know damn well, what's up?" Karen shouted with her hands on her hips.

"No, why don't you enlighten me!" Teddy said nonchalantly. "Why don't you relax and have another drink?"

Teddy turned away and went to get a beer out of the refrigerator. Just as he was about to take a sip, Karen came charging into the kitchen and slapped the bottle out of his hand.

"I pay the mortgage, the light bill, the phone bill, and buy the groceries!" she said with her finger in his face. "I'll be damned if you're going to disrespect me in my own house."

"There's no need to get violent," he said while trying to put his arms around her. "I would never do anything to jeopardize our relationship. You know I love you."

"Don't try to charm me, Teddy. It's not going to work this time. I want to know how these panties got into my house."

"Maybe they just floated in through the window and buried themselves in the bottom of your drawer."

"That shit ain't funny," she said as she shoved him.

"Okay, baby, let me explain what happened so we can put this behind us." He was trying to sound serious. "Remember the show I had at Club Obsession Thursday night?"

"Yeah, and?"

"Well, while I was performing, one of the waitresses came backstage and slipped a pair of panties inside my pocket as a joke."

"How does that explain how they got into my house?"

"It was hot that night so I threw my jacket in the backseat. It wasn't until I was looking for the car keys this morning that I realized they were in my pocket."

"I'm still waiting for you to explain how they found their way into the bottom of my drawer."

"You were coming upstairs at that exact moment and I panicked. So, I put them somewhere I figured you wouldn't look."

"Why didn't you put them in one of your drawers?"

"Like I said, I put them somewhere you wouldn't look," he said sarcastically. "We both know you go through my shit every chance you get?"

Karen wanted to laugh because she knew he was right. She took a long sip of wine then tapped her finger on the glass as if contemplating her next question. Teddy's explanation was weak but it was believable. She knew his job attracted fast women.

"Maybe you are telling the truth," she said calmly. "But if you knew they were in there, explain to me why you didn't take them out before you left this morning."

"I had my mind on something more important."

"Something more important, like what?"

"Like going by the jewelry store to pick this up."

He pulled the Tiffany's box out of his pocket and handed it to her.

She paused, "Is this what I think it is?"

"Open it up and see," he said.

She lifted the top of the small velvet box slowly. Inside was a diamond engagement ring. "Oh, baby, it's beautiful."

"I wanted to get you something bigger, but business has been slow lately."

"That's okay, sweetheart. It's the thought that counts." The tears began to roll down her face. "Please forgive me for not trusting you."

"Don't worry about it, baby, everybody makes mistakes."

She gave him a wet kiss and ran upstairs screaming like a child on Christmas Day. "I'm going to call my mom and my sister, Lisa, to tell them the good news! And when I come back, we're going to the most expensive restaurant in town to celebrate, my treat!"

Teddy got another beer out of the refrigerator and kicked back on Karen's plush leather sofa. While he sipped on his drink, he pulled the pawnshop receipt out of his pocket. When he looked at the two-hundred-dollar charge for the ring, he shook his head and laughed.

"That ought to keep a roof over my head for at least another year."

CHAPTER 9

THE MAINTENANCE MAN

Malcolm checked out of the Four Seasons Hotel in Buckhead at one o'clock. While he waited on the elevator, he thought about going up to Helen's room to say good-bye, but when the doors opened, he pushed the button for the lobby instead. After what had happened the night before, he figured she wouldn't answer the door, let alone talk to him. Before leaving the hotel, he stopped at the front desk and wrote her a short letter. When he finished, he gestured for the clerk who was working the front desk.

"Do you have an envelope?"

"Yes, sir, Mr. Tremell, here you go!"

Malcolm wrote Helen's room number on the front and handed it to her. "Make sure she gets this!"

"I'll take care of it personally, Mr. Tremell," the blonde clerk replied. "It's always a pleasure having you with us. See you next time."

Malcolm handed his bag to the valet and followed him outside to where his driver was waiting. Just as he stepped inside, his phone rang. It was Simon.

"Wassup, partner, I'm just checking out. Are we still meeting up at Gladys Knight's Famous Chicken and Waffles? My treat!"

"You're not getting off that cheap, Mr. Big Shot! The last time I paid for lunch you ran up a two-hundred dollar tab; let's make it The Capital Grill on East Paces Ferry Rd."

"Sounds like a plan!"

"By the way, I've got a new manager I want you to meet later tonight. Her name is Ariel."

"What the hell is an Ariel?" he joked. "Sounds like a laundry detergent."

"She's the new manager of the club, fool." Simon went on. "I fired Darren Thursday night after I caught him stealing."

"I hope you whipped his ass!"

"You know I did!"

"Glad to see you haven't forgotten you're from the South side of Chicago!" Malcolm said while throwing up his hands. "Southsiii-eeed!" they yelled in unison.

The conservative white driver turned red, probably thinking he was throwing up gang signs. Malcolm wanted to tell him it was a black thing, but after noticing the Republican Tea Party button swinging on the rear view mirror, he thought to himself, fuck'em.

"Man, I can't tell you how much I miss hanging out with you," Simon said. "How long has it been, anyway?"

"Too long, bro. We've got a lot of catching up to do."

"And a lot of eating to do to," Simon laughed. "I'm starving!"

"I've got a taste for a nice rib eye steak."

"I thought you stopped eating red meat."

"I didn't say I was a Muslim," he told him. "A juicy steak

every now and then won't kill me."

"Yeah, but it can clog up your arteries like a motherfucker!" Simon laughed. "I'll meet you at The Capital Grill in fifteen minutes. Last one there has to foot the bill."

"That's a bet!"

• • •

Malcolm entered the restaurant with his usual air of confidence. The hostess, who was a tall, thin woman with short locks, smiled as he approached her desk.

"May I help you?"

"Table for two, please!" Malcolm said while scanning the room to see if Simon had arrived before him.

"Expecting the missus?" she smiled.

"I'm not married."

"Really?"

"What about you," Malcolm flirted back.

"No, I'm into women, but I would make an exception for you."

"I'm flattered."

"You should be," she joked. "You know how many men and women I turn down every day?"

"I could only imagine."

"Follow me!"

She grabbed two menus and escorted Malcolm into the dining area. Just as he was feeling confident that he had won the bet and was eating free, he noticed Simon sitting at the end bar flirting with a beautiful Asian woman. One of them was writing something on a napkin and then she walked away with her drink. As she walked away, Simon was looking at her ass. The dress she had on was hugging her hips so tightly he could see the dimples in her lower back. Malcolm snuck up behind him hoping to surprise him.

"You want some of that sweet Asian poo-nanie, don't you?" he said in Simon's ear.

"Malcolm, you scared the shit out of me!" He turned around holding his chest. "I was just admiring her, uh, her outfit?"

"It's good to see you, partner," he said as they embraced.

"It's good to see you, too, Mr. Gigolo," Simon said punching him playfully in the chest. "I see you've been pumpin' iron."

"My body is my business," he told him. "You can't have a potbelly and flabby ass and expect women to pay top dollar."

"Refresh my memory, Malcolm, how much do these women pay you?"

"Two thousand dollars an hour, plus expenses!"

"I remember when you were struggling to make two hundred dollars a week."

"Thank God those days are over," he said. "I was afraid I might have to get a real job."

"I'm just glad your mom never found out what you do for a living; it would break her heart."

"Come on, Simon, don't start up with that again."

"I'm just saying, man, you're so talented. Nobody I know plays those ivory keys like you do."

"Yeah, but Lil Wayne can make a rap CD with lyrics I don't even understand and make ten million dollars. You can't drop it like it's hot to John Coltrane."

"I can't argue with that," he replied. "Now, let's have lunch."

"You sure you don't want to invite your new girlfriend? Asians need love, too!"

"Very funny. She was giving me her contact number for a job opening at the club for a bartender; she was just getting off her shift here at the bar."

"I'm sure it was only her mixing skills you were interested in, right?"

"Hey, man, a little eye candy at work never hurts," Simon said. "I may be in love with Cynthia, but I'm only human. I like to look at the menu sometimes."

"Amen, brother, but I like to order every chance I get." Malcolm laughed and they slapped five.

After being seated, the waitress came over to take their order. Malcolm's stomach growled as he sipped on his water.

"Damn, you must really be hungry," Simon said.

"I haven't eaten since yesterday afternoon, and that was lousy airplane food."

"Wait a minute, I thought you flew in today."

"Actually I got in last night," he confessed. "I was going to surprise you but I got a call from a client to attend the UNCF benefit."

"Oh, yeah, I heard the advertisement on the radio last week. How was it?"

"It was nice. As a matter of fact, I met one of the dancers in the show. Her name is Antoinette. And man was she fine! Smooth brown skin, long pretty legs, and the most beautiful light brown eyes you'd ever want to see. And talk about talented! I've never seen a woman move with such style and grace."

"She sounds like a keeper."

"Yeah, that's what I thought, too, until she told me she was engaged."

"Since when did that stop you? Back in the day, you would mack a woman down on her wedding night. Don't tell me you're starting to get a conscience."

"It's not always about sex," Malcom told him. "It's possible for men and women to just be friends."

"In other words, she didn't give you any play."

"Exactly," he laughed. "But she did promise to come to the club tonight."

"I can't wait to meet her. Any woman who can put Mr. Smooth in the 'friend zone' has got to be something special."

"She's something special, all right," Malcolm said. "If she wasn't already taken, I might consider putting in some serious time with her."

Simon almost choked on his iced tea. "Where in the hell did that come from?"

"Maybe my biological clock is ticking," Malcolm said with a serious look on his face. "I am almost 40 years old with no kids to carry on my name. Hell, I haven't taken a woman home to meet my mom since high school."

"That's the first time since I've known you that you've mentioned settling down," Simon said sounding surprised. "You sure you're not on drugs?"

"I'm just getting tired of the games, man. The money is great but dealing with these emotionally scarred women is wearing me out. Lately, I've been giving some serious thought to hanging it up."

"Why don't you come into business with me? I've already made plans to open another club in Marietta. You could be the manager."

"No offense, but there ain't no way in hell I'm working as a nightclub manager. I wouldn't give a damn if Donald Trump was the owner."

Simon's face turned as red as a black man's could. "Fuck you, Malcolm!" he said, raising his voice. "If you want to die of AIDS or end up shot in the head like your old man, be my guest."

Malcolm sat back in his seat to absorb his statement. Simon knew how deeply Malcolm felt about what had happened to his father. It was the first time in ten years either of them had brought it up.

"Hey, man, I'm sorry," Simon took a deep breath. "You know I didn't mean that the way it came out. It's just that you're like a brother to me and I don't want anything to happen to you. These diseases out here don't discriminate. And it's only a matter of time before one of these crazy and insecure husbands finds out you're laying the pipe on his sweet little wife, then what?"

"Simon, I realize that you're only trying to help, but this is something I've got to work out for myself."

"I understand, partner. But—"

The waitress coming over to take their order interrupted them.

"Hello, my name is Karen," she said cordially, "would you gentlemen like to hear about the specials?"

"Can I get a crown and cranberry?" Simon asked.

"Make mine a double!" Malcolm added.

Once she was gone, Simon leaned forward and looked Malcolm in the eyes.

"Look man, I love you, and whatever you want to do with your life is fine with me. Hell, I'm the last person that needs to be giving advice. I've got bills up the ass, crooked employees that are robbing me blind, and a girlfriend you can't stand!" He paused. "So why don't we just have a good meal, a stiff drink, and enjoy hanging out together tonight. It'll be like old times."

"I'm down for that," Malcolm said. "I can't wait to see the new club!"

"Well, if it will make you feel any better, Cynthia won't be able to make it. She's in New Orleans for the weekend."

"Man, that's the best news I've heard all day!"

CHAPTER 10

The Marriott Hotel in New Orleans was buzzing with activity. Hundreds of people gathered in the lobby waiting for the shuttle buses to take them over to the convention center where the seminars and book signings were being held. Cynthia and her girlfriend Debra were killing time at the bar sipping on Coronas.

"Girl, look at all these phony women," Debra said. "I haven't seen a woman yet who has her own eyes, hair, and breasts."

"We all can't be blessed with natural beauty," Cynthia said with conceit as she threw back her long brown hair.

"I guess not." Debra lifted her perfectly round 36DD breasts. "Who needs a boob job?"

They gave each other a high five and toasted with their Coronas. "Here's to a week away from work, the traffic on Interstate Eighty-five, and our men," Debra said.

"I'll drink to that!"

"Excuse me, ladies and gentleman!" a short, chubby woman wearing a bright orange vest yelled. "The shuttle buses have been delayed. There seems to have been some sort of car accident on Canal Street and traffic is backed up for miles. So please be patient and we'll get you over to the convention center as soon as possible. Thank you."

"That's fine with me," Cynthia said. "It's too damned hot out there anyway."

"Hey, bartender, another!" Debra yelled.

"I'll have a Long Island Iced Tea this time. I still don't have a buzz!"

"Girl, it's only three in the afternoon!"

"And?"

Debra looked at Cynthia and smiled. "Hey, bartender, make that two Long Islands. I'm not gonna let my girl get shit-faced by herself."

After the bartender brought over the drinks, they continued to criticize and break down every woman who walked by, making fun of their outfits, body shapes, and what they called project-penitentiary hairstyles. But their signifying came to an abrupt end when a group of five men came strutting in from the parking garage. They were all wearing sandals and shorts, which showed off their thick, hairy legs.

The entire room suddenly got quiet as the men walked up to the front desk to check in.

"Now, see, that's the kind of shit that can get a woman in trouble," Debra said as she stared shamelessly.

"You need to get a grip. Remember you have a man at home."

"Cynthia, why are you fronting? You know damn well you want to break off some of that dark meat."

"That was the old Cynthia. I'm engaged now," she said while

admiring the five-carat diamond ring Simon had given her. "My hoein' days are over!"

"Bitch, please," Debra laughed. "Just last month you were fuckin' that light-skin brotha from accounting. Now all of a sudden you're Ms. Goody Two-Shoes?"

"This time I'm going to be faithful to Simon," Cynthia said in a serious tone. "I want to settle down and raise a family. I'm not getting any younger you know."

Debra got quiet realizing that Cynthia was serious. She reached over and held her hand. "I hope everything works out for you and Simon. He's a damn good man and he really loves you."

"I know," Cynthia replied somberly. "Sometimes I don't think I deserve him."

Just then, two of the five men who had attracted all the attention, walked up behind them. One of them was tall and muscular with a fraternity symbol branded on his right arm. His shirt was unbuttoned halfway, exposing his hairy chest. The other was five-ten with piercing brown eyes and short wavy hair. He wore a well-groomed beard that reminded Cynthia of Teddy Pendergrass.

"Excuse me, are these seats taken?" the one with the brown eyes asked Cynthia. His voice was deep.

"Hell no...I mean...I don't think so," she replied.

The two men sat down and ordered orange juice and water. All eyes were on them as they drank and chatted with each other. Debra wanted to say something to the tall one but she was nervous. Cynthia decided to instigate just for fun.

"Excuse me, gentlemen, my name is Cynthia and this is my best friend, Debra."

"Pleased to meet you, ladies," the tall one said as he shook their hands. "I'm Randall."

"And my name is James," the other said. He shook their

hands, too. "Are you ladies here for the Essence Festival?"

"Yes, we are," Cynthia joined in. "We come every year."

"This is our first time," James said. "But it won't be our last. I've never seen so many beautiful women in my entire life. Present company included."

"Why, thank you." Cynthia blushed. "You gentlemen look quite handsome yourselves."

James smiled as he took a sip of his orange juice. His eyes never left Cynthia.

"So, are you ladies here with your husbands?" Randall asked.

"I'm not married!" Debra said promptly.

"That's a shame," he said as he walked over and sat on the stool next to her.

Debra turned around on her stool and talked with Randall in private.

"What about you, Cynthia?" James asked. "Where is your husband?" he asked, while looking down at her engagement ring.

"I'm not married. Not yet, anyway," she said sounding dull.

"Congratulations! When is the big day?"

"We haven't set an exact date yet."

"Well, I wish you all the best," he said while looking deep into her eyes. "Marriage can be a wonderful thing...with the right man."

"What about you, James, are you married?"

"Yes, I am."

That response made Cynthia's heart skip. Although she was engaged, she enjoyed the idea of him being available.

"So, how long have you and your wife been together?"

"I'm not married to a woman, I'm married to the Lord." He reached inside his pocket and pulled out a business card.

"Reverend James Young, marriage and substance abuse counselor, Atlanta, Georgia," Cynthia read off the card. "That's where I live."

"I know," James said while stroking his beard. "I watch you on the five o'clock news every night. You're very talented."

"Thank you, Reverend."

"Do me a favor and call me James. 'Reverend' sounds so formal."

"Okay, James," she said then handed the card back to him.

"No, keep it," He closed her hands around it. "Give me a call if you ever need marital advice. The first appointment is on the house."

"I'm sure I won't be in need of any counseling, but thanks anyway." She tried to pass the card back again.

"Keep it just in case," he said and then stood up from his stool. "You never know when you might need someone to talk to."

He placed twenty dollars on the bar to pay for his drink, then he shook her hand and walked away. Randall said good-bye to Debra and followed behind him.

"Girl, I've got his room number!" Debra said while waving the napkin he wrote on.

"He's sanctified," Cynthia said, staring at James's card.

"So what! He has needs just like any other man."

"Well, I don't know about you but I don't do church men." Cynthia took a long sip of her drink. "Besides, I'm happily engaged."

"I guess that's why you just slipped his card inside your purse. You ain't slick!"

"I was just saving it for a friend."

"Friend, my ass!" Debra replied. "Girl, take my advice, don't even think about getting married. You still have HP!"

"What's HP?"

"Ho Potential!"

CHAPTER 11

Malcolm was lying in the guest bedroom at Simon's house tossing and turning. He was dreaming about his father being shot by the next-door neighbor's husband. Ever since Simon mentioned the incident over lunch earlier that day, he couldn't block the vivid images of his father being murdered. He imagined the expression on his father's face just before the bullet penetrated his skull. In his dream, Malcolm saw his father reaching for his pants while begging for his life. The wife took the first two bullets, then the husband walked up slowly to Malcolm's father, and said, "Before I blow your fuckin' brains out, I want you to ask yourself, was it worth it!" Bang! The sound of the gunshot exploded in his mind and woke him up. "Dad!" he yelled.

Once he collected himself, he walked into the bathroom. He leaned over the sink and then splashed cold water on his face. "Pull it together, Malcolm! Don't let this get to you...not again!" He wiped off his face with a towel and popped a couple of aspirin in his mouth. After he slipped on his pants and shoes, he walked towards Simon's bedroom. "Yo, Simon!" he yelled, expecting to find him sleeping, but his bed was empty. There was a letter sitting on his nightstand next to an 8x10 photo of Simon and Cynthia wearing pointy hats at a New Year's Eve party. Malcolm picked it up and stared at it with a frown on his face. "Uggghh!" he said with disgust. "What in the hell does he see in this woman? I know it's not good to hate, but I really do hate you!" he said looking at Cynthia's fake smile.

Malcolm picked up the envelope, which had his name on it, written in bold black letters with a marker. "Damn, I guess he wanted to make sure I saw it!" he laughed.

Malcolm,

I had to leave early to handle some business at the club. If you're hungry, there's leftover curry chicken and rice in the fridge. The bar is stocked with beer, wine, and your favorite Vodka. Try not to get too drunk before I see you. Lol

By the way, I need you at the club before ten o'clock tonight. I want to show you around before the crowd gets too thick. If you need to reach me, my new office number is on the back of this letter along with the directions, just in case you forgot how to get there. See you there!

Your Homie,
Simon

"You sly old fox," he said with a wide grin. "What are you up to?" Malcolm went to the bar and pulled out the bottle of

Stoli and mixed it in with cranberry juice. "Ahhh," he sighed as he took a long sip. He walked over to the stereo system and sat down on the floor to look through Simon's old album collection. He had some real classics like, "Love Rollercoaster" by Ohio Players, and "Footsteps" by the Isley Brothers. Finally, Malcolm ran across the perfect song for the occasion, "Trouble Man," by Marvin Gaye.

He pushed the power button to the five-hundred-watt digital Denon receiver and turned the speakers toward the bathroom. He carefully brushed the dust off the needle and laid the record down gently on the turntable. When the song began to play, he turned the knob on the volume until the walls vibrated. "The neighbors can go to hell," he said. "It's Saturday night!" When Marvin began singing, Malcolm picked up his hairbrush and pretended like it was a microphone.

I come up hard, baby, but now I'm cool
I didn't make it sugar, playin' by the rules
I come up hard, baby, but now I'm fine
I'm checkin' trouble sugar, movin' down the line

That was the only part of the song he knew by heart and he sang the shit out of it. While the rest of the album played, he took a shower then slipped into his Versace suit. He sprayed his neck and hands with cologne and snapped his watch onto his wrist. By nine o'clock he was dressed to kill.

On his way out, he stopped in front of the mirror in the hallway to check himself one last time. "I'm a trouble man, baby, don't get in my way," he sang as he licked his fingers and ran them over his goatee in the hallway mirror. Then he strutted out the door, ready to raise hell.

It was just after 9:30 when Malcolm arrived at the club. A dark blue van with 107.5/97.5 colorfully painted on the sides was parked out front. Two men were passing out T-shirts and CDs, mostly to women wearing short, tight skirts. A gold awning with the name Club Obsession, emblazoned in bold black letters, covered the entrance to the club.

"Good evening, sir," the valet said while cordially opening his door.

"How much do I owe you?"

"It's on the house, Mr. Tremell."

"How do you know who I am?"

"Mr. Harris said you would be arriving in a Black Lincoln Town Car. He's expecting you," he said with a noticeable grin.

"Thank you," he told him and slipped him a twenty-dollar bill.

Malcolm walked through the double glass doors that led into a lavish foyer. Two burly security guards directed him over to a small booth where the receptionist was collecting money.

"Excuse me, I'm looking for Mr. Harris."

"He's busy right now, can I take your name?" she asked politely.

"Malcolm Tremell."

"I'm sorry, Mr. Tremell, I didn't know it was you," she said excitedly. "Mr. Harris is waiting for you upstairs in the Jazz Room."

"Where is that exactly?"

"Just go inside and you'll see the stairs to your right. The Jazz Room is on the second floor."

When he walked inside the Jazz club, he was impressed by how classy the place was laid out. The room was filled with round tables covered with white cloths. The bar was circular with a brass footrest and high-back leather stools. And on the back wall across from the deejay's booth was a built-in aquarium. It was twenty feet long and had an assortment of tropical fish swimming about.

As he made his way up the winding staircase, he noticed a dim light coming from the Jazz Room. When he got to the door, it suddenly went out. Malcolm put his ear to the door but there was no sound. "Simon, you in there?" he yelled. He pushed the door open slowly and entered the dark room. Suddenly the lights flashed on and the room erupted with cheers.

"Surprise!" a crowd of people yelled. Over 200 people were clapping and screaming.

Simon was standing on the stage with a microphone leading the crowd in song. "Happy birthday to you. Happy birthday to you. Happy birthday, dear Malcolm. Happy birthday to you."

"Now, this is awkward!" Malcolm said under his breath.

And to make matters worse, Antoinette was in the corner singing right along. They made eye contact briefly before Simon called Malcolm to join him onstage.

"Malcolm, over the years, we've gone through many wars together. Sometimes we agreed to disagree; other times we fought like hell. But in the end, we always remained best friends," he said with his hand on Malcolm's shoulder. "As a token of my friendship, I want to present you with a special gift."

Simon signaled one of his employees to draw the long velvet stage curtain. As it slowly drew back, Malcolm felt like a contestant on "The Price Is Right." When the gift was revealed, Malcolm gasped.

"Is this what I think it is?" he asked nervously.

"I don't know what you're talking about," Simon said, trying not to grin.

Malcolm walked up slowly to the polished black Steinway

piano. When he saw the initials M.T. engraved on the face, he knew it was the same piano his father had given him on his eighteenth birthday.

"I thought it was destroyed in the fire," he said while gently running his finger across the keys.

"It was burned pretty bad, but I had it restored."

"I don't know what to say."

"Don't say anything, just play something."

"What do you want to hear?" Malcolm asked, still trying to stay composed.

"It's your night, partner, you decide."

The house band joined him onstage and took their places next to their instruments. Malcolm used to play with them back at Simon's old club, The Oasis, before it burned down. There were four members: Big Johnny on the upright bass, Jimmy on guitar, Ricky on saxophone, and the vocalist Francine. But Malcolm called her Billie because she sang like Billie Holiday. They exchanged emotional hugs and then prepared to turn the joint out.

While the band warmed up, the crowd took their seats and began ordering drinks. Simon escorted Toni to the front table where he had a bottle of champagne chilling in a bucket of ice. The strapless white cocktail dress she wore draped perfectly over her shapely frame. Her hair was pulled back in a tight bun, which showed off her long neck and soft shoulders. As Malcolm looked into her brown eyes, she seemed even more beautiful than she did the night before. Now he was the one on stage and she was a part of his audience.

When the band was warmed up, Simon signaled for the engineer to dim the floor lights. The audience suddenly faded behind the bright glare of the stage lamps. "I want to dedicate this piece to a beautiful and gifted woman whose passion and talent are limitless," he said while looking at Toni, "and the man who changed my life by introducing me to music. This one is for you, Dad." The song he chose was a jazz version of "If I Ain't Got You," by Alicia Keys.

As he pressed down on the familiar ivory keys, Billie stepped into the spotlight wearing a fitted red-sequined dress and matching pumps. She gently stroked the microphone in a circular motion as if making love to it. The crowd applauded wildly as her soft, smooth voice filled the room. "Sing that song, baby!" one man yelled. It had been months since Malcolm had performed in front of an audience and he was a little nervous. He took a deep breath to settle down. When it was time for his solo, he pretended like his father was in the audience. His father had always brought out the best in him.

The room was quiet except for the sound of his piano keys striking their chords. Malcolm closed his eyes and allowed the spirit to move him. He wanted to play it perfectly, just in case his father was listening. As his fingers glided across the keys, he felt the emotions building up inside of him. There was too much pain and unresolved issues. He missed his best friend and his inspiration. Even after twelve years, he hadn't forgiven his father for dying.

He poured his innermost feelings out in front of a room full of perfect strangers, not giving a damn if they appreciated it or not. He played that solo piece like never before. His eyes watered as he pressed down on the keys with the final note. The audience erupted with applause. "Encore! Encore!" Even the band members were clapping. Malcolm stood up and took a bow. "Thank you," he said while inconspicuously wiping his eyes. "Thank you very much."

He exited the stage and went over to the table where Simon and Toni were seated.

"That was incredible!" Toni said and then gave him a firm hug. "I've never seen anyone play with such passion."

"I was just trying to impress you."

"Mission accomplished!" she said still holding on to him. "You were great!"

"All right, that's enough with the compliments. His head is big enough as it is," Simon said while aiming his camera. "Now put your arms around that fine woman and say 'cheese.'"

"Speaking of big heads, whose bright idea was it to invite Toni?" Malcolm asked.

"It was mine," Ariel said, coming out of nowhere. "I told her about the party when she called for directions."

"And who might you be?" Malcolm was still trying to adjust his eyes from the flash.

"Allow me to make the formal introductions," Simon said cutting in. "Malcolm Tremell, this is my new manager, Ariel Daniels."

"So, this is Ariel?" Malcolm looked her up and down. "Simon didn't tell me you were so lovely."

"And he didn't tell me you were so handsome and talented."

Ahem. Toni cleared her throat.

"I'm sorry, I hope I didn't step on any toes," Ariel apologized.

"No, it's not that," Toni said, reaching for her purse. "I just wanted to say good-bye. I've got to be leaving."

"Could you excuse us for a moment?" Malcolm said to Simon and Ariel.

"No problem!" Simon said. "It was a pleasure meeting you, Toni. Hope to see you again."

"I'm sure you will." She smiled, then gave him a hug. "Thanks for the hospitality."

Once they were alone, Malcolm sat down with her at the table and poured them both a glass of champagne. "The least you could do is join me for a birthday toast."

"Okay, just one drink then I have to be going."

"What's the hurry? The night is still young."

"I would love to stay but I've got to get up first thing in the morning to drop a friend off at the airport."

"So, am I going to see you again? I still owe you that rose, you know?"

"Tell you what—" She pulled out a business card and handed it to him. "If you take me out to brunch next week, we'll call it even. That is, if you're still in Atlanta."

"I'll be here all right," Malcolm said as they tapped glasses. "Here's to friendship."

They sat and talked for a few minutes and then she left. Once she was out of sight, Ariel came over to the table with another bottle of champagne.

"You mind if I join you?" she asked.

"Be my guest."

"I hope I didn't get you into trouble," she said.

"It's not that serious. Toni and I are just friends," he said unconvincingly. "As a matter of fact, she's engaged."

"Engaged?" she said looking puzzled. "That's strange. She was the first one here for your party, and—" She stopped abruptly.

"And, what?"

"Look, Malcolm, I don't know you well enough to get into your business, so I think I'll just keep my big mouth shut."

"It's too late for that now, spit it out!"

"Look, Malcolm, a woman who is in a good relationship wouldn't be hanging out at the club at eleven o'clock at night with a man she just met the night before."

"How did you know that?"

"We had plenty of time to talk before you arrived. Like I told you, she was the first one here."

"That doesn't mean anything. Maybe she was already in the area."

"Okay, then explain to me why she wasn't wearing a ring," she said with an attitude. "If I had an engagement ring, I would be sporting that bad boy for the whole world to see!"

"Maybe she just forgot to put it on. She is a dancer, you know."

"Yeah right or maybe she took it off to change a flat tire. Give me a break!" She stood up from the table. "When a woman is excited about getting married...she represents! Just think about it, Malcolm, she's reaching out in her own way!"

She took one last sip of her drink and walked away. Malcolm knew Ariel was right. Toni wasn't happy and she damn sure wasn't in love. At least not in the way a woman should be before she gets married. He was just trying to be a gentleman. His job was to temporarily fulfill women's needs and keep it moving, not to become an emotionally attached home wrecker. But this was different; he and Toni had a connection, and above all else, he was curious.

Malcolm figured her fiancé was just another rich asshole that got comfortable once he put that ring on her finger. Men do it all the time, he was thinking. They stop dating, stop complimenting, and they stop fucking. That's the reason why I get paid the big bucks, to do what another man won't do or can't do.

Whatever the reason, Malcolm wasn't sympathetic. Toni's fiancé had something he wanted and it was every man for himself. He decided the best approach was to stay friends, stay available, and wait for the fiancé to slip up. Men always do!

CHAPTER 12

ⅲ MAINTENANCE MAN

"Damn, it's hot!" Ariel said as she stepped outside barefoot to get her Sunday morning paper. "No wonder they call it Hotlanta," she said while hopping from one foot to the other. She rushed back into her living room to finish chatting with her friends on Facebook. She was chatting, tweeting, and shopping on Amazon.com all at the same time. She belonged to a book club and was looking for a new title to suggest for their meeting in August. Lately, they had begun reading books by male authors like Eric Jerome Dickey and E. Lynn Harris. She almost choked on her food when she ran across a novel called *Men Cry in the Dark*. "They should cry in the fuckin' light with all the hell they put us through," she yelled at the computer.

Just as she was sending the link to the book to her friends on Facebook, the phone rang. She looked at the caller ID to see who it was.

"Oh, no, I'm not in the mood today," she said as she picked up the phone. "Hello, Mother."

"How did you know it was me?"

"It's called caller ID, Mom. Get rid of that old rotary phone and come out of the Stone Age."

"I just called to see how my baby girl is doing. I hope I'm not interrupting anything."

"Anything like what?" Ariel asked. "It's eleven o'clock in the morning."

"I thought you might have company."

"Mama, please don't start preaching to me about finding a husband. I keep telling you, I'm not ready to share my space. And besides, these immature men can't handle a strong woman."

"That's exactly your problem; you need to stop being so damned strong!"

"What's that supposed to mean?"

"It means that your older sisters have good jobs and college degrees. And they've been married twice."

"Joyce and Sheila are just settling," Ariel said with an attitude. "I'm not going to spend the rest of my life with some overweight postal employee or an underpaid elementary school teacher. I need someone who challenges me."

"Ariel, you know I love you with all my heart, and I'm proud of you for accomplishing so much on your own, but, baby, you ain't all that!"

"Excuse me?"

"You heard what I said. Stop holding yourself up as if you're better than everybody else," she told her. "You're from the streets like all these other uppity Negroes. And I should know, I raised your nappy-headed behind."

"I don't think I'm better than other people. I just want someone who accepts me for who I am," Ariel said trying not to get upset. "Why should I have to act like an airhead just to make a man feel secure?"

"Sweetheart, I'm not asking you to play dumb, but you've got to learn how to relax and let the man lead. Or at least let him think he's leading," she said. "Men have to feel a sense of power. They have to feel needed."

Ariel got up from the sofa and walked over to the fireplace where her college degrees and certificates were on display. "Why do women always have to be the one in the relationship to submit, even when they have more education?" she asked emotionally. "It's just not fair, Mama!"

"Baby, listen to what I'm about to say, and don't ever forget it. When you find a God-fearing man who is worthy, you won't even see it as submission," she said in a motherly tone. "It will happen naturally."

"Thanks for the pep talk, Mom, but I'm going to do things my way…and on my terms. If these weak men can't keep up, it's their loss. Goodbye, Mama!" she said angrily and slammed the phone down.

When she got back to her computer to finish sending out the link to her Twitter and Facebook friends, she noticed a party posted in a group she created called, Professional Men and Women of Atlanta. It read:

Are you sick and tired of meeting men who are either broke, uneducated, or on the down low? Well, join us tonight at Justin's Lounge from 7-10:00 P.M. for drinks, great conversation, and speed dating. Please RSVP if you plan to attend.

Jeff

"Now, this sounds like my kind of crowd," she said while quickly sending an RSVP back to Jeff. Afterwards, she began tweeting and copying the link of the invitation to her friends on Facebook. Before she could press share, Jeff texted back.

Hey, you! Looking forward to seeing you tonight!

Jeff

So, she texted him back.

I'm excited; I already copied all my friends on it! Great idea you came up with!

Ariel

I've been an admirer of yours for a while, why don't we hook up when we get there?

Jeff

Ariel went straight to his profile to see what he looked like. And just as she figured, he didn't have a photo, just a large banner of a Los Angeles Lakers Jersey. She wanted to amuse herself, so she texted back.

So, Jeff, what do you look like? So I'll recognize you when I see you.

Ariel

There was a pause, then a couple of minutes later, a reply.

I'm about six-three, 200 pounds, and muscular. Women tell me I'm a cross between Denzel Washington and Wesley Snipes. Also, I own a landscaping company. And yes, I'm straight and single. Lol

Jeff

"Yeah, right!" she laughed as she wrote back. If this fool was all that he wouldn't be single! But she had already decided to go, and having someone to meet there would make it less awkward, so she played along.

Okay, Jeff, I'll meet you there between 7-7:30 P.M.

Ariel

She shut her laptop and immediately started looking through her closet for something to wear. "I swear, if this date doesn't work out, I'm going to buy an economy pack of double A batteries and practice being submissive to my vibrator," she laughed.

• • •

It was 7:30 P.M. when Ariel arrived at Justin's. She left her car with the valet and went inside to look for Jeff. She was hoping he was at least being honest about owning a landscaping business. With all the single women buying homes in Atlanta, she figured he was making a killing, especially if he looked like Denzel.

When she didn't spot anyone who fit his description, she reserved a table with the host and went to the bar to get a drink.

"What can I get you?" the bartender asked.

"Mojito, and make it strong!"

"Coming right up."

While Ariel waited for her drink, the men at the bar began raping her with their eyes. Even the ones who had dates sitting right next to them were giving her flirtatious smiles. Like any other woman, Ariel loved attention, but her baby face and large breasts always seemed to attract knuckleheads, mostly the ones under 30. It wasn't long before one of them made his move.

"Excuse me, is anyone sitting here?" a short man wearing a loud red jacket asked. He looked like a Puerto Rican, but he moved and talked like a brother.

101

"No, but I am waiting for someone," Ariel said.

"I'll be happy to leave when he arrives," he said politely as he sat down. "My name is Chris, what's yours?"

"I'm Ariel. Nice to meet you, Chris." She extended her hand.

Ariel was surprised by how comfortable she was with him. She preferred to be left alone, especially when she was waiting for a date. But Chris had one of those bubbly personalities that made her feel relaxed. It didn't hurt that he was cute and smelled good. Ariel loved men who wore nice cologne.

"So what brings you out on a Sunday night, Chris?"

"I got the invite on my Facebook page, and since I was dropping my daughter off down the street from here, I decided to stop in for a bite before heading home."

"How old is your daughter?"

"She's seven," he said while reaching for his wallet. "This is a picture of her when she was six."

"Aw, look at her. She's a real cutie."

"Yeah, that's my little princess. I don't know what I would do without her."

"It's always nice to see men taking care of their kids."

"For me, it wasn't even an option," he said passionately. "When her mother and I divorced, I made a commitment to be there for her, no matter what."

"I'm sorry it didn't work out," Ariel said compassionately. "You think you'll ever get back together?"

"Excuse my French, but hell naw! That woman drove me crazy. Every time I turned around she was spending money, mine and hers," he laughed. "Worst of all, she couldn't cook worth shit! Her idea of cooking from scratch was Hamburger Helper, and she burned that half the time."

"I'm glad to see you have such a positive attitude. Most men would be carrying around a lot of emotional baggage."

"The way I look at it, she did me a favor. I have a renewed appreciation for being single," he told her. "Now, that's enough about me, what's your story."

"Well, I'm single, no kids, no debt, and I just received my master's degree in business management."

"Don't tell me you're one of those strong, independent black women who doesn't need a man?"

"For your information, Mr. Know-It-All, I'm here on a date tonight," Ariel said with her face frowned up.

"So, where is he?"

"That's a good question," Ariel replied while looking down at her watch. It read 7:45 P.M.

Jeff was supposed to meet her between 7-7:30. With the exception of bad hygiene, promptness was her biggest pet peeve. After waiting another fifteen minutes, Ariel wrote him off. When her table reservation was called, she invited Chris to join her for dinner, her treat. Although she wasn't attracted to him in a sexual way, she enjoyed his conversation.

By 9:00 P.M. Ariel and Chris were carrying on like old friends. She was surprised by how much they had in common. They had both graduated from Howard University. And they both grew up in Cleveland. Chris had her cracking up when he talked about basement parties and blue-light posters back in the '70s. She almost peed on herself when he reminded her of the zodiac poster with the different sex positions. "I almost killed myself trying to imitate that Scorpio position," he joked. They even ordered the same dish off the menu, catfish and grits.

The evening was going perfectly until Ariel noticed a man glancing around the room as if he were looking for someone. She had a strange feeling it was Jeff. He was six-three, 230 pounds, but she didn't see any muscles. His stomach was protruding out of his slacks and his hairline was receding.

"Oh, shit!" Ariel said sounding distressed. "It's him!"

"Who is he?" Chris asked.

"My blind date."

"You mean the fat, baldheaded guy in the tight suit?" Chris said, looking over his shoulder trying not to laugh.

"Yeah, that's the one. Stop looking, maybe he won't notice me."

When the hostess pointed in her direction, she was sure it was Jeff. Luckily, the picture she had posted on her page was old, her hair was cut short and she had just come back from Jamaica so her skin was really dark.

"Oh, my God, here he comes," Ariel whispered while shielding her face.

Jeff approached the table apprehensively. First he stood there like an idiot trying to figure out what to say. Chris and Ariel ignored him and went on with their conversation. Finally, he worked up the courage to speak.

"Ah, excuse me, is your name Ariel?"

"Naw, my name is Aquanita," Ariel said, sounding ghetto. "And this is my man, Rico."

Chris had to cover his mouth to keep from spitting his food out. Ariel reached over to pat him on the back.

"You all right, baby?"

"Yeah...Aquanita, I'm fine," Chris said as he wiped the tears from his eyes with his napkin.

"You're sure your name isn't Ariel?" Jeff asked again. "You look an awful lot like her."

"Look, I know what my name is!" Ariel said getting loud. "Don't make me call secuur-rity!"

"I'm sorry to have disturbed you." Jeff backed away. "Have a nice evening."

Chris was still wiping his face when Jeff walked away, then he eventually left the restaurant.

"Now that's what I call an Oscar-winning performance!" he said while still laughing. "Two thumbs up!"

"What can I say? I'm a woman of many talents."

"You don't seem to have any talent when it comes to dating. Where did you meet that loser?"

"I told you it was a blind date. How was I supposed to know he was lying about his looks? When he messaged me on Facebook, he said he was a cross between Denzel Washington and Wesley Snipes."

"He looked more like a cross between Fat Albert and Cee Lo, if you ask me," Chris joked.

"Very funny. Now stop talking for a minute so I can give you something," Ariel leaned over and kissed him on the cheek.

"What was that for?"

"For rescuing me and for being so much fun to hang out with. I really enjoyed your company."

"Does that mean I'll be seeing you again?"

"Please don't take this the wrong way, Chris, but you're not exactly my type," Ariel said reluctantly. "But I would like to stay in touch."

"That's fine with me," he said as he pulled out his business card. "Give me a call when you get some free time. Maybe we can get together and rent a video. I'll even bring the popcorn."

"Don't be surprised if I take you up on that offer," Ariel said. "With all the bad luck I'm having with men, it's probably the best offer I'll get all year. No offense."

"None taken."

PART III

WOMANOLOGY

CHAPTER 13

Monday afternoon Teddy arrived at the Foxy nightclub to pick up his paycheck. The club was a hole in the wall, but it was one the most profitable strip joints in Atlanta thanks to Teddy. His dance group Hot Chocolate performed there weekly to standing-room-only crowds. When he walked inside the double-glass doors, the club manager, Claudia, was standing behind the bar doing inventory. Teddy knelt down before she could see him and crept up on her.

"Boo!" he shouted as he sprung up.

"Oh, my goodness," she said as she spun around grabbing her chest. "Teddy, you scared the shit out of me! You should know better than to frighten a woman my age. I could've had a heart attack!"

Claudia reached over the bar and gave Teddy a hug. She was a burly 45-year-old black woman, standing six feet. Her hair was dyed blonde and she walked with a slight limp.

"Stop whining, you old lesbian, and give me my money," Teddy said, laughing.

"I may be a lesbian, but at least I'm a good one," she told him.

"Yeah, so I've heard. That's why I don't bring my women around here. You might turn them out."

"You know what they say, a hole will outlast a pole anytime."

"That depends on the pole," Teddy said holding his crotch. "I've been known to transform lesbians with one stroke."

"You're an arrogant little so-and-so, aren't you?" she said while handing him his check. "If I mixed business with pleasure, I would try you."

"You can't handle this sweet young meat. I'd have your old ass walking around like *Dawn of the Dead*."

"That's exactly your problem; these naive little girls are giving you a big head. One day you're going to run into a mature woman and she's gonna put a mojo on you."

"The woman that I'm shacking with is forty-five and a successful attorney. But I've got her educated ass sprung so bad that if I told her the sky was green, she'd believe it," he boasted. "Just last week she confronted me about a pair of panties she found in her drawer. By the end of the night she was giving me a bath and a blowjob. So, who's putting the mojo on whom?"

"That's why so many women are walking around so angry!" she said getting irritated. "All men do is use women up and throw them away like garbage."

"Don't get mad at me! She knew what she was getting into," he said adamantly. "What the hell did she expect from a thirty-year-old stripper? When we met, I didn't have an apartment or a car, and I was dating three other women. It's not my fault if she wants to play Mother Teresa and try to reform me."

"That doesn't mean you have to take advantage of her."

"Any woman who is stupid enough to give a perfect stranger

credit cards and keys to her house deserves to be played," he told her. "I'm going to ride this horse until it goes lame or until a better one comes along."

"You mean a richer one, don't you?" Claudia asked.

"Whatever!" He turned and began walking towards the restroom. "Now if you will excuse me, I'm going to use the little boys' room."

Suddenly there was a loud knock on the glass door. Claudia pulled back the curtains and noticed a sheriff's vehicle parked out front. "Come in, it's open!" she yelled.

"Good afternoon, ma'am. I'm looking for Mr. Theodore Simmons," he said. "Is he employed here?"

"Yes, he is, officer. Is he in some kind of trouble?" she asked, sounding concerned.

"That's for the judge to decide." He handed Claudia a clipboard with a pen and white envelope attached to it. "I need you to sign here."

"What's this?"

"It's a summons for him to appear in family court."

Claudia signed on the dotted line and handed him back his pen. "Is there anything you want me to tell him?" she asked.

"You can tell him that if he doesn't show up, I'll be back with a warrant and handcuffs. Have a good day, ma'am." He tipped his cap and walked out.

Right after he drove off, Teddy came out of the bathroom and sat down at the bar. He buried his face in his hands for a moment then burst out laughing.

"What's so funny?" Claudia asked. "Didn't you hear what the officer said?"

"I heard him," he said calmly. "Excuse me for a second, I need to make a call."

Teddy scrolled through his numbers until he found the listing for Club Obsession. After dialing the number, he took a deep breath and cleared his throat.

"Hello, this is Teddy Simmons, may I please speak to Mr. Harris?"

While he waited to be connected, he whistled like he didn't have a care in the world. Claudia watched him, totally perplexed by his attitude.

"Hello, Mr. Harris. How are you? I just called to let you know I'm interested in that gig on Thursday nights," he said cheerfully. "I just have one condition; I need to be paid in cash. Is that a problem?"

He paused for a second while Simon answered. "You've got yourself a deal! Me and the fellas will see you Thursday. Nice doing business with you." Then he hung up.

"I can't believe you're so calm considering what just happened."

"I knew it was coming," he said casually. "The woman has been trying to track me down for months trying to tell me I had a baby to support."

"Why didn't you get a blood test to see if the baby was yours?"

"I already did, and it's mine. I have a son."

"So why are you being served with papers?"

"Because I told that bitch she wasn't getting a single, solitary dime of my money, that's why!"

"That's not right, Teddy," she said. "No matter what you think or feel about the woman, your child shouldn't have to suffer."

"Look, I never asked for this baby," he said, agitated. "Hell, I hardly even know that heifer. I met her last year after I stripped at her bachelorette party."

"You mean she's married!"

"No, she *was* married. That love affair was over nine months after the honeymoon. I wish I could have seen the look on her husband's face when his son came out brown, not white," he laughed.

"Get the hell out of here, you no-good bastard!" Claudia yelled. "I don't want your kind around here. I don't give a damn how much money you bring in!"

"I was tired of this rundown dump anyway," he said arrogantly as he walked backward toward the door. "Besides, I got a better offer."

"You need to grow up and stop running away from responsibility."

"Fuck you, Claudia, you pussy-eating dyke."

"I may be a dyke, but at least I'm not a deadbeat parent." She tossed the summons at him. "One day all the pain you cause is going to come back on you. Karma is a bitch."

CHAPTER 14

M alcolm was pacing back and forth and looking down at his watch. It read 6:30 P.M.

"Where is that knucklehead?" he said while staring out the living room window. "I'm going to kill him if I miss this flight."

After waiting another two minutes, he dialed the number to Yellow Taxi. "To hell with this!"

"Hello, Yellow Taxi," the dispatcher answered.

"Yes, I need a pick up from—," he paused when he heard the sound of Simon's car pulling into the driveway. "Never mind!"

"Let's go!" Simon yelled as he blew the horn. Malcolm rushed out the door and threw his bags into the back seat of the White Range Rover.

"Where have you been?" he asked while strapping on his seat belt. "My flight is at 7:30."

"I had a few things to straighten out at the club," he said, burning rubber into traffic. "But don't worry, I'll get you there in plenty of time."

"You'd better!" Malcolm said. "If I miss that flight, I'm going to keep your ass up all night complaining."

"In that case, hold on. I know a shortcut."

Simon slid on his shades and stepped on the gas, sending Malcolm slamming back into the headrest. He swerved in and out of traffic like a mad man, with Malcolm holding onto the dashboard. Once they reached I-85, Simon merged into the HOV lane trying to make up time. People were blowing their horns and cursing them out. "Watch where you're going, you dumb son-of-a-bitch!" an old woman yelled as she gave them the finger. Malcolm was laughing so hard tears were running down his face. Once they reached the I-20 merge, traffic began to lighten up.

"Now, that's what I call driving," Malcolm said, slapping Simon five.

"Man, that was a piece of cake compared to rush hour on the Dan Ryan in Chicago."

"A piece of cake? You damn near got us killed," he laughed. "What's gotten into you?"

"I'm having one of those exceptional days where everything is going right," Simon said with a wide grin. "The revenue from the club is up; Ariel is working out perfectly as manager, and I just booked this stripper named Teddy Bear for Ladies' Night, every Thursday. Too bad you can't stick around to see him perform."

"Why would I want to watch some guy swinging his dick in front of a room full of sexually deprived women?"

"This guy has talent; he put on one hell of a show last week. I've never seen professional women act so rowdy!"

"Well, you can tell Teddy Bear, Yogi Bear, or whatever the hell his name is, that I said good luck," Malcolm joked. "I've got my own hustle to deal with."

"Speaking of your hustle, does Toni know what you do for a living?"

"No, she doesn't. And she never will, not if I can help it."

"That's like trying to keep it a secret that the pope is Catholic," Simon said.

"What's your point?"

"My point is, there must be at least twenty women in Atlanta that you've escorted professionally—or fucked casually. It's only a matter of time before your name comes up. This town is not as big as people think!"

"Toni is new to Atlanta. And I doubt that she's the type to listen to gossip."

"Yeah, right! I haven't met a female yet that didn't listen to a rumor or two," Simon said wisely. "They can't help it. They're nosey by nature."

"I probably won't have to worry about her finding out anyway," Malcolm told him. "I left her a message yesterday and today and she never returned my calls."

"Maybe she had an emergency. You never know. Why don't you give her another call, just in case." He tried to hand Malcolm his cell phone.

"Are you crazy? Didn't you hear me say I already left two messages."

"And?"

"Rule number one in the Player's Handbook, never ever call a woman more than twice," Malcolm said while holding up two fingers. "If she doesn't return your call after two messages, she's not interested."

"Fine, have it your way, I just hope your stubbornness doesn't backfire on you."

By the time they arrived at the airport, it was ten after seven. Simon pulled up to the American Airlines curbside check-in and unlocked the doors.

"Thanks for making the trip to see me, partner," Simon said

as he walked over and gave Malcolm a brotherly hug.

"I'm the one who should be thanking you; that piano was the best gift I've ever had," he told him. "Just make sure it doesn't get burned up before I can have it shipped to Miami."

"Don't worry, I'll keep a fire extinguisher right next to it this time," Simon said while getting back into the truck. "And by the way, I'll be sure to tell my fiancée you said hello."

"Oh, I almost forgot about the love of your life," Malcolm said sarcastically. "Isn't she supposed to be back from New Orleans today?"

"Yeah, but she called me this afternoon and said she was staying an extra night. I told her I didn't have a problem with that."

"Do you honestly think she would have come home even if you did have a problem with it?"

"Of course," Simon said confidently. "Cynthia would never do anything to disrespect me."

"That's rule number two in the Player's Handbook," Malcolm said as walked backwards into the automatic terminal doors.

"What's that?" he yelled.

"Never say never!"

CHAPTER 15

ᴛʜᴇ MAINTENANCE MAN

I t was half past midnight. The dimly lit tavern on Bourbon Street was still overflowing with intoxicated tourists. Cynthia and Debra blended in perfectly as they sipped on Coronas and turned over shots of Patron. "Happy Fourth of July!" they yelled. Technically it was July third, but that was close enough.

"Girl, I'm drunk as hell," Debra said while checking herself in the dingy mirror behind the bar. "I hope we don't get pulled over for WWI."

"What the hell is WWI?"

"Walking while intoxicated," Debra joked.

They burst out laughing and tried to give high fives, missing each other's hands twice before finally connecting. The white patrons sitting next to them moved down a stool. Cynthia and Debra thought it was funny. They laughed in their faces and kept on clowning.

"It must be my perfume," Cynthia laughed.

"Excuse me, ladies," the bartender said, "could you please keep it down?"

"I didn't come all the way to New Orleans to keep it down," Debra replied. "And besides, I don't see you asking those rowdy white boys at the end of the bar to keep it down and they're twice as loud as us!"

"Look, Miss, I don't want any trouble." He tried to sound more cordial. "I'm just trying to do my job."

"Well, do your job and get the hell out of my face before I have a Rodney King flashback!"

"Calm down, Deb, it's not worth it," Cynthia said.

"Fuck that!" Debra said getting louder. "I paid my money just like everybody else."

The bouncer, who was six-five and as wide as a refrigerator, came over and stood behind Debra, trying to be intimidating. He had a baby face and wore an old Texas Rangers baseball cap and a dingy white T-shirt that read Cowboys Do It Best.

"Is there a problem?" he asked in a strong Southern accent.

"You're damn right there's a problem," Debra stretched her neck to look him in the eye. "You're in my space."

"I'm going to have to ask you ladies to pay for your drinks and leave."

"On what grounds?" Cynthia asked.

"I don't have to give you black bitches any explanation. Now get out, before I throw you out!"

"No, you didn't call me a bitch, you redneck motherfucker." Debra swung her glass of beer with all her might, barely missing his face.

The customers sitting at the bar quickly ran for cover as beer went flying everywhere. The bouncer grabbed her by the arm and picked her up like a rag doll. He put her in a bear hug and began carrying her toward the door.

"Let her go!" Cynthia yelled as she pounded on his back with her tiny fists.

"You want some, too?" he asked as he turned toward her with his fist balled.

"I wouldn't do that if I were you," a deep voice said out of nowhere.

It was the Reverends James and Randall, the two men they had met at the Marriott.

"Mind your own business, nigger!" the bouncer said.

"If I weren't a man of God, I would make you sorry for using that word. But since I am, I'm going to ask you again to put that woman down, and I'm not going to ask you a second time!"

"And if I don't, then what?"

"Let's just say, I'll be praying for forgiveness tomorrow," he said.

Although the tavern was more than ninety percent white, the other patrons wanted no part of this standoff. Some were afraid but most felt the bouncer was out of line. It didn't take him long to realize that if he took it any further, he was on his own.

"You're lucky I'm in a good mood tonight," the bouncer said as he let go of Debra.

Debra straightened her clothes and gave him the finger.

"You're not so cocky now, are you, Baby Huey?" she said while picking up her purse off the floor.

"Just get the hell out before I call the police."

Cynthia walked over to the bar and sipped down the last of her beer. Then she slammed down a twenty-dollar bill. "Thanks for the warm Southern hospitality," she said. "Keep the change."

They strutted out of the tavern with their heads held high, feeling like queens who had been rescued by their black kings. The moment they made it outside they laughed and slapped five.

"Girl, that was some shit right out of a Shaft movie," Debra laughed.

"Did you see the look on that white boy's face when he saw

all those brothas," Cynthia added. "I bet he's never been in the same room with that many black folks in his entire life."

James and Randall didn't find it amusing. Neither did the other ministers who walked away shortly after the altercation.

"Now, what was that all about?" James asked urgently.

"We were just having a little fun, that's all," Cynthia said.

"I think that's enough fun for one night," Randall said. "Let's go."

"Where are we going?" Debra asked.

"Back to the hotel, that's where. You two are in no condition to be walking around these streets."

"Okay, I'll go peacefully, Reverend," Debra said as she pressed her large breasts against him. "But first I need to stop at the store for some aspirin."

"Good, now let's go," James said, leading the way.

"Hold up." Debra pulled James in the opposite direction. "It doesn't take four people to buy a bottle of Tylenol. Randall will take care of me. We'll meet you back at the hotel."

"I don't know, Debra," Cynthia said nervously. "Are you sure?"

"Yes, I'm sure!" Debra winked at Cynthia and led Randall away by the hand. "Don't wait up!"

Cynthia was as nervous as a teenager on her first date as she stood alone with James. She tried not to make eye contact with him knowing her eyes would reveal how much she was attracted to him. She tried looking down at his feet but that didn't help. James had on a pair of shorts that showed off his hairy, muscular legs. Cynthia couldn't help getting moist.

"So what do we do now?" she asked timidly.

"We're going home!" James said.

Although Cynthia wasn't expecting anything but an escort to her room, she loved the way home sounded.

● ● ●

Early the next morning, Cynthia awoke to the voice of a radio personality on Q93 FM. He was on the phone with a female caller who admitted to having an affair.

"So why did you cheat on your husband?" he asked.

"He wasn't giving me any attention," she said. "When we first met, he would take me everywhere, to the movies, to dinner, and out dancing. I love to dance. But now he's so preoccupied with running his business that we hardly ever see each other."

"Why not get a divorce instead of cheating?"

"Because I love my husband. And he's a good man. But a woman has needs!" she emphasized. "Every now and then you need a little maintenance."

"I heard that!" Cynthia agreed.

She was tempted to call the radio station to tell her story. She had experienced the same problem with Simon over the years. Although he tried to include her in functions at the club, she felt left out. It was only a matter of time before another man filled the void. As she watched James get dressed, she knew she had gone past the point of no return.

"You okay?" he asked, while pulling on his underwear.

"Sorry. I was just listening to the program. Kind of ironic, isn't it?"

"Yes, it is," he said. "You think God is trying to tell us something?"

"Could be. The Good Book says He works in mysterious ways."

Suddenly the phone rang. James grabbed the rest of his clothes and went into the bathroom to give Cynthia some privacy. She turned down the radio and picked up the receiver.

"Hello?"

"Good morning, sweetheart."

"Oh, good morning, Simon. Where are you?" she asked nervously.

"I'm downstairs in the lobby, I wanted to surprise you!"

"Oh, shit!" She covered the phone with her hand. "I mean, oh really."

"I'm only kidding," he laughed. "I'm at the club. I had to come in and take care of some paperwork. How's everything in New Orleans?"

"It's going great." Cynthia put her hand over her chest, trying to calm herself.

"So what time are you flying in today?"

"Debra booked us on the eleven o'clock."

"Where is old loud mouth Debra, anyway? I'm surprised she's not yapping as usual in the background."

"She's in the bathroom."

At that moment, James decided to take a piss. The sound of him hitting the water echoed through the room.

"What's that noise I hear?" Simon asked.

"What noise?" Cynthia said as she rushed over to close the bathroom door.

"That splashing sound I hear in the background."

"Oh, that's just Debra running bathwater."

Simon paused as if he was trying to decide whether or not to accept that explanation.

"Well, be sure to tell her I said hello. I'll see you in Atlanta at the airport. Have a safe flight, sweetheart. Love you."

"I love you, too. Bye."

Cynthia covered her face with a pillow and screamed. "That was too close." James came out of the bathroom fully clothed with his Bible in hand.

"Was that your fiancé?"

124

"Yes, it was."

"Sorry about that. I guess I wasn't thinking."

"I don't believe either one of us was thinking last night," she said with her hand on her forehead. "This was a big mistake."

"I agree."

"If you thought it was such a big mistake, why did you go through with it in the first place? You're supposed to be able to resist temptation. At least I have an excuse, I was drunk!"

"First of all, I'm imperfect just like any other man. Being involved in the church doesn't magically remove lust from your heart," he said sounding convincing. "And as far as your excuse goes, alcohol only makes you do what you don't have the courage to do when you're sober. So don't try to lay all the responsibility on me."

"You're right. We both should have known better," she said while putting on her robe. "The best thing to do is put this behind us and go on with our lives."

"That's a good idea. And I'll be sure to pray for both of us." He kissed her gently on the forehead and walked toward the door. "By the way, you're still my favorite reporter. See you on TV tomorrow night. I'll never watch the news quite the same." Then he left.

No sooner did the door close behind him than Debra burst into the room with a big smile on her face and singing, "I shot the sheriff!"

Cynthia was staring out the window shaking her head.

"What's wrong with you?" she asked, putting her arms around Cynthia. "I know you got some last night. I can smell sex in the air." Then she sniffed comically.

"I got some all right, and I'm already starting to feel guilty."

"Girl, you need to stop trippin'. Men do this kind of shit all the time and they get married with a clear conscience. Just consider it your last fling, your bachelorette party," Debra said.

"Maybe you're right."

"I know I'm right. Now get dressed so we can get something to eat before we fly out. All those orgasms last night made me hungry."

"I guess I could use a bagel and a glass of orange juice myself," Cynthia said while untangling her hair. "But you know we're going straight to hell for what we did last night."

"Yeah, I know, but at least we'll go on a full stomach."

CHAPTER 16

Ariel was feeling like a million bucks as she drove down Lenox Road listening to "Joy and Pain" by Frankie Beverly and Maze. "Sing that song, Frankie!" she shouted as she snapped her fingers to the music. It was the Fourth of July and the weather was gorgeous. Her hair was freshly cut and she was enjoying her first full day after resigning from Coca-Cola. She was living her dream working as manager of Club Obsession. This was as far from corporate America as she had been and she was determined never to go back. As she looked over at the passenger seat, her old office ID was sticking out of her purse. She quickly let down the window and flung it out, "Free at last, free at last. Thank God almighty, I'm free at last!" she screamed.

To celebrate, she had gone on a shopping spree. The backseat of her Mercedes was packed with all kinds of goodies from Lenox Mall: a Coach bag, a Versace dress, and four boxes of Donna Karan shoes. She even bought two sets of white lace bras and panties from Victoria's Secret and she already had a drawer full.

She was still singing and bouncing in her seat as she approached the stoplight at Buford Highway. Suddenly, a white Lexus pulled up beside her. Two men waved their hands frantically, signaling her to let down her window. They appeared to be young. About 25, she estimated. She turned down her music and cracked the window to hear what they were trying to say.

"Excuse me, baby. Can I talk to you for a minute?" the driver screamed.

"Come on, shorty, don't be like that. I just want to get those seven digits," the passenger hollered.

Ariel couldn't believe they had the audacity to even speak to her. They looked like two escapees from a bad rap video. The man driving had bumps on his face and was cross-eyed. And the scrub on the passenger's side had a row of gold teeth and the wildest hair she had ever seen. He could put Busta Rhymes to shame, she was thinking.

She rolled up her window, put on her Gucci sunglasses, and turned up the volume on her music. It was just another harsh example of the lack of quality men in Atlanta. Since she moved from D.C. four years ago, she had been trying to find all the wonderful men her cousin bragged about. The same cousin who became so frustrated with men that she turned to women. Ariel wasn't about to start bumping nipples. Having a man wasn't that serious, not as long as she had a vibrator and a strong middle finger. And when that didn't work she positioned herself underneath the spout in the bathtub and let the water do the job. She called it The Waterfall Technique.

While she waited impatiently for the light to change, her cell phone rang. She checked the Caller ID to make sure it wasn't her mother.

"Ms. Ariel Daniels," she answered sounding proper.

"Good afternoon, Ms. Daniels, this is Simon Harris," he said with perfect diction making fun of her. "Are you having a bad day or are you always this stiff?"

"Sorry, boss. I guess I'm used to answering the phone at my office. It's going to take me a while to adjust."

"While you're adjusting, I need a couple of favors. One, I need—"

"Not again," she interrupted. "I've only been on the job four days and you're already asking me to work overtime twice?"

"Well, you know what they say, you have to work eighteen hours a day for yourself if you don't want to work eight hours a day for someone else," Simon said.

"All right, Tony Robbins, now that you've motivated me, what do you want?" she said to him.

"I have to pick up Cynthia from the airport, so could you please stop by the club and sign for a shipment? The liquor vendor is going to make a special delivery today. It should be there at one o'clock."

"No problem. I'm in Buckhead right now," she said. "What's the other favor?"

"The stripper I told you about is going to stop by to drop off some costumes and props. Just show him where the green room is."

"You mean Theodore?"

"Yeah, that's him. But he prefers to be called Teddy, or Teddy Bear."

"I don't care what he prefers to be called," she said with an attitude. "His mama named him Theodore and that's what I'm gonna call him."

"I wish I could be there to see you two go at it," Simon said to her. "This should be better than Ali and Frazier."

"It'll be more like Ali and Sammy Davis, Jr.," Ariel replied. "These strippers may have great bodies but some of them are dumb as a doorknob."

"Try not to break him down too badly, okay? Remember, he works for us now."

"Don't worry, boss, I'll leave him enough self-esteem to shake his ass on Thursday," Ariel said. "But if he steps out of line, I'm gonna put him in check, hard!"

• • •

The vendors were waiting outside the club when Ariel arrived at 12:45. She turned off the building alarm and let them in the back door to unload the cases of liquor. "Put the Heineken over there," she directed. "And you, stack those cases of Courvoisier over here!" The vendors knew the routine but Ariel got a kick out of bossing the burly men around.

Within twenty minutes everything was unloaded and signed for. Ariel locked the back door and put the paperwork in Simon's office. "Now where is Mr. Theodore?" she wondered aloud while looking down at her watch. "I've got to get ready for my date." The club was stuffy, so she waited outside in her car to take advantage of the beautiful weather. She turned on her Frankie Beverly and Maze CD and started singing like she was in concert. Joy and pain, like sunshine and rain. She was seriously getting her groove on, snapping her fingers and clapping.

Suddenly a black Lincoln Navigator pulled up beside her with the music blaring. Lil Wayne drowned her smooth Frankie Beverly out. She knew it could only be one person: Theodore.

"Wassup?" he yelled while rocking back and forth to the beat.

"Wassup, nothing. Turn that damn music down," she yelled back.

"What?" He pretended like he didn't hear her.

"I said turn that music down before you wake the dead."

He gave her a conniving smile as he turned off the ignition.

"I'm looking for Mr. Harris. Is he in?" he asked.

"He couldn't make it," Ariel got out of her car. "He asked me to meet you. My name is Ariel Daniels. I'm the new manager."

"Well, hello, Ariel. It's nice to meet you," he said while checking her out.

He was wearing a pair of long white shorts and a tight body shirt that showed off his muscles. Ariel couldn't believe how incredible his physique was. His bald head was cleanly shaven and shiny. Ariel was impressed but she wasn't about to let him know it.

"You can call me Ms. Daniels, Theodore."

"Oh, so it's like that, huh?"

"It's exactly like that, Theodore." She emphasized his name to annoy him. "Now get your things out of the car and I'll show you where the green room is."

Teddy's ego was bruised. When he flexed his biceps, even the strongest of women would bow down. Ariel's attitude was intriguing and challenging. He was determined to break her down.

"You mind if I ask you a personal question, Ms. Daniels?" He followed closely behind her carrying two large boxes.

"What is it, Theodore?"

"Are you married?"

"No?"

"Have any kids?"

"No."

"Do you have a man?"

"None of your business."

"Ah-hah!" he said sounding excited. "So that's why you're so tense. You haven't had your annual tune-up!"

"Are you always this obnoxious?"

"Look, I'm just trying to get to know you. I mean, I'm single, and you're single, what's the problem?"

Ariel didn't say a word; she just pointed him in the direction of the storage closet. Teddy set the boxes down and closed the door. By the time he turned around, Ariel was already walking toward the front.

"Look, I promise I'll never bug you again if you'll give me one good reason why we can't hook up," he said.

"Okay, I'll give you two reasons," she told him. "One, I don't sleep with the help. And two, you're not my type."

"Why, because I don't wear a suit and tie to work?"

"No, because you're arrogant and self-centered. But the biggest reason is you're a player."

"Who me?" he asked, playing innocent. "I'm the most monogamous man in America."

"Look, brotha, I grew up with two brothers and three uncles who were the biggest whores in D.C. So I know a player when I see one," she said with conviction. "Now some women may see you as a challenge, and believe they can change you. But one look at you and any sane woman could see that you're a bona fide player for life."

Teddy burst out laughing and gave her a high five. "Well, you can't blame a guy for trying."

"I ain't mad at you. It's not your fault these women are stupid."

She gave Teddy a friendly handshake and escorted him outside to his car.

"See you Thursday, Ariel—I mean, Ms. Daniels," he said as he stepped inside his truck. "I might even treat you to a personal lap dance."

"Bye, Theodore," she said as she waved. "Try to go easy on these country girls. I know you're breaking their hearts."

"Their hearts and their wallets!" he laughed.

Ariel watched as Teddy drove off in his Navigator with his music blasting away. Once he was out of sight, she shook her head, still trying to get over how incredible his body was.

"What a waste of good meat," she said, while locking the doors to the club. "Why can't I find a man with a body like that and a brain to match?"

CHAPTER 17

Later on that afternoon, Ariel was getting dressed to meet Lawrence at his home for a barbecue. She met him on Facebook and was determined to give it another try after Jeff struck out at Justin's.

"Lord, please don't let this man look too much different from his picture!" she said while putting on her makeup. "You've got to kiss a helluva lot of frogs to find a prince in this town."

This time she took precautions. She insisted on seeing a photo, a recent one. She made him take a photo with today's paper before she agreed to the date, but she still wasn't comfortable. She had it propped up on her bathroom sink while she was putting on her makeup, along with other photos he sent of himself visiting Cancun over the summer. He was wearing a pair of swim trunks and sandals. Ariel was pleased with what she saw: no love handles, no flabby ass, and most importantly, no beer belly. He was the perfect height, too, six-one. Although looks weren't number one on her list, Ariel wanted a man she was sexually and financially attracted to. In his profile he listed his occupation as engineer. She didn't know too much about how much engineers were being paid, but she was sure she didn't know any broke ones.

By 5:30 she was dressed to kill and ready to make her grand entrance. She checked herself one last time in the full-length mirror, then grabbed her purse off the kitchen counter. Just as she was reaching for the doorknob, the phone rang. Something told her not to answer it, but she did anyway.

"Hello?"

"Hi, sweetheart, hope I'm not interrupting anything."

"Mama, how do you always manage to call me at the most inopportune times?"

"I guess I'm psychic."

"If you're psychic, then you should know that I'm late for a date."

"Glad to see you're getting out more often. Before you know it, I'll have another son-in-law and some grandbabies."

"I wish you would stop putting so much pressure on me to get married and knocked up." Ariel was getting frustrated. "It's hard enough to find a man to date, let alone to marry and have kids with."

"It's not so hard to find a good man if you know where to look. There are plenty of nice men out here ready to settle down."

"They're nice all right—nice and boring. I need a man who is romantic but knows how to handle himself on the streets. You know, a combination of Brian McKnight and Jay-Z."

"What the hell is a Jay-Z, is that a new car?"

"I meant, a combination of Nat King Cole and Teddy Pendergrass, Mama."

"Aw, I understand, a pretty boy and a roughneck."

"Something like that," Ariel laughed. "Look, I've got to get going. I'll call you later in the week, okay?"

"Okay, baby, have a good time. And don't forget what I told you."

"Yeah, yeah, I remember. Don't be so strong!" she replied. "Bye, Mama."

• • •

The drive out to Lawrence's home took a little more than 35 minutes. He lived in Alpharetta, a suburb just north of downtown Atlanta. Ariel was impressed as she drove through the well-manicured gated community. Many of the homes were still under construction and had For Sale signs on the lawns that read new homes starting at $350,000.

The navigation system had her turned around inside the subdivision, but finding his house was easy. There was a line of cars two blocks long parked along the sidewalk and on the grass, and the unmistakable beat of Parliament Funkadelics' "Knee Deep" jammin' from the last house on the corner.

After parking three blocks down the road, she grabbed her Fendi bag and strutted towards the lavish two-story home. As she got closer, she noticed a group of four women standing in the driveway. They were drinking out of paper cups and talking loud. Ariel wanted to walk by without speaking but she knew that was asking for trouble. So, she took a deep breath and walked into the lionesses' den.

"Excuse me, ladies, do you know where I can find Lawrence?" Ariel asked cordially.

They turned in her direction but didn't say a word. They suddenly got quiet and checked her out from head to toe. Not this childish nonsense again, she was thinking. Three of the women were average looking, the shortest one had on a thong bikini exposing her wide stretch marks on her stomach and behind. The fourth woman was attractive but didn't carry herself well. She was wearing too much makeup and her hair was a mess. The tension in the air was thick enough to cut with a knife. Without even knowing her name, they had already judged her. It wasn't her fault that she was looking cute in her bright yellow shorts and matching halter-top. Her waistline was a firm 24 inches, which made her 34-inch breasts look even bigger. "Bitch!" she could practically hear them thinking.

"Lawrence ran to the liquor store to pick up some more beer, sweetheart," the woman with the stretch marks said with an attitude.

"He'll be back in a little while," another woman said, seeming more polite. "You can wait around back by the pool. That's where everybody is hanging out."

"Thank you very much," Ariel said.

"You're welcome."

The minute Ariel turned the corner, she could hear the ugly comments and snickering.

"Who does that trick think she is?" one woman said.

"She needs to go take off that loud-ass yellow outfit," another remarked. "Looking like a damn yield sign!"

Ariel just kept stepping. She understood how some women could be; they feel threatened when a more attractive woman comes on the scene. Thank God they didn't see me drive up in the 500 SL Mercedes, she was thinking. I would have been run out of the place. But this was exactly why she and other educated and classy women were catching hell in Atlanta. Sistahs were constantly competing with one another and breaking each other down. The men were sitting back enjoying the show. With the ratio of twenty to one they could pick and choose from women with Ph.D.s to hood rats. And women allowed it. It was a classic case of divide and conquer.

She received a better reception in the backyard from the men. They were giving her compliments left and right. Several guys came over to cordially introduce themselves the minute she walked in. One guy even brought her a plate of food and a cold beer. Of course, all that attention only made the women even more jealous.

Ariel was so turned off by the hostile atmosphere that she decided to leave after taking a few bites of barbecue. Just as she was gathering her things and was about to stand up, a strong hand pressed down on her shoulder from behind.

"And where do you think you're going?" a deep, sexy voice asked.

Ariel looked up and saw a tall and tanned man towering over her. It was Lawrence. He was even more attractive than his picture. And his thighs seemed more muscular than in his Cancun pictures. Um, um, good, she was thinking.

"I guess I'm not going anywhere." Ariel was blushing.

"Good, now let me go put this beer in the fridge and I'll be right back," he said. Then he walked inside the patio door.

"I'll be right here!" she said, barely able to keep from gloating as the other women watched with envy. There's nothing that pisses women off more than the woman they hate getting the man they want. She knew it and was playing it for all it was worth. She made sure to make eye contact with every woman who was giving her attitude.

When Lawrence came back out, he pulled a chair next to hers and sat down.

"So, did anybody give you a hard time?" he asked.

"No, everybody has been very nice," Ariel lied.

"Well, you be sure to let me know because I'll kick their asses," he said in a casual tone. "I'm not going to have anybody bothering my baby." Then he kissed her on the cheek and took a sip of his beer.

Ariel was somewhat disturbed by what he said. She didn't

139

know him that well and he was already staking a claim. But she brushed it off figuring he was just kidding. Besides, she was flattered that he was being so protective. After dealing with so many wimps, she needed a man who would take charge.

Theodore was right; I need a tune-up, she was thinking as her eyes kept dropping down to his crotch. If Lawrence plays his cards right, I might get my tires rotated and my oil changed, too.

CHAPTER 18

It was the Fourth of July and Malcolm was sitting on the balcony of his South Beach penthouse watching the fireworks. From his view he could see the skies illuminating from Aventura to as far south as Coral Gables. The exploding rockets in the distance and the sounds of the waves crashing against the beach created the perfect symphony. "What a life!" Malcolm said as he took a deep breath. "There's no place like South Beach!" As he sipped on his cocktail, his phone lit up. It was a text message from his mother. He tapped the tab on his iPhone and pulled it up.

Happy Fourth of July, son. I hope Ms. Ruby is taking good care of you. I gave her my recipe for your favorite lemon cake. I hope you like it. You know it won't taste as good as mine, but don't tell her that, ok? lol Also, tell Simon I appreciate what he did for you on your birthday.

— Love Mama

P.S. When are you going to start making me some grandbabies? lol

"There you go again," he said nodding his head. He was about to text her back when his phone vibrated. It was Simon. When he answered, all he could hear was loud music playing in the background and the sound of people chatting.

"Hey, partner!" Simon shouted. "I'm not going to keep you, I just wanted to wish you a happy Fourth of July!"

"Thanks, bro! Malcolm yelled back. "It sounds like another busy night at the club!"

"Yeah, man, this place is jam-packed and the hoochies are out in full force! I'm on the roof now watching these lame fireworks in downtown Atlanta. At times like this I miss Chicago. Remember how we used to picnic at The Taste of Chicago and watch the fireworks on the lakefront?"

"That's funny, I was thinking the same thing while I was watching these tired fireworks here in Miami." He laughed. "Those were the good ole days!"

"So, what you got up for tonight? I'm sure your calendar is full with sexy clientele from all over the world, Mr. Ladies' Man."

"Believe it or not, things are always slow around this time of the year. Even rich women who cheat stay at home with their husbands during the holidays," he laughed.

There was a pause. Malcolm knew what was coming.

"So, uh, have you heard from Toni?"

"No, bro, I think that ship has sailed."

"I'm sorry to hear that," he sounded disappointed. "Well, you know what they say, if it was meant to be, it would happen, right?"

"Yeah, that's what they say!"

"Well, try not to do anything I wouldn't do better," he joked. "By the way, Cynthia told me to tell you hello."

"Simon, you know damn well Cynthia didn't say shit to me!" Malcolm laughed. "That woman can't stand me and I can't stand her, so stop lying."

142

"Hey, a man can dream, can't he?" They both laughed. "Enjoy your night, bro, I'll chat with you later."

After Malcolm hung up the phone, he thought about calling Toni to leave another message but his pride wouldn't let him. He had a picture of her on his bedroom dresser, the one they took at Club Obsession. But he still tried to convince himself she was nothing special. He looked at it every day to remind him of how stunning she was. He couldn't get her out of his mind and that made him even more uncomfortable. "Fuck it!" he said while slamming his drink down. "Time to stop acting like a chump and get back in the game!"

He headed for his closet and flung the doors open to his massive closet that resembled a men's boutique. The top row was lined with designer and tailored suits, the second tier was a rainbow of colors of casual and dress shirts, and the bottom rack had an assortment of shoes and sandals, every top designer from Ferragamo to Berluti. While he laid out his wardrobe on his bed to match up outfits, he phoned Melvin to let him know he was on his way. When nobody picked up, he left a message.

"Hey, Old Man, it's me, I'll be there in forty-five minutes, set aside my usual spot, see you there!"

He pushed the play button on his home audio system to get in the right frame of mind. He thought about old school, but he was in a rebellious state of mind, so he clicked on his hip-hop playlist and scrolled down to a song by Drake. While he listened to the thumbing bass and hard lyrics, he slide into his black Canali slacks and Egyptian cotton short sleeve shirt. He looked through his case of watches and grabbed a black Bvlgari, which was a Christmas gift from Helen. As he snapped the watch around his wrist, he pressed the valet button on his phone. "This is Mr. Tremell, bring the Lamborghini around front. I'll be down in five minutes."

On his way out the door, he looked over at Toni's picture on the dresser. "What are you looking at?" he said with contempt. "I can't wait around for you. I've got bills to pay."

• • •

The drive from South Beach to Melvin's Jazz Club only took fifteen minutes. As he approached the club, he could see the long line of scantily dressed groupies that stretched nearly a block long. He cruised past just slow enough for them to get a good look at the freshly waxed black Lamborghini. The gigolo game was all about appearances and facades, and Miami was the materialistic capital of the world. If a man had a few dollars, drove an expensive car, and was halfway decent-looking, he could have practically any woman he wanted. Sometimes he didn't even need money, just the appearance of money. In Miami it was all about knowing how to advertise and perpetrate.

When he rolled up to the front entrance, it was blocked off with orange cones and a sign in bold letters that read, Valet Parking Full. Some of the jealous men waiting in line were laughing because they assumed he had to park two blocks down the street like everybody else.

Malcolm let them have their laugh for a minute, then he blew the horn and flashed his headlights three times.

The valet removed the bright orange cones and directed him to pull up to the curb. "Ain't that a bitch?" he heard one of them say.

"Good evening, Mr. Tremell," Rosco said as he opened the door. "I can see you drove the Batmobile tonight."

"It was time to take old Betsy out for a spin," Malcolm said to him. "How's it going this evening?"

"It's crazy as usual. I'll be glad when it's time to go home."

"Hang in there," Malcolm slid him a fifty-dollar bill. "The night's still young."

His adrenaline was pumping the moment he walked through the door. He was on the hunt to get paid, and he was determined not to leave with empty pockets. The deejay was playing "Mr. Magic" by Grover Washington, Jr., and a few people were on the dance floor trying to step. He wanted to cut in and show them how to do it Chicago style, but he was too busy scoping out the ladies. Melvin's was packed with beautiful women of every race: black, white, Hispanic, and Asian. It was a man's paradise. Not surprisingly, most of the men were holding up the wall sipping on empty drinks, too chicken to strike up a conversation. "Look at those pussies," he said to himself. "No wonder women have to pay for sex!"

As he walked towards his usual table, he scanned the room for prospects. He made eye contact with an attractive woman seated in the VIP section on the opposite side of the club. She had light brown skin, short black hair, and slanted green eyes. She appeared to be mixed with Asian. He had seen her somewhere before, either on television or on a magazine cover, but he couldn't recall. They stared at each other without losing eye contact as he made his way over to his table. She winked, he winked back and then she took a sip of her drink and began tying a knot in the cherry with her tongue. "Looks like we got a winner!" he said to himself.

Just as he was about to make his move, he felt a heavy slap on the shoulder.

"What the—" he said as he spun around.

"Melvin wants to see you in his office," Scottie said. He was head of security and Melvin's personal assistant.

"You scared the shit out of me, Scottie," he said. "Next time, how about a simple, hello?"

"Melvin needs to see you, it's important."

"What's wrong now? Don't tell me he got another heart attack chasing around all those young girls?"

"It's serious, Malcolm, I've never seen him like this before."

"Come on, Scottie, I was just kidding."

"I'm not!" he said in a serious tone.

The woman in the VIP section followed Malcolm with her eyes across the crowded club as he followed closely behind Scottie. "I'll be right back," Malcolm mouthed to her. She read his lips and mouthed back, "I'll be here."

Malcolm stopped outside the door to Melvin's office and knocked three times.

"Who is it?" Melvin shouted in his deep, raspy voice.

"It's Malcolm."

"Come on in, Cool Breeze."

Melvin pushed the security and Malcolm walked inside expecting Melvin to be his usual brash self. But Melvin was leaning out the window with his shirt unbuttoned, gasping for air.

"What's wrong, old man?" he said rushing over and holding Melvin up. "And this time, don't tell me it was something you ate."

"I'll be fine. I just need to catch my breath." He began to breathe easier.

"That's it! You're going to see a doctor!"

"Those doctors don't know shit," he said angrily. "According to them, I was supposed to be dead ten years ago."

"Well, if you don't stop smoking those cigars and working so hard, you won't last another ten months."

"I didn't ask you to come back here to give medical advice. I have something for you."

He pulled a box from under his desk and handed it to Malcom. It was wrapped with a large bow on it.

"What's this?"

"It's your birthday present," he said. "I wanted to give it to you last week but you were in too big a hurry."

"What is it?"

"If I told you what it was, it wouldn't be a surprise, now would it?"

Malcolm began to unwrap it but Melvin stopped him. "Don't open it now!" he shouted. "Wait until you get home."

"Why? Is it going to explode?" he joked, trying to cheer him up.

"I just prefer that you wait. Is that too much to ask?"

"Okay, you old grouch, I'll wait."

Malcolm walked him back to his chair behind his desk and sat him down gently. He noticed that Melvin was holding him tighter than he had ever done before. That only made him more concerned. As he tried to sit Melvin down, he wouldn't let go. When he finally stepped away, tears were rolling down Melvin's face. It was the first time Malcolm had ever seen him cry.

"Goddammit, what's wrong, Melvin," he shouted. "You're fuckin' scaring me!"

"I'm fine, Cool Breeze. Really, I am."

"I know you're lying, you stubborn old bastard!"

"Hey, watch your mouth! I can still whip your young ass with one hand tied behind my back," he said while throwing punches in the air.

"You old fool, you couldn't hit American Airlines Arena if you had a map and a Seeing Eye dog!" They both laughed as the tears rolled down both their cheeks. "I know you're too stubborn to tell me what's really going on, so I'm not going to press you. So, why don't you let me play something special for you tonight."

"Now, you talking, Cool Breeze," he said, trying to get up from his seat.

"You sure you're alright?" Malcolm rushed over to help him.

"I'm fine, son, just help me get my shirt buttoned up and hand me my jacket. You know I like to look good for the ladies."

"Same old Melvin."

Malcolm escorted Melvin from his office and sat him directly in front of the stage. Since there was no band performing that night, he hopped onstage and started warming up on the piano. He didn't even bother making an announcement. "Testing, one, two," he said into the mic. The deejay finally caught on and the music abruptly stopped.

"Excuse me, ladies and gentleman. Can I please have your attention?"

The crowd suddenly got quiet, and all eyes were on the stage. Scottie signaled the engineer to pull down the lights in the club and put the spotlight on the stage.

"Tonight I want to recognize a man who has supported me through some pretty hard times. He picked me up when I was down, slapped some sense into my hard head when I was young and rebellious. A man who taught me not only to love music but also to appreciate the talent God gave me to allow me to share it. Most of all, he was the man who took me into his home and treated me like his son. This one's for you, Melvin. I love you, old man."

The song Malcolm chose was the classic "My Favorite Things" by Oscar Hammerstein II. It was an upbeat song. And it was old school, like Melvin. When he began to play, you could feel the positive vibes blanket the room. It was like family. Some of the old timers began singing along. And those who didn't know all the lyrics faked it. Before long the whole room was serenading Melvin. It was an emotional experience.

During the song, Malcolm gazed deep into Melvin's weary

old eyes and expressed his love as much as he possibly could through those piano keys. His face lit up as he improvised on the notes and made the song his own, just like Melvin had taught him to do.

When the song ended, the crowd gave him a standing ovation. Melvin's face was completely red and covered with tears. He didn't bother trying to hold them back. Malcolm took a bow and rushed over and embraced him. This time it was Malcolm who didn't want to let go. "Thank you, Cool Breeze," Melvin said, crying. "That was the best gift you could've ever given me."

He and Melvin said their good-byes and Scottie escorted Melvin outside to his car and drove him home. Malcolm was so emotionally spent he forgot all about the woman he was flirting with earlier, but she hadn't forgotten about him. Before he reached the exit, she came up behind him and grabbed his arm.

"Hey, I hope you're not leaving without me," she said.

"That depends," he said.

"On what?"

"On how much money you have to spend. I'm tired and in no mood for games!" He was expecting his assertiveness to scare her away. But she didn't scare easily.

"Is this enough?" She pulled out a piece of paper with the amount 3,000 written on it. "I hope this will get me more than a church hug."

"Trust me, for this amount, you'll be repenting and speaking in tongues by the time I'm done with you," he told her. "Now, where do you want to go, I'm on your time now?"

"I own a beach house not too far from here," she said while pulling out the keys to her Bentley. "You can follow me there... if you can keep up in that raggedy Lambo I saw you drive up in."

"I always like a challenge; lead the way."

While he waited outside for the valet to get his car, it finally dawned on him where he recognized her from; she was on a popular reality series.

She never told him her name or asked him his. It was simply a business transaction. That's the way they both wanted it.

CHAPTER 19

Early the next morning Malcolm made it home from Coconut Creek. He put the gift Melvin had given him inside his closet, peeled off his clothes, and jumped into the shower. After washing off the scent of perfume and sex, he collapsed into bed. An hour later, the loud humming of the vacuum cleaner woke him up. He glanced over at his clock. It read 8:00 A.M. "This is some fragernackle bull," he said while slipping on his robe. He stormed into the living room with his hands over his eyes to block out the sunlight.

"Ms. Ruby, why are you torturing me?" he shouted.

"Oh, Lord, you almost gave me a heart attack," she said with her hand over her chest.

151

"Now we're even!" he said angrily. "Why are you vacuuming at eight o'clock in the morning?"

"I didn't know you were here," she explained. "I came by to drop off your mail and make my grocery list but when I saw the curtains open, I figured you weren't here. You always close your blinds when you sleep."

"Look, I understand you have a job to do, but could you please take care of the housework that doesn't involve making noise?"

"No problem, sir. Sorry I woke you."

Ms. Ruby put away the vacuum cleaner and began collecting the trash to dump in the incinerator.

As Malcolm turned to go back to his bedroom, he noticed a FedEx envelope on the kitchen counter. When he looked at the name on the air bill, he was surprised to see Antoinette Grayson at the top of it. He sat down at the dining room table and opened it.

Dear Malcolm,

I know I'm the last person on earth you wanted to hear from, but please allow me to explain before you tear up this letter. Ever since I met you at the Fox Theatre, I haven't been able to stop thinking about you. Even choreographing new routines has become a challenge. I haven't created a single dance step in three days. Even my fiancé, Eric, has noticed a change in how I respond to him. No, I'm not trying to tell you that I'm in love with you, but you've definitely had an impact on me. I was moved by your confidence and your passion. Not many men have the ability to inspire me.

I guess what I'm trying to say is, I'm afraid. Afraid because I don't understand what I'm feeling. At first I thought it was infatuation, but since I'm a little too old for that, I'm sure it's something more. If you're interested in talking about it, call me before Friday. I'll be leaving for Chicago to do a show at the DuSable Museum on Saturday afternoon at 2:00 P.M. If I don't hear from you, I'll understand.

Yours truly,
Antoinette Grayson

P.S. I realize a phone call would've been simpler, but I'm much better at communicating on real paper. I'm not an e-mails or texting type of girl. That's so impersonal.

He read it over again to make sure he wasn't dreaming, then he shouted, "I'll be damned!"

"What's wrong, did I miss something?" Ms. Ruby asked.

"No, actually everything is just fine!" Malcolm said enthusiastically while checking his calendar. "I'm going to need you to book me a flight to Chicago; looks like I'm going home!"

"That must've been one heck of a letter!"

"For your information, it's from a very special lady."

"Excuse me, but did I hear you call her special?"

"Yeah, and—?"

"That's the first time in six years you've ever expressed any interest in a woman. And it's definitely the first time you've ever called a woman special," she said adamantly. "To be honest with you—," she stopped abruptly.

"What?"

"I'm sorry, I'm getting way too nosey in my old age."

"Too late now, you've already stuck your neck out!"

"I'm sorry, Mr. Malcolm, but let's be honest, I've been working for you for over ten years and I have yet to see you invite a woman over!"

"Are you trying to imply that I'm gay?" Malcolm laughed and

began walking towards his bedroom. "I'm about as gay as Hugh Hefner."

Just before he closed his door, he paused. "And by the way, I'm sorry for raising my voice at you," he told her. "You know I couldn't manage without you."

"It's okay, Mr. Malcolm. I know you work hard and need your rest," she said. "But I'm not going to be around forever. Hopefully that special lady will be here to take care of you when I'm gone."

"Now, you're starting to sound like my mother." He walked back to her and kissed her on the cheek. "But maybe you're both right. At some point I've got to trust someone enough to let them in."

CHAPTER 20

Simon woke up horny as hell. Two weeks had passed since he and Cynthia last had sex and he was ready to explode. She was lying next to him naked, except for a pair of panties. He brushed up against her to give her the hint that he wanted some. When that didn't work, he kissed her on the back, then the neck. When that didn't work, he began fondling her breasts.

"Come on, baby," he whispered in her ear. "I need some lovin'."

"Not now, Simon, I'm tired." Cynthia rolled over onto her stomach.

After a few more attempts, Simon became frustrated. He jumped on top of Cynthia's back and tried to pry her legs open.

"What are you doing, Simon!"

"I'm skydiving. What the hell does it look like I'm doing?"

155

"Get off me!" she screamed. "I can't have sex right now."

"Why not?"

"Because it's close to my period and I've got bad cramps."

Simon rolled off her and sat on the edge of the bed. He covered his face with his hands trying to calm himself.

"Since you got back from New Orleans, we haven't even kissed. When you got off the plane, you said you were tired. Last night you said you had a headache. Now you're telling me it's cramps. I know damn well your period isn't for another two weeks!" he said furiously. "Now do you want to keep playing games or do you want to tell me what the hell is going on?"

Cynthia was speechless. Simon had never spoken to her so forcefully. She had to come up with an answer, and fast.

"I'm sorry, sweetheart. Don't get upset," she said, while leaning over and stroking the back of his head. "Nothing is going on. I'm just getting a little nervous over this whole idea of being married. You know how emotional women can get."

Simon was a sucker for an apology. He was in love with Cynthia. Any decent explanation was good enough for him.

"I wish you would talk to me instead of leaving me in the dark. I was beginning to think there was someone else."

"You know I would never do anything to disrespect you," she said, convincingly. "You're the only man I ever want inside of me."

Cynthia led him back into the bed and laid him down on his back. Then she stripped off her thong panties and jumped on top. She really didn't want to have sex with him, but she knew Simon would forgive her for anything after she gave him a little pussy.

"Is it good?" he asked.

"Yes, it's good, baby," she moaned unenthusiastically.

"Is it mine?"

"Sure, it is."

Simon moaned and squirmed for a few minutes, then he climaxed. Cynthia looked over at the clock and shook her head. It lasted ten minutes flat. Right on schedule, she was thinking. Cynthia immediately got up and went to the bathroom.

"Where're you going, baby?" Simon asked. "I want to cuddle."

"I'll be right back," she told him. "I have to pee."

Simon lay back against the pillow with his arms behind his head feeling like Don Juan. Meanwhile, Cynthia was looking at herself in the bathroom mirror trying to decide if she was making the right decision marrying a man who couldn't satisfy her sexually. Simon had his moments when the sex was great, but those moments had become few and far between.

When Cynthia came out of the bathroom, she planned to tell Simon a lie about needing to go home to do extra work. But before she could tell him, the phone rang.

"Hello?"

"Mr. Harris, this is Ariel. I know it's early to be calling you at home, but I need to call in that favor."

"What is it, Ariel?"

"I scheduled a private party at the club this evening, but something has come up. Can you handle it for me?"

"Hold on, Ariel. I've got to consult the boss." Simon put his hand over the phone.

"Cynthia, do you mind if I run over to the club for a few hours?" he asked.

"No problem, sweetheart," she said while rushing to get dressed. "Take care of your business."

He took his hand away from the phone. "I've got you covered, Ariel. Enjoy your evening."

"Thanks, boss."

After he hung up with Ariel, Simon walked Cynthia to her

car. She gave him a peck on the cheek and quickly jumped in her car.

"You sure you don't want to come hang out with me at the club?"

"No, I would only be in the way," she said while turning on the ignition. "Besides, I have a ton of work to do."

"How about dinner tomorrow night?"

"I would love to, honey, but I promised Debra I would go to church with her."

"Since when did you turn religious?"

"Since today," she told him. "When I woke up this morning, I finally realized the importance of a strong spiritual foundation."

"Well, make sure you say a prayer for me."

"Oh, don't worry, sweetheart, I will."

CHAPTER 21

Teddy gathered his most recent pay stubs and his tax returns and rushed out the door. The hearing for his child-support case was at nine o'clock at the Broward courthouse. The drive was only twenty minutes from his girlfriend's house, but he left an hour early to make sure he wasn't late.

As he drove down I-95, the traffic was heavy and moving slowly. He tuned in to 105.1 on the radio and tried to relax. Ironically, the topic of the day was "Deadbeat Dads." "This is definitely a bad omen," he said to himself.

He turned up the volume and listened as a man and woman argued over the issue of child support.

"Whether a man pays child support or not, he should have access to his kids," the man said. "Why should money be a factor?"

"Because kids cost money, that's why!" the woman angrily replied. "Men don't realize how expensive it is to raise a child. I pay five hundred a month just for day care. What about diapers, and food, and the days I have to take off work for doctors' appointments and PTA meetings? Men have no idea how expensive kids are!"

They bickered back and forth for a few minutes, then the radio personality jumped in.

"Both of you have valid points. But I have another question," he said. "Should a man have to pay child support even if he tells the woman up front that he doesn't want kids?" he asked. "Call in and tell us what you think." He gave the number to the studio line and then went to a commercial break.

Teddy couldn't resist. He picked up his cell phone and dialed the radio station as fast as he could. The first few times the line was busy, but eventually he got through. He reached into the glove compartment for a napkin and placed it over the receiver to help disguise his voice.

"Hot 105, what's your comment?" the producer asked.

"Yeah, uh, I want to respond to the question about men paying child support to women who trapped them."

"Are you being sued for child support?"

"Hell, yeah," he said. "As a matter of fact, I'm on my way to court right now!"

"Perfect!" she said excitedly. "I'm going to put you on hold and we'll come right to you after the commercial break. Give me your name."

"My name is, uh, Tyrone."

"Okay, Tyrone, hold on."

When the commercials ended, the radio personality repeated the question to get the listeners stirred up. Teddy cleared his throat and tried his best to disguise his voice.

"On the phone, we have a man who claims he was trapped. And he's on his way to court for child support as we speak. Are you there, Tyrone?"

"Yeah, I'm here."

"So, what's your story?"

"Well, I was hired to strip at this bachelorette party and I met this very attractive woman. We talked, had a few drinks, and one thing led to another," he said. "Now she expects me to pay child support."

"Let me get this right," the female co-host joined in. "You met a perfect stranger at a party and you had sex with her that same night...without a condom? Haven't you heard of AIDS?"

"For your information, I had on a condom, but it broke. That happens sometimes when you're well-endowed," he said, arrogantly.

"But the question is, did you tell her up front that you didn't want kids?"

"That should've been understood."

"And why is that?"

"Because she was the bachelorette who was getting married."

"Now that's a trifling wench," the male personality said. "Let's go to the phones and see what the listeners have to say. Hot 105, what's your question or comment."

"I'm so upset with Tyrone I don't even know where to begin," a woman said.

"Just take a deep breath and say what's on your mind."

"First of all, you're right about the woman; she played herself by having sex with a complete stranger on the night before her wedding. Second, it doesn't matter what the circumstances were; it's all about the welfare of the child. After all, that baby didn't choose to be born," she went on. "And lastly, I'm fed up with these tired-ass men running away from their responsibilities. If you don't want kids, practice celibacy or get a vasectomy."

"I heard that, sistah!" the female jock said.

"Let's not turn this into a *Real Housewives* episode," the male jock joked. "Let's take another caller. What's your question or comment?"

"I agree with Tyrone!" a male caller said. "The problem with the child-support system is that it rewards women for having babies out of wedlock. All these lazy tramps have to do is get pregnant by a man with money and they can lie on their asses and collect a paycheck for eighteen years."

"So, what's your solution?" the jock asked.

"They should pass a law stating that if a man doesn't sign an agreement to have children, then he's not liable for child support. I guarantee you the birth rate would drop by ninety percent overnight," he asserted. "And if I were you, Tyrone, I wouldn't pay that heifer one red cent. Maybe next time she'll think twice before she tries to trap another brotha!"

"Whew! It's getting hot up in here," the jock said.

"Thank God, neither one of you fools is my daddy," the female jock said, laughing. "I'd be on the Dr. Phil show trying to get therapy."

"Well, Tyrone, thanks for your call. And good luck in court today."

"Good luck, my ass," the female jock added. "I hope they take the shirt off your back, you old deadbeat."

"Go to hell!" Teddy screamed into the phone!

Then he hung up and turned off the radio.

• • •

Teddy parked his Navigator in the back of the lot and took off his diamond earring and Rolex watch. His lawyer advised him not to come into court looking too prosperous. When he walked into the building, there were three deputies standing by the entrance directing people through a metal detector.

"What's up with the tight security," he asked one of the officers. "I thought this was a courthouse, not a prison."

"It's just a precaution," the officer said. "You'd be surprised how violent people can get in family court."

"No, I wouldn't," Teddy said while emptying his pockets then walking through. "I'm surprised you're not wearing a bullet-proof vest."

After he collected his belongings, Teddy walked toward the courtroom where his lawyer, Steve Grundy, was waiting. He was a short, thin white man with a long scar on the left side of his face. Rumor was he got it from a ballplayer after winning the wife a large alimony settlement. Steve had on his trademark drab gray suit and scuffed-up shoes. His hair was unkempt and his shirt had a ring around the collar. Although he wasn't much to look at, he had a reputation for winning big cases. Teddy was hoping he could work his magic for him.

"Wuz up, counselor?" Teddy said as they shook hands.

"Good morning, Mr. Simmons. Do you have a copy of your pay stubs and tax returns?"

"You get right down to business, don't you?"

"That's what I get paid for."

"So, what's next?"

"Just wait here," Steve told him. "I have to let the judge know you're here. We should be out of here in no time."

"That sounds good to me."

Shortly after Steve left, Teddy noticed a woman with long blonde hair walking towards him. From a distance he could tell she was well-built and was preparing to pass her one of his business cards, but as she grew closer, he realized it was his son's mother, Donna. She looked him dead in the eye and walked past him and into the courtroom without saying a word. A few moments later, Steve came out of the courtroom and signaled for Teddy to come inside. It was nine o'clock, the moment of truth. Teddy sat in the back of the courtroom to avoid attention. Donna took a seat in the front row, directly across from the bench. Once the court was brought to order, Steve finally worked up the courage to give Teddy the bad news.

"We may have a slight problem," Steve whispered.

"What do you mean by...slight?"

"Well, the judge who was supposed to hear our case had a family emergency."

"And?"

"And he was replaced by Judge Harris."

"So what's the problem?"

"Judge Harris is the toughest judge in the state on deadbeat parents. I mean, really tough!"

"Can't we get a postponement?" Teddy asked nervously.

"That's what I've been trying to do for the last few minutes," Steve told him. "We're going to have to see this one through."

"Something told me this wasn't going to be my day."

As the door to the judge's chamber opened, the bailiff turned toward the gallery. "All rise, the Honorable Judge Ann Harris presiding," he announced.

The second Teddy laid eyes on her, he knew he was in trouble. Judge Harris was a black woman in her late 50s; she wore eyeglasses that rested crookedly on her nose. He knew his charm and good looks weren't going to do him any good. He leaned back against the hard wooden bench and prayed for a miracle. But like everything else that day, his situation was going from bad to worse. His case was the first one called.

Teddy looked awkward as he made his way toward the front of the courtroom. At six-five, he stood out like a sore thumb. Everyone was staring and making comments, especially the women. "Isn't that the guy who strips at the Foxy?" one of them whispered. That made him even more uncomfortable.

All the attention didn't go unnoticed by the judge, who quickly used it to give him a hard time.

"Good morning, Mr. Simmons," she said. "I can see you're quite the celebrity."

"Not me, Your Honor. I'm just trying to get by like everybody else."

"Is that right?" she said while looking at him over the top of her glasses.

Teddy was sworn in, then he stated his name for the record.

"So what's the situation here?" the judge asked Steve.

"Your Honor, my client has cooperated by taking a paternity test, which proved he was the father of the child," Steve said. "However, the five hundred dollars a month that the state is asking for is unreasonable. As you can see by his tax returns, Mr. Simmons only earned twelve thousand dollars last year. Even at the highest rate of twenty percent of his gross income that would only be equivalent to two-hundred-forty dollars a month."

"I know how to do math, Mr. Grundy," she said curtly. "However, the court has an affidavit by your client's previous employer stating that his income from tips is much greater then he reported. And from what I understand, these tips constitute the majority of his income as a stripper."

"I prefer to be called an exotic dancer," Teddy said sarcastically.

"Whatever!" the judge snapped back.

"Before you make a ruling, we would like to bring it to the court's attention that Mr. Simmons also has two other children that he provides for," Steve added. "A five-year-old daughter in Texas and a two-year-old son in Oklahoma."

"Just because his name is on the birth certificates doesn't mean he's providing support," she told him. "Do you have proof?"

Teddy was speechless. He didn't have any proof because he wasn't providing support. Steve advised him not to include that information but Teddy insisted, hoping the judge would be sympathetic.

"Unless you have any additional information, I'm going to make a ruling for the five hundred per month."

"But, Your Honor, I don't even know this woman," Teddy said, getting loud. "Why should I have to give her five hundred dollars of my hard-earned money?"

"Because it's the law, Mr. Simmons. And furthermore, you'd better watch your tone in my courtroom. Do you understand?"

Teddy just gave her an angry stare.

"Now, according to the record, your son is six months old," she went on. "Have you been providing support during that time?"

"Yes, I have."

"You're a damned liar!" Donna shouted from the gallery.

She easily stood out in the mostly black gallery with her long blonde hair and blue eyes.

"Calm down, Ms., this is a courtroom not a cathouse!" the Judge lamented. "You're Ms. Donna Riley, the child's mother, is that correct?"

"Yes, ma'am, and this jerk hasn't given me a single, solitary dime!"

The room was abuzz with chatter. The black women in the back stood up to get a better look at Donna.

"I can't wait to get home and call my girlfriend," one woman said.

"Sellout!" another yelled.

The judge slammed her gavel down on the bench to get order.

"Mr. Simmons, you'd better have proof that you are providing support," she said angrily, "Or I'll make you wish you had never set foot in my courtroom!"

"I do have proof. I just don't have it with me."

"Your Honor, he hasn't given me a penny since my son was born. Not even when I asked him for twenty dollars for a bag of

Pampers," Donna said. "I know I should have taken him to court sooner, but he threatened to kill me."

The room erupted with chatter again. The expressions on the women's faces in the courtroom were fierce. Although Donna was white, they could relate to her predicament. It was a woman thing.

"I've heard enough!" the judge shouted. "My judgment is for seven hundred dollars a month, retroactive from the date of the paternity test. You will provide proof of health insurance for this child within thirty days. And if you don't begin payments immediately, Mr. Simmons, you will be held in contempt and sent to jail."

"I'm not a brain surgeon, for Christ's sake," Teddy said, looking distressed. "How am I supposed to pay that kind of money?"

"Stop shaking your ass for a living and get a real job!" she said, then she slammed her gavel down. "Next case!"

Teddy was furious. He stormed out of the courtroom with Steve trailing closely behind. On his way out, he saw Claudia, the manager of Foxy strip club. She was sitting in the back of the courtroom with a big smile on her face.

"You fuckin' lesbian traitor!" Teddy said to her.

"I told you Karma was a bitch, didn't I?" she snapped back.

Once they were out in the hallway, Steve assured him that he would win on appeal. A few minutes later, Donna and Claudia came out of the courtroom.

"Teddy, I don't want your money," she said sincerely. "I just want you to take care of your son and try to be a father to him."

"Look, you poor white trash, I can hardly remember your name. What makes you think I want to play daddy to your mutt-ass child? Now leave me alone and go back to your lily-white world," he said viciously. "And by the way, I ain't paying you a dime. I don't give a damn what that tight-ass judge says."

Teddy looked her up and down with disgust, then walked toward the exit.

"I hope you burn in hell, you cold-blooded bastard," Donna screamed with tears rolling down her face. "I wouldn't want my child anywhere near you anyway!"

"Lower your voice, Donna. Court is still in session," Claudia said, trying to calm her down.

"I don't care," she screamed. "And I may be poor white trash, but at least I'm not running away from my responsibilities as a parent like you are. You fuckin' coward!"

Teddy gave her the finger and dangled the keys to his Navigator and smiled back at her like he didn't have a care in the world.

"Keep smiling motherfucker; your day is coming!" Claudia yelled at him.

CHAPTER 22

A riel arrived at Sylvia's just before seven o'clock. She was wearing four-inch pumps and a black halter dress that showed off her shapely figure. When she walked through the door, all eyes were on her.

"How many?" the hostess asked.

"Table for two, something near the front."

The hostess grabbed two menus and escorted her to the corner table next to the window. Ariel wanted to get a good look at Lawrence's tight buns when he showed up. It had been a long time since she had had a man to lust over and she wanted to make the most of it.

When the waitress came over to take her order, Ariel asked for her usual Mojito; she wasn't really in the mood for a drink, but it was a helpful prop to ignore all the unwanted stares from the men surrounding her. Some were totally disrespectful. They continued to stare even though their dates were sitting right next to them.

The man at the table across from her was more discreet. He waited until his date went to the restroom, then he sent the waitress over with a complimentary drink and his phone number. Ariel sent it back without even looking in his direction.

While she waited impatiently for Lawrence to come to her rescue, she pulled out her compact to check her makeup. When she looked into the mirror, a man's face appeared out of nowhere over her shoulder. It was Chris. She hadn't seen him since they had met at Justin's, but she recognized him right away.

"Hello, stranger," he said.

"Chris, you startled me!"

"Sorry about that. I saw you sitting over here and I wanted to say hello."

"How did you know it was me with my back to the door?"

"Not too many women can wear a short haircut and look as fine as you."

"Don't try to make up by complimenting me. I'm still shaking," Ariel joked.

"Well, I didn't want to bother you," Chris said as he began to back away. "Enjoy your food."

"Oh, no you don't. Come back here and protect me from these vultures." Ariel waved for him to come back. "Unless, of course, you're here with a date."

"No, I come here alone every Thursday after work to get my grub on."

"Well, pull up a chair and hang out with me for a minute," she said.

As soon as Chris sat down, the jealous stares began. Half the men in the room were checking him out as if he were sitting with their woman.

"Next time you might want to consider wearing a pair of coveralls," he said, laughing. "Those legs could get a brotha killed."

"I don't usually dress like a hoochie so early in the day, but I thought my friend would like it."

"Don't tell me you're here on another blind date?" he said. "I'm not going to play Rico the killer pimp again."

"No, I had enough of that drama," she said. "I've already met this one. And he seems pretty cool."

"I'm happy everything is working out for you, but I hope this doesn't mean we can't still be friends. I'm still waiting on that Netflix movie night you promised me," he smiled and reached out to hold her hand.

"I'm sorry, Chris, I've just been so busy at the club. You know how it is with a new job. But I give you my word we'll get together soon."

"I hope you're into action movies like *The Bourne Identity* and *A Long Kiss Goodnight*."

"That's one of my favorites," Ariel excitedly replied. "Samuel Jackson and Geena Davis were great together on that movie; I'm still waiting on the sequel."

At that moment Lawrence walked into the restaurant. He glanced around the room until he saw Ariel. He saw Chris, too. And he didn't appreciate his hand on Ariel. He rushed over to the table and lifted Chris up by his arm."

"Get your hands off my woman," he shouted.

"Hey, man, what's your fuckin' problem?" Chris yelled back.

He got in Lawrence's face and shoved him. Although he was only five-six and fifty pounds lighter, he didn't back down.

"Stop it, Lawrence!" Ariel stepped between them. "Chris is just a friend."

By now, everyone in the restaurant was watching; even the waitresses stopped serving food to see if it was going to escalate.

"Chris, I'm so sorry," Ariel apologized. "Please let me handle this. I'll talk to you later."

"You should do a better job of choosing who you go out with," he said, while fixing his clothes. "Your boyfriend isn't playing with a full deck."

He stared Lawrence down then he walked away.

Ariel sat down at the table and tried to act normally. She took a sip of her drink and took a deep breath. Lawrence was still standing as if he were waiting for an invitation to sit.

"Would you please sit down?" she asked. "I think you've already attracted enough attention, don't you?"

Lawrence picked the chair up from off the floor and sat down.

"Look, Ariel, I apologize for what happened with your little friend, but a man has got to protect what's his."

"I don't need protection when I'm in a crowded restaurant talking to a friend."

"I know, baby. And I'm sorry for overreacting," he said, looking pitiful. "It's just that men today don't have any respect for another man's woman. They will stare at your woman and even grab her ass if you don't put them in check."

"Every woman wants a hero, Lawrence," she told him, "but I'm a strong, independent woman who can take care of herself."

"I know you can, Ariel. But maybe it's time you let someone else be strong," he said. He took her hand as if he were proposing. "I've got a great job, a big house, and enough money so that you don't have to work unless you want to."

"Lawrence, I'm flattered, I really am." Ariel was smiling. "But as romantic as that all sounds, you don't even know me. And I don't know you. Why don't we give it a few months and see what happens?"

"Maybe you're right. It probably is a good idea to slow down and get to know each other better. After all, you're not going anywhere, right?"

"Right, baby," she said apprehensively.

"Good, now let's get out of here. I want to go to the mall before it closes and look at some rings." He stood up from the table.

"I thought we agreed to slow down."

"I was just kidding," he laughed. "But I would like to go to the mall. Maybe we can catch a movie."

"That sounds like fun, but don't you want to eat first?"

"No, I lost my appetite," he said.

Ariel put twenty dollars on the table for her drink and began walking toward the door.

"I got it, baby," Lawrence said while pulling a wad of bills out of his pocket. "No woman of mine has to spend her own money."

Ariel didn't argue. She gladly picked up her hard-earned money and put it back inside her purse. There had been too many occasions when her dates stuck her with the bill. Any act of chivalry was greatly appreciated.

Before they left, Ariel noticed Chris was in the dining area in the back.

"Lawrence, wait for me outside. I want to go say good-bye to Chris," she told him. "That's the least I can do after what happened."

"Go ahead. And tell the little fella I said I was sorry for the misunderstanding," he said sarcastically.

Ariel made her way through the thick crowd, trying to avoid brushing up against the horny men who were watching her every move. When she finally made it to the back dining area, she walked over to Chris's table and pulled up a chair.

"I can't tell you how embarrassed I am for what happened. I don't know what got into him," she said. "He's very protective of me."

Chris kept eating without even looking up at her.

"Anyway, we're getting ready to leave," she went on. "I'll give you a call later this week to see how you're doing, okay?"

When he didn't respond, she stood up from the table and began to walk away.

"Wait a minute!" He stood up and walked toward her. "Look, Ariel, I know you don't know me from Adam, but I like you and I think we have a lot in common. If you ever need someone to talk to, or just a shoulder to lean on, don't hesitate to call. Even if it's only for a Netflix movie night."

"Thanks for being so sweet, Chris." She gave him a kiss on the cheek, then she began walking towards the door, "I'll see you later."

"I hope so," he whispered to himself. "If that psycho doesn't kill you first."

CHAPTER 23

Malcolm's flight arrived into Chicago's O'Hare airport at 3:15 Saturday afternoon, two hours later than scheduled. He grabbed his garment bag from the overhead compartment and hurried through the terminal to meet his driver. While he waited outside of the baggage claim area, he pulled out Antoinette's letter to confirm the time of her performance was two o'clock. "These damn planes are never on time, unless you're rushing to catch one," he said to himself. "What else could go wrong?" No sooner did he mumble those words than his phone rang. He could see by the caller ID it was from the limousine service.

"Hello."

"Mr. Tremell, this is the dispatcher at Boston Coach. Your driver had a flat tire on the Kennedy Expressway; we're sending another car to you right away."

"How soon will it get here?"

"The closest driver is at Midway Airport; he should be there in thirty to forty-five minutes."

"That's not going to work for me; I'll just hop in a taxi."

"Sorry for the inconvenience!"

The line at the taxi stand was long and moving slowly. Malcolm rushed to the front of the line and offered one hundred dollars to the man who was next in line. He gladly accepted.

"DuSable Museum, Seven-forty East Fifty-sixth Place," Malcolm shouted at the driver, "and step on it!"

While the driver sped towards the airport exit, Malcolm called the museum to confirm Antoinette's event was still on time.

"DuSable Museum, how may I direct your call?" a woman's voice answered.

"I'm looking for information about a dance recital this afternoon. Can you tell me what time it starts?"

"I don't believe we have any recitals scheduled today, sir. But if you'll hold on for a moment, I'll double-check."

While he waited for her to return, he slapped himself on the forehead.

"Godammit! I knew I should have called first before I flew all the way from Miami!"

"You talking to me buddy?" the taxi driver asked

"No, I'm talking to myself. How long will it take us to get there?"

"In this traffic, we'll be lucky to get there in an hour!"

"That's just great, more good news!"

"Hello, sir?" the receptionist cut in.

"Yes, I'm here."

"We don't have a dance recital today, but there is a youth group scheduled to use the auditorium for dance lessons between two and four this afternoon."

"That has to be it," he said to her. "Thank you very much for your help."

After he hung up the phone, he tried to relax by looking out of the window at the CTA trains as they emerged from the tunnel underneath the airport. When he was a kid, he and his friends used to ride those same trains downtown to watch Bruce Lee movies at McVickers Theater. He laughed out loud when he thought about how they kicked and punched each other all the way to Ninety-fifth Street. Those were the good old days, he thought.

But those childhood memories didn't last long. He was stressing over the idea of coming all the way from Miami only to miss Toni by a few minutes. He looked down at his watch a hundred times as if he could make time stand still. Even the elderly taxi driver seemed to be working against him. He was driving slowly and letting other cars cut him off. Finally, after getting frustrated, Malcolm knocked on the glass and pressed a hundred-dollar bill against it.

"I'll add this to the fare and pay for any traffic tickets if you can get me to the museum in less than an hour!"

The taxi lunged forward and onto the shoulder passing the slow-moving cars. "Hold on tight, my brotha," the driver said in a heavy Indian accent. "I need all the cash I can get in this bad economy."

By the time the taxi came off the ramp at Fifty-fifth Street, it was 3:59 P.M. They turned east and headed toward Cottage Grove Avenue, driving like a bat out of hell. The driver ran two red lights, three stop signs, and almost hit an old lady crossing the street with her grocery cart.

When he finally made it to the museum, Malcolm jumped out of the car and rushed toward the entrance. Once inside, he approached the receptionist booth to get directions. An elderly black woman with long gray hair was sitting inside reading an *Essence* magazine.

"Excuse me, could you tell me where the auditorium is?"

"It's around that corner and to your left," she said. "Are you the gentleman who called earlier?"

"Yes, ma'am."

"Well, you'd better hurry, there are only a few people still inside."

"Thanks again," he said as he hurried off.

The closer he got to the auditorium, the faster his heart pounded. He was excited at the thought of seeing Toni again, but he dreaded the possibility of her not being there. As he got closer to the door, he could hear classical music playing softly in the background. He slowly pushed the door open and peeked inside. And there was Toni, looking more beautiful than he had remembered. She was standing onstage giving dance lessons to a group of young girls.

He wanted to rush over and surprise her, but he didn't want to interrupt their lesson. So he crept upstairs to the balcony and watched from the back row. He admired the way Toni handled the energetic young girls. She was trying to teach them how to pirouette but they were getting discouraged. "You can do it," she

178

told them. "Just pretend like you're a top and spin." The little girls turned as fast as they could, while balancing themselves on their toes. The parents, who were sitting near the stage, applauded as though their daughters had just won Olympic gold medals.

After another ten minutes, the lesson was over. The children collected their belongings and left with their parents. Toni turned off her music and began packing up her large duffle bag. He was ready to rush downstairs to meet her at the door, but she suddenly stopped. She stood in the middle of the stage and looked around as if she were checking to see if anyone was still inside the auditorium. Malcolm slid down in his seat as low as possible to avoid being seen.

When she felt comfortable that she was alone, she put on her leggings and ballet slippers and began stretching. She did a series of splits then stood up and touched her head to her knees. Malcolm had never seen a woman so limber. After she was warmed up, she pulled another CD out of her bag and placed it inside the player. Then she rushed to center stage to get set.

Malcolm was expecting to hear something classical or possibly a modern dance song. But his guess wasn't close. The song was "Makeda" by Les Nubians. It was a popular song by two black French women. The beat was hypnotic and smooth. He sat up in his seat and watched as Toni swayed to the rhythm of the music. Her motions were fluent and precise and her facial expression was intense. It was obvious that the song had a special meaning. He couldn't help feeling like he was trespassing on a private moment.

As the song continued to play, Toni stopped ballet dancing and began bumping and grinding like she was at a nightclub. And she was doing it so nasty. "Um, um, um," he said to himself. "God is good." He decided the time was right to make his move. He rushed down the balcony stairs and made his way backstage.

Toni was so deep into the music that she didn't see him coming as he danced his way toward her from the shadows. But she must have sensed him coming because she suddenly turned in his direction. She was startled at first, but once she saw it was him, she kept dancing and waved for him to come closer.

"Aw, sookie, sookie, now!" he said moving in towards her.

When he got right up on her, she put her arms around his neck, pressed up against him, and began to grind while singing in French.

La reine de Saba vit en moi
Makeda vit en moi.
Oh, oh, oh, oh.

Malcolm spoke back to her in French.

"Quelle belle vue est toi—mon amour"

"So you speak French, too!"

"I'm a man of many talents, Ms. Grayson."

"So, I see."

"What else are you good at, Mr. Tremell?"

The pace of their dancing slowed down and then came to a complete stop.

"I'm really good at this—"

As they moved toward each other, they met lips at the same time. She smiled. He smiled. Then they kissed. It was the first time in twelve years that he was affectionate with a woman without getting paid for it. When they finally separated, she kept her arms around his neck and leaned against his chest.

"I see you got my letter," she said.

"I got it, all right, but you could've saved us both a lot of time and stress by calling."

"I felt you were worth the wait and the effort."

180

"I hope I don't disappoint you."

"I hope you don't, either," she said then she kissed him again. "So now what?"

"Well, we could run off and get married," he said jokingly. "Or we can get something to eat."

"As much as I would love to take you up on the marriage proposal, I'll have to take door number two."

"Oh, well, you can't blame a guy for trying. Let's get outta here."

"I have a few people I have to see before I can leave," she said. "Why don't I call you in a couple of hours and you can tell me where you want to meet?"

"Actually, I wanted to invite you over to my mom's house for dinner; she makes the best peach cobbler in Chicago."

"Sounds like a plan! Will eight o'clock be too late?"

"Eight o'clock it is."

They hugged and Malcolm gave her a final kiss on the forehead as they were walking toward the exit.

"By the way, did you come all the way to Chicago just to teach this class?" Malcolm asked, "Or was it an excuse to see me?"

"As much as I would love to stroke your gigantic male ego, I came as a favor to a good friend. She had a last-minute engagement and she didn't want to disappoint the girls."

"You're one hell of a friend."

"No, baby, I'm one hell of a woman."

"I heard that!" he said with a smile as he wrote down his mom's address. "See you at eight."

When Malcolm made it back to the taxi, he hopped in and called his mother on his cell phone. The phone rang five times, which was unusual. When she finally picked up, he understood what was keeping her. She had "Love and Happiness" by Al Green blaring in the background.

"Love will make you do wrong," she sang loudly in his ear. "Hello!"

"Mama, it's me, Malcolm."

"Who?"

"It's Malcolm!" he yelled. "If you turn down that music maybe you could hear me."

"Hold on, baby."

She turned down the stereo and came back to the phone, still singing.

"Love will make you come home early, make you stay out all night long," she sang.

"I can see you're in a good mood today."

"Of course I am. The Lord blessed me with another day and my favorite son is coming home to have dinner with me."

"I'm your only son, Mama," I reminded her. "Now, stop singing for a minute so I can ask a favor."

"The last time you asked me for a favor, I had to bail you and Simon out of jail," she laughed. "Remember when you got caught with those guys in the basement back in—"

"Mama, please, can we not go down memory lane today?" He told her, "I called to ask you if it's okay to bring a lady friend over for dinner?"

He heard what sounded like a large skillet dropping in the background.

"Ouch!" Mama yelled.

"Are you all right?"

"I'm fine, son. I just need to make sure I heard you correctly. Did you say you were bringing a woman over for dinner?"

"Yes."

"Is this woman a friend, or a girlfriend?"

"I guess you could call her a girlfriend."

"Hallelujah!" she screamed.

"Why are you making such a big deal out of this?"

"I'm sorry I got carried away, sweetheart, but you haven't brought a girl home since you were in high school. I was beginning to think you were gay."

"I'm not gay! I'm not gay!" I hollered.

"All right, son, I believe you," she said. "Now let me go so I can make something special for your guest. What time will you be over?"

"About eight."

"Okay, I'll see you then," she said, sounding excited. "This is a young lady I've got to meet." Then she abruptly hung up.

The phone was dead, but that didn't stop him from venting. He looked at the taxi driver through the rear view mirror and yelled, "What are you looking at? I'm not gay, dammit!"

CHAPTER 24

Malcolm arrived at his mother's house in Hyde Park at 7:30. When he pulled into the driveway, he could hear "Let's Stay Together" by Al Green blaring from her living room window. He rang the bell and pounded on the door for nearly two minutes before she finally heard him. "I'm coming!" she yelled. "Hold your horses!"

When she opened the door, he was greeted with the aroma of collard greens and peach cobbler.

"Is dinner ready yet?" he asked and walked right past her.

"Boy, you better come back here and give your mama a hug."

"I was just kiddin', Mama. How's my favorite girl?" he lifted her up by the waist and gave her a kiss.

"Malcolm, you're so crazy. Put me down, boy!"

"Look at you, did you lose weight?"

"You noticed, huh? she said while modeling her new figure. "I've been working out at the gym and I dance every Thursday and Friday night."

"You look good, Mama, not bad for a 65-year-old."

"Shoot, I'm not bad for a 45-year-old. You see how fat these young girls are today?" she laughed. "Now, enough about me, where is your lady friend?"

"Her name is Antoinette, and she should be here any minute."

"Oh, my goodness, I look a mess," she said trying to fix her hair. "Watch the food while I go freshen up." Then she ran off to the bathroom.

"Mama, stop making such a big fuss. She's just a friend, not the President of the United States."

Malcolm took his bags into his old bedroom and started unpacking. His mother hadn't changed his room since he left after high school. He smiled as he looked around at the old furniture and old Parliament and Funkadelic posters hanging on the wall. There was also a shelf with all of his first-place trophies from talent shows.

"Too bad they didn't have "American Idol" back then; I would have blown them away!" he boasted while holding the biggest trophy.

While he was taking his trip down memory lane, the doorbell rang. "I'll get it!" Mama yelled. Malcolm quickly sprayed on a fresh coat of cologne and checked himself in the mirror.

"Good evening, Mrs. Tremell," he heard Toni say.

"Malcolm, it's your friend Antoinette!" she yelled. "Come in, sweetheart."

Malcolm couldn't believe how anxious he was as he waited for Toni to turn the corner from the hallway. Although he had seen her just three hours earlier, Toni had a presence about her that

186

made every encounter feel like the first time. When she walked into the living room, Malcolm stepped back to admire her outfit. She had on high heels and a white skirt that showed off her toned legs. Her hair was pulled back into a tight ponytail that came down just past her shoulder.

"Well, look at you," he said while holding her hand and spinning her around. "Umm Umm, Umm."

"Don't I get a hug or something?" Toni asked.

"Most definitely!"

At first he held her gently, trying to be respectful in front of his mother. But Toni was feeling so good that he tightened his grip until he could feel her heart beat. "Um," they both sighed.

"All right, you lovebirds, break it up," Mama said while taking Toni by the hand. "I think you better come with me, young lady."

"Where are you taking her?"

"Away from your hormones," she said as she led Toni toward the kitchen. "Can you cook, Chile?"

"Yes, ma'am," Toni said.

"Good, come on in here and give me a hand with these greens."

While Malcolm finished unpacking and checking on his clientele, Toni and Mama stayed in the kitchen for nearly thirty minutes yapping it up like mother and daughter. Mama came out to grab the family album and then retreated back inside the man-free zone.

The next thing Malcolm heard was his mother bursting out in laughter. "Aw, look at him. He's so cute!" he heard Toni say.

"Ok, that's it!" Malcolm barged into the kitchen to see what was going on. To his embarrassment his mother was showing Toni his baby pictures, and the photos from his grammar school graduation.

"Aw, Mama, please tell me you didn't."

"Shush, boy, you look adorable with you little shag hair cut."

"Yeah, shush, Bam Bam, you look adorable in those diapers, too." Toni laughed.

"Mama, I can't believe you told her that nickname."

"Don't worry, Baby, I won't tell anybody," Toni told him. "I just wish I could've seen you banging away on that toy piano when you were a baby. I bet you were cute."

"See what you started, Mama? I'll never live this down."

"Alright you two, let's put these away," Mama said while collecting the photo albums, "dinner is ready."

They sat down to a delicious dinner of red beans and rice, collard greens, neck bones, corn bread, and of course, her famous peach cobbler. They laughed and talked about his childhood and anything else his mother could think of to embarrass him.

"Malcolm was a real lady-killer," Mama said. "All the girls in the neighborhood had a crush on him."

"Tell me more, Mrs. Tremell," Toni said as she rested her arms on the table.

"When he graduated from high school, five different girls asked him to the prom."

"So how did he manage his little harem?"

"He charged them fifty dollars each and made them pay for his tuxedo and a limo."

"Did they pay?"

"Oh yeah! They were lined up, Chile. And if they didn't have the money, their parents were happy to foot the bill."

"Sounds like he had a nice little enterprise going on."

"I told him he should've gone into the escort business instead of real estate," Mama said. "He could've made a fortune."

When she made that comment, Malcolm nearly choked on his sweet tea.

"Are you all right, Baby?" Toni asked while patting him on

the back.

Malcolm nodded yes and went to the kitchen to get a paper towel to wipe his face, making sure to leave the door cracked so he could hear what else his mother was going to say to make him feel even more awkward.

"I thought Malcolm was a musician," Toni said. "I heard him play at Simon's club in Atlanta and he sounded great!"

"I've been trying to convince him to pursue his music full-time, but he won't listen," Mama said. "Maybe you can talk some sense into him."

"I'm surprised that someone with so much talent would have to be convinced. It seems like such a part of who he is."

"It is a part of him. A very important part," Mama said. "But when his father died, something inside of Malcolm died, too."

"I didn't know his father was dead," Toni said.

"Malcolm didn't tell you what happened?" Mama said getting emotional.

"No, ma'am. But we don't have to talk about it if it's going to upset you."

"It's okay, Sweetheart. Maybe it's time I talk about it," she told her. "I've been holding on to this for over fifteen years."

Mama reached for the family album and opened the page with her black-and-white wedding picture. It was taken back in 1971. Toni moved in closer and put her arms around Mama.

"He was such a handsome young man, wasn't he?" Mama said.

"Yes, ma'am. Did he die of natural causes?"

Mama chuckled as tears began to roll down her cheeks. "I guess you could call it natural. He was shot while screwing the next-door neighbor's wife."

"Oh, my God!" Toni sighed. "I'm sorry, Mrs. Tremell, I didn't know."

MICHAEL BAISDEN

"The painful part is that I still blame myself for what happened. I knew what was going on and I didn't do anything to stop it."

"It's not your fault, Mrs. Tremell. You can't control a man's behavior."

"But I had a choice not to put up with it!" she said getting upset with herself. "If I had taken a stand, I believe my husband would be alive today. But like so many women raised back in those days, we were taught to hang in there no matter what. A man is going to be a man, my mother would preach."

"That's not right, Mrs. Tremell. And it's not right for you to torture yourself," Toni said. "I know there's someone else out there for you who can make you happy. You're so beautiful and full of energy."

"Thanks for being so sweet, Antoinette," Mama said, wiping her tears away with her hands. "But you don't understand how deeply I loved this man. He was truly my soul mate. I remember the first time I ever saw him. We were at a high school sock hop and he asked me to dance. All the other girls were so jealous," Mama said with a smile. "When I looked into his eyes, I knew we would spend the rest of our lives together. It's the same way you look into Malcolm's eyes."

Mama gave Toni a hug and kiss on the forehead. "Sometimes true love only comes around once in a lifetime, Sweetheart. When it comes around for you, don't ever let it go," she told her. Then she said goodnight and went upstairs to her bedroom.

Malcolm waited inside the kitchen for a couple of minutes trying to give Toni a chance to get composed. When he finally came out, he tried to act as if he hadn't heard a word of their conversation.

"So, where's Mama?"

"She went upstairs to lie down," Toni said sounding depressed.

190

"Maybe this would be a good time to say good night."

"Don't be ridiculous. It's not even ten o'clock yet. Besides, we haven't had a chance to talk."

"Well, can we at least go outside? I could use some fresh air."

"I've got a better idea. Why don't we walk over to the lake front? I could use some fresh air myself."

They walked across the steel bridge on Lake Shore Drive over to the beach. The gentle breeze coming off the lake and the full moon created the perfect atmosphere. But Toni's mind was on the other side of town. She hadn't uttered a single word since they left the house. She just gazed off into the stars seemingly full of thought.

"Are you all right?" he asked her.

"To be honest with you, I'm pretty shaken up."

"Was it the conversation you had with Mama? I heard what she told you."

"Malcolm, why didn't you tell me what happened to your father?"

"What was I supposed to say: Hi, my name is Malcolm, and by the way, my father was shot in the head while fucking the next-door neighbor?"

"No, but you could've told me he was dead, especially if you were taking me to meet your mother. That's something that just might come up in casual conversation, don't you think?"

"You're right, I guess I'm out of dating practice. Believe it or not, I haven't brought a woman home to meet my mother since I was in high school."

"Why has it been so long?"

"Because I haven't met anyone special enough, that's why. You don't just bring any old woman home to meet your mother."

"Amen to that."

As they continued to talk, they took off their shoes and walked onto the cool sand. There were couples everywhere, holding hands and walking along the shoreline. Toni and Malcolm grasped hands tightly and walked toward the water.

"Malcolm, why haven't you asked me about my situation with Eric?"

"I didn't want to force the issue. I figured you would tell me when you were ready."

"Well, I think this would be a good time," she said.

They sat down on the sand near the water and leaned back resting on their arms.

"I've known Eric since college," she went on. "We dated for a while, but after we graduated, we sort of grew apart. About a year ago we ran into each other at a fund-raiser and we started dating again. The night before I met you, he asked me to marry him. I didn't officially accept but I didn't turn him down either."

"Now I'm even more confused."

"What I'm trying to say is I love Eric, I really do. But not in the way a woman should love a man she's going to marry," she said. "I struggled with my feelings all that night. Finally, I just put it in the Lord's hands and prayed. I asked God to give me a sign, any sign that would tell me if I was making the right decision. The very next day I met you. There you were sitting in the front row at the Fox Theatre smiling at me with that handsome face. Through all the bright lights, loud music, and hundreds of people in the audience, something made me look your way. At first I dismissed it as simply a physical attraction. But when you showed up with those eleven roses after the show, I knew I was about to set off on another journey with someone special."

"I don't know what to say."

"Don't say anything unless you feel the same way I do. I don't want to feel this way by myself."

"I do feel the same way, Baby. It's been a long time since I

192

truly cared about someone. Maybe too long."

"Just promise me one thing, Malcolm," she said as she held his face gently in her hands. "Promise me that we'll always be honest with each other. That's very important to me. I don't ever want to experience the pain your father put your mother through. I could never forgive you for that."

"I promise," he told her.

Then they kissed and held each other until the sun came up. It was the first time in his life that he had felt that close to a woman.

CHAPTER 25

A riel woke up Sunday morning and immediately went into her ritual. She brewed a fresh pot of coffee, retrieved her Sunday morning paper, and curled up on the sofa to watch the recording of *Baisden After Dark* on TV One. The show focused on books about relationships and self-improvement. "What a coincidence," Ariel said as she ran to get a notepad and pen. "A sistah could use a little advice right about now." Just when they were about to interview Iyanla Vanzant, the phone rang. Ariel checked the Caller ID to see if it was her mother, but the number was blocked.

"Hello?"

"Hello, Ariel, this is Lawrence. I know it's a bit early to be calling, but I wanted to make sure you were okay. I was getting worried since I hadn't heard from you in a while."

"Lawrence, I need time out from this relationship."

"Time out for what?"

"Time out to get my head together, that's what! Things are moving way too fast."

"Can't we sit down and talk about this like adults?" he asked.

"There's nothing to talk about," she told him.

"I hope you're not still upset with me about what happened with your little friend at The Cheesecake Factory."

"My little friend's name is Chris," she said defensively. "And it has nothing to do with him. I just need time to sort things out."

"Have it your way," he said. "But I'm not going to stop calling unless you accept these flowers as a token of our friendship."

"What flowers?"

"The ones I'm holding outside your door."

Ariel walked over to the window and pulled back the curtains. Lawrence's black Lexus was parked in her driveway.

"I'll be damned," she said to herself. When she opened the door, Lawrence was holding a gift basket filled with whipping cream, condoms, and other sexual paraphernalia.

"Surprise!"

"Surprise, my ass!" she said. "I don't appreciate you coming over here unannounced. And what the hell is that basket for?"

"I just wanted to show you how much I've missed you."

"Well, you've shown me, now good-bye!" she said, then she tried to shut the door.

"Damn, baby, don't be so cold," he said while putting his foot in the doorway. "Can I at least set this basket down and get a glass of water?"

Ariel thought about it for a second then reluctantly let him. She made him stand in the hallway while she poured him a glass of water from the faucet. She wasn't about to treat him to her bottled spring water.

"Here!" she shoved it at him. "And don't take all day sipping on it. I want to get back to my program."

Suddenly the phone rang. Ariel was hoping it was her mother.

196

She wanted to let someone know Lawrence was there, just in case he turned violent. She excused herself and rushed into the bedroom to answer it.

"Hello!"

"Good morning, Ms. Daniels. How's my favorite manager?"

"Simon, you won't believe who just showed up at my front door," she whispered.

"Who, Michael Jordan?"

"No, you smart aleck. It's Lawrence!"

"You mean the guy who went off on your friend at The Cheesecake Factory?"

"That's the one."

"I thought you dumped him."

"I've been trying to cut him loose since last week, but he's persistent."

"Well, if he starts choking the shit out of you, make sure you scratch him so the police can get a DNA sample," Simon joked.

"That's not funny. I think this guy is really crazy."

"You want me to call the police?"

"No, I think I can handle it," she told him. "But if you don't hear back from me in ten minutes, dial nine-one-one"

"Alright, Ariel, but be careful. I don't want to see you on *CSI*."

When she went back into the living room, Lawrence was sitting on the sofa with his shoes off. His feet were propped up on her glass cocktail table.

"Lawrence, what the hell are you doing?"

"I was just watching *Baisden After Dark*," he said with a smile. "I love this program, the comedian George Willborn is hilarious!"

"Well, the show is over." She turned off the television with the remote.

MICHAEL BAISDEN

"Okay, okay," he said while standing up. "I know when I'm not wanted. Just let me use your bathroom and I'm outta here."

Ariel didn't want to make matters worse, so she showed him to the bathroom. While he handled his business, she wiped off the table where he had smudged her glass with his sweaty feet. "You trifling bastard," she said to herself. Then she took his glass into the kitchen and washed it out in hot water.

While her back was turned toward the sink, Lawrence came out of the bathroom buck naked, wearing a bright green condom, and holding a can of whipped cream.

"Here's Johnny!" he said.

Ariel was so stunned the glass slipped out of her hand and shattered on the floor.

"What the hell do you think you're doing?" she asked.

"I thought you might want some meat with your breakfast," he laughed. "And this is one hundred percent beef Polish sausage!"

"Lawrence, you've got about ten seconds to put on your clothes and get the fuck outta my house!"

"Come on, baby. Stop fighting it. You know you want some of this sweet meat." He walked toward her while stroking his penis.

Ariel pulled a butcher's knife out of the drawer and swung it at him.

"If you take another step, I'm going to cut that little crooked motherfucker off."

"All right, I'm leaving!" he yelled as he ran into the bathroom and grabbed his clothes. "Just stop making dick threats."

Ariel followed him to the door waving the knife like a samurai. She didn't even give him a chance to put on his clothes before she pushed him out. "And stay out, you fuckin' lunatic!" she yelled as she locked the door.

A few minutes later, Lawrence drove off. Ariel collapsed on

the sofa and tried to calm herself down long enough to call Simon back.

"Simon, this is Ariel," she said nervously. "I just wanted to let you know that he's gone and I'm okay."

"Are you sure? You sound terrible."

"I always sound like this when a deranged man comes to my house first thing in the morning and pulls out his dick."

"I'm glad that's all he pulled out," Simon said.

"Don't worry, I've got protection and I know how to use it," she said, sounding cocky. "By the way, why were you calling me this morning?"

"With all the drama going on I almost forgot," Simon told her. "I called to remind you about Ladies' Night on Thursday. I promised Teddy that you would personally take care of him."

"Thanks, boss. That's all I need in my life is another lunatic," she said.

CHAPTER 26

The line outside Club Obsession stretched two blocks down Peachtree Street. The crowd was so unruly the security guards had to set up barricades to keep the overly eager women from cutting the line. Thursday nights had become chaotic since Teddy and his dance group, Hot Chocolate, began performing. It was the third consecutive sellout week and the crowds were becoming unmanageable. Ariel and Simon watched from the second-floor window trying to decide what to do.

"You think we should cancel the show?" Ariel asked Simon.

"Are you crazy? That would cause a riot," he said. "But we've got to come up with something fast. We don't have enough seats for all those people."

Ariel looked around the club with her hand on her chin.

"I've got an idea," she said. "Why don't we open the balcony area and place more chairs along the back wall? If we move those old boxes, we can accommodate another two hundred people."

"That could work, except for one problem," Simon said. "The view is obscured by partitions."

"Believe me, those horny women will look around a building to see a naked man."

"You're pretty sharp for a rookie," Simon said as he gave her a friendly peck on the cheek."

"What's that for?"

"For thinking fast on your feet," he told her. "If we get through this night in one piece, I might even give you a raise."

While he hurried to get the chairs in place, Ariel went to the dressing room to check on Teddy. She knocked on the door twice, but he didn't answer. "Theodore, you in there?" she yelled. When she put her ear to the door, she heard a smacking sound. She knocked again, this time harder. When he didn't answer, she used her key to unlock the door.

"Theodore, I know you're in—"

She was too stunned to get out the rest of her sentence. Teddy had one of the waitresses bent over against the wall banging her doggie-style.

"Didn't your mama ever teach you to knock?" Teddy said with a sly grin.

"I'm sorry, Ms. Daniels," the waitress whined as she pulled down her skirt. "I came to give him a glass of water and, well, one thing led to another. It was an accident!"

"Yeah, right. I guess you accidentally slipped on a wet spot and fell on his dick," Ariel said sarcastically. "Go collect your belongings, you're fired!"

"But, Ms. Daniels, I need this job."

"You should've thought about that before you bent over against that wall and played yourself," she told her. "Now get to steppin'."

She stormed by Ariel and mumbled, "Stuck-up bitch."

"Excuse me?"

"I didn't say anything."

"I know you didn't," Ariel said looking fierce. "If you open your filthy mouth again, they'll be carrying your ass out of here!"

Teddy was getting a good laugh out of the situation. He had a wide grin on his face as he pulled up his pants.

"You shouldn't have fired that sweet young thang," Teddy said. "Good help is hard to find."

"I would fire your arrogant ass, too, if it weren't for all the money Simon invested in you."

"Well, since I still have a job, I'm sure you won't mind closing the door so I can get dressed. My public is waiting," he said smugly. "Of course, you're welcome to stick around and watch."

"That's quite all right. I've already seen your little show, and frankly, I'm not impressed." Then she slammed the door shut.

Ariel tried to compose herself as she walked out into the club. The doors had opened for business and hundreds of women were rushing in to get front-row seats. Ariel maneuvered her way over to the bar where Simon was standing. He had the phone in his hand and was signaling that she had a phone call.

"Who is it?" she asked

Simon put his hand over the receiver.

"I think it's Lawrence," he whispered. "You want me to tell him you're not here?"

"No, I'll take it in the office," she told him. "I need to put this behind me once and for all."

Once Ariel was inside the office, she closed the door, and picked up. Simon muted the phone and listened.

"Hello?"

"Hello, Ariel. This is Lawrence."

"Didn't I tell you not to call me again?"

"I know, but I just wanted to talk."

"Talk about what?"

"About working things out."

"There's nothing to work out. So please stop stalking me, otherwise I'm going to call the police."

"I'm harmless, baby. But if you call the cops, I might have to get ugly," he said, sounding crazy. "Now stop playing hard to get and tell me what time I should pick you up tomorrow. My mother is having us over for dinner at eight o'clock. I told her all about you."

"Lawrence, I don't want to meet your mother, your father, or your damned dog. I just want to be left alone!"

"I'm not going anywhere until I get some pussy," he said. "I invested time and money in you."

"Look, you sick bastard, you heard what the lady said, now leave her alone!" Simon said, cutting in.

"Is that you, Mr. Big-Shot Club Owner?"

"It's me," Simon said. "You got something to say, tough guy?"

"Yeah, mind your own damned business!"

"Ariel is my business! If you have anything else to say, you can say it to me!"

"Now I see what's going on," he said. "You and Ariel have been mixing business with pleasure. Well, I've got something for both of your asses!" Then he hung up.

Simon rushed to the office to see how Ariel was doing. When he opened the door, she had her head down on the desk.

"This is like a bad dream," she said. "Why can't I find a straight black man in Atlanta with a good job, who's not on Prozac?"

"He's just trying to scare you," Simon said. "Guys like that are all talk."

"I don't know, Simon. I've got a bad feeling about this," Ariel said. "And now that you're involved, you'd better watch your back, too."

"Don't worry about me, I'm from the Southside of Chicago."

"Being from the Southside of Chicago doesn't make you bulletproof," she told him.

• • •

By 10:00 P.M. the club was jam-packed. Hundreds of women waited impatiently for the show to begin. "We want Teddy! We want Teddy!" they yelled. Simon gave the signal for the deejay to start the music. The lights dimmed and clouds of artificial smoke rose from the stage. The crowd erupted in cheers. "Bring on the meat!" one woman hollered.

When the smoke cleared, a mock toolbox was sitting in the center of the stage. Suddenly, four muscular men burst out of the cardboard box dressed like maintenance men: a plumber, an auto mechanic, a painter, and the short stocky one as an electrician.

Teddy came out last dressed in construction worker gear. When they stripped off their costumes, hundreds of women rushed the stage to get a touch of their muscular physiques.

"How much for a tune-up, baby?" a woman yelled, while flashing a twenty-dollar bill.

"I need my pipes unclogged," another screamed. "Can you help a sistah out?"

The security guards rushed onto the stage to keep the situation under control. One woman got hold of the penis of one of the mechanics and wouldn't let go. "You can rotate my tires anytime, you fine motherfucker!"

Teddy was grinding and collecting money in his thong and loving all the attention.

He licked out his tongue and massaged his penis working the crowd into a frenzy. Simon and Ariel stood on the upstairs balcony and watched in disbelief as professional women in business suits climbed over one another like teenagers to stuff the strippers' thongs with cash.

"I'm in the wrong line of work," Simon said. "I might have to put on a tight pair of drawers and get out there and shake it up myself."

"Don't even think about it," Ariel said while patting him on his slightly protruding stomach. "They don't make G-strings that hold nickels and dimes."

The evening was going better than Simon expected. The bartenders were selling drinks left and right and the customers were having a ball. Even the women sitting upstairs with the obstructed view were enjoying themselves.

"Looks like we're going to survive another wild-and-crazy night," Simon said to Ariel as he looked around the crowded room. "You might get that raise after all."

"Don't be so quick to count your chickens. The night's not over yet."

Suddenly, there was a loud crashing sound near the front entrance. The music abruptly stopped and the crowd began to panic. "Somebody is shooting!" a woman yelled. People scattered in all directions running for the emergency exits. Ariel and Simon ducked into the Jazz Room to keep from being run over.

"I hate it when I'm right," Ariel said.

"Me, too. And by the way, you can forget about that raise."

Once the commotion settled down, they came out to check the damage. It wasn't as bad as they had thought. Most of the tables and chairs were knocked over, but the glass to the aquarium wasn't damaged.

That was Simon's biggest concern. There were a few people lying on the floor hurt, some of them bleeding. "Call 911," Simon told Ariel. "I'm going to go see what the hell happened."

When he made it to the club's entrance, he noticed the large picture window was completely shattered. Glass was everywhere. The police had a man outside in handcuffs lying facedown on the ground. He was wearing flannel pajamas and a pair of flip-flops.

"Is this the son-of-a-bitch who did this?" Simon asked.

"Yes, sir," the officer said. "He threw a brick in the window and tried to make a run for it."

"Turn him over so I can see his punk ass."

"Wuz up, Mr. Big-Shot Club Owner?" the man said. "I hope I didn't ruin your little party."

"Lawrence?"

"In the flesh," he said. "Maybe that'll teach you not to fuck with another man's woman."

Ariel saw what was going on and came running. When she saw Lawrence covered in his muddied pajamas and wearing flip-flops, she didn't know whether to laugh or cry.

"Don't just stand there, Baby, come over here and give Big Daddy a kiss," Lawrence said with a smirk on his face.

"Lawrence, you need professional help," she said to him.

"All I need is you. And if I can't have you, nobody will."

"Get him outta here," Simon said to the officer.

"It ain't over!" Lawrence yelled while being carried away. "I know where you live you two-timing bitch!"

Ariel broke down in tears and began to tremble. Simon walked over and held her in his arms. "It'll be all right," he said, stroking her shoulders. "I won't ever let him hurt you."

Just then, Teddy came out of the club with his bag slung over his shoulder.

"I heard about what happened," he said. "Are you all right, Ariel—I mean, Ms. Daniels?"

"I'll be fine, Theodore. Thanks for asking."

"So does this mean the show is canceled next Thursday?"

"It's hard to say right now," Simon said. "I'll get in touch with you after I evaluate the damage."

"I'm glad I made a few dollars before this shit got out of control."

Teddy pulled out a fat roll of money and began to walk toward his car in the parking lot. But he couldn't leave without making a wisecrack.

"You must have some good pussy to have a brotha trippin' like that," he laughed.

Ariel walked up to him and slapped the grin off his face.

"You'll never know, smart ass!"

CHAPTER 27

The next morning Simon awoke just in time to watch Cynthia on the twelve o'clock news. She was interviewing a famous bodybuilder at a local health club. Simon couldn't help noticing how friendly they were. Too friendly for a television interview, he thought. The muscle-bound man inconspicuously stroked Cynthia's breast while showing her the proper way to bench press. It may have seemed innocent to most people, but Simon knew he was getting his feel on. "Don't make me come down there and hit your big ass with a dumbbell!" he shouted at the television.

Just then, the phone rang. He glanced over at the Caller ID to make sure it wasn't a pesky telemarketer. When he saw the 305 area code, he knew who it was.

"Wuz up, fool?"

"It's all good!" Malcolm said. "How's everything in Hotlanta?"

"Not so good, partner. Last night Ariel's psychopathic boyfriend threw a brick through the front window of the club."

"What did he do that for?"

"He thought Ariel and I were fooling around."

"I wonder what gave him that idea?" Malcolm said sarcastically.

"Don't even go there, I'm a one-woman man, not a big-time player like you."

"Well, my playing days might be over. I just got back from my little rendezvous with Toni in Chicago."

"How did it go?"

"It was great! We had dinner at Mama's house and chilled out on the lakefront."

"And?"

"And what?"

"Did you hit it?"

"No, I didn't hit it, you old freak," Malcolm said to him. "We just hung out for a few days and enjoyed each other's company. Sex wasn't a priority."

"Now, that's a first. I guess you're ready to settle down and get married."

"I don't know about getting married, but I'm definitely ready for a change! This gigolo game is getting played out," he told him. "As a matter of fact, Toni hooked me up with an agent friend of hers in New York. If I get a deal with a major record company, I'd seriously consider settling down, maybe even having a few kids."

"That's great news about the agent. I always told you, you could make a fortune in the music business!" Simon sounded excited. "But aren't you forgetting about Toni's fiancé? I do recall her mentioning that she was engaged."

"That's no big deal. Toni is giving him the boot as soon as she gets back to Atlanta."

"And I bet you don't feel an ounce of guilt, do you?"

"Hell, no! Why should I? He had his chance and he blew it. Or as my father used to say, if you snooze, you lose."

"That's cold-blooded. Whatever happened to brothers sticking together?"

"In the love game, it's every man for himself," Malcolm said. "I'm looking out for my own interests."

Simon was still watching Cynthia flirt with the bodybuilder. He wasn't the type to get intimidated by another man, but listening to Malcolm brag about stealing Toni had made him paranoid.

"You think Cynthia would dump me for another man?" Simon asked.

"I'm the wrong person to ask about Cynthia."

"Just answer yes or no," Simon said sounding concerned.

"Anything is possible," Malcolm told him. "I mean, you're not exactly the easiest man in the world to be in a relationship with."

"What's that supposed to mean?"

"You're a workaholic! As much as I dislike Cynthia, I have to sympathize with her. You probably don't have sex unless it's on your itinerary."

"Unlike you, I have a business to run. I can't lie up in bed all day," he said getting defensive. "Sometimes all I have time for is a quickie."

"Women need romance, not some guy slamming against her for five minutes like he just got out of prison," Malcolm told him. "It's the little things that matter to women, caressing, a gentle kiss on the neck and stomach, and sending them flowers when it's not a special occasion.".

"All right, Mr. Ladies' Man, what do you suggest?"

"Try something different like surprising her with a hot bubble bath by candlelight. Women love that kind of shit," Malcolm told him. "But most importantly, you've got to lick that clit until her toes curl."

"You know I don't take nosedives," Simon said.

"When it comes to satisfying your woman, the word *don't* shouldn't exist in your vocabulary."

"Look, I don't eat pussy and nothing you say is going to change my mind."

"It's men like you that keep men like me in business. All you care about is making money! Meanwhile, your woman is home alone with a vibrator and her little black book," he said to him. "It's only a matter of time before she steps out for some maintenance."

Simon was speechless. For the first time in his life he was faced with the truth about his obsession with money. His relationship with Cynthia was deteriorating because he hadn't made her a priority.

"You're right," Simon confessed. "But it might be too late to make things right."

"What do you mean?"

"I haven't talked to Cynthia in almost a week. Since her trip to New Orleans she doesn't return my calls. And when I do manage to reach her, she's on her way to church."

"Why don't you hire a private investigator? I have a contact in Atlanta who owns a detective agency. He's eccentric, but he's good."

"Maybe I'm just overreacting." Simon was trying to avoid dealing with the issue. "I mean, what could she possibly be getting into at church?"

"Don't be so naïve, Simon. Church is a player's paradise. I know men who go to service every Sunday just to meet desperate and lonely women."

"Okay, you've made your point."

Simon rummaged through his briefcase for a pen and something to write on.

"Now, tell me where I can find this associate of yours."

• • •

Late that afternoon, Simon arrived at the detective agency on 62ⁿᵈ Street not far from Liberty City. The office was on the second floor of a dilapidated building that sat between a liquor store and a barbecue joint. Simon glanced down at his notepad hoping he'd written down another address. Unfortunately, it was a perfect match. He grabbed the large brown envelope off the passenger seat and made his way across the street.

The building was a haven for derelicts and drug addicts. The hallways reeked of urine. Simon covered his nose with the handkerchief from his suit pocket and rushed to the second floor, stepping over an intoxicated bum along the way. The investigator's office was the third door on the right, directly across from the janitor's closet. PRIVATE DICK DETECTIVE AGENCY was awkwardly painted on the door. Simon took a deep breath and knocked.

"Who is it?" a man with a deep voice yelled out.

"It's Simon Harris, Malcolm's friend."

The door made an annoying squeaking sound as it opened. And the slower Simon tried to open it, the louder it squeaked. The detective was trying to crack the door just enough to peek out. Once he was convinced the coast was clear, he directed Simon to come in. He was clutching a nine-millimeter pistol, which he quickly tucked into the back of his trousers.

"Sorry for the tight security, but I make a lot of enemies in my line of work."

"I can imagine."

The detective was a tall, thin black man. But his dark complexion couldn't disguise the jagged scar on the right side of his face. It was the type of scar made by a knife with a dull blade or broken glass. He must have really pissed someone off, Simon was thinking.

The inside of the drab office was filled with all kinds of '70s paraphernalia. It was like walking through a time warp. The walls were covered with blue-light posters and old album covers. The living room was a shrine to the so-called black exploitation movies. Huge theater posters from movies like *Claudine, Foxy Brown, Cleopatra Jones,* and *J.D.'s Revenge* were everywhere. Taped to the refrigerator door was a mint-condition Ohio Players cover, the one with the woman pouring honey on her chest.

The detective was a throwback to the '70s himself. He wore a pair of tight polyester pants and was sporting a short, unkempt Afro. Simon damn near fell out when he saw the Afro pick with the retracting red-and-green handles sticking out of the back of his head. Simon would've paid anything for that antique.

"I guess we haven't been formally introduced. My name is Ricky," he said, while extending his hand, "but everybody calls me by my last name, Roundtree. You know, like Richard Roundtree in the movie *Shaft.*"

"Yeah, I remember," Simon relied. "He's a bad mother—"

"Shut your mouth," Roundtree cut in.

It was impossible for black folks to say *Shaft* without throwing in the lyrics to the song. It was one of those black things. The humor was unexpected but it helped to relax the mood.

"So, Mr. Harris, what can I do for you?"

"As I told you briefly on the phone, I'm getting married and I want to find out if my fiancée is cheating."

"Sounds simple enough," Roundtree said while popping open a can of Old English 800. "Did you bring the information I asked for?"

"I've got everything right here."

214

Simon emptied the contents of the brown envelope onto an old scarred-up wooden table that sat in the corner of the dimly lit room. There were several pictures of him and Cynthia, Debra and Cynthia, and one picture of Cynthia's Range Rover.

"Can I offer you a brew?" Roundtree asked.

"No thanks. The last time I drank some Old E, I woke up in a vacant lot wearing nothing but my drawers."

"Suit yourself."

Roundtree sat down on the dingy black leather sofa and looked over the pictures carefully. He grunted a few times then took a long sip of his beer.

"Nice-looking lady you got there," he said casually.

"Thanks."

"Have you considered a prenuptial agreement?" he asked out of nowhere.

"What made you ask that?"

"Just curious."

"You sound as if you expect to find something negative."

"Let's just say, I'm intuitive about these things."

He looked at Simon and smiled uncomfortably. Then he stood up and began pacing.

"Okay, this is the deal," he said with his hand firmly pressed against his chin. "I'll follow her for the next thirty days to see what I can dig up. When I put together enough evidence, I'll give you a call."

"That sounds fair enough. So how much is this little investigation going to cost?"

Roundtree wrote down a figure on a piece of paper towel and handed it to Simon. The amount read $2,999.95.

"What's up with the ninety-five cents?"

"It's marketing," he explained. "I got the idea from watching those Tae-Bo infomercials. The workout video sells for nineteen ninety-five because it sounds cheaper than twenty."

He escorted Simon to the door.

"I assume you want to be paid in cash?"

"If it's not a problem," Roundtree said. "I don't want Uncle Sam in my pocket, if you know what I mean."

"Any particular denominations?"

"How about twenty-nine hundred-dollar bills, one fifty, two twenties, nine singles, three quarters, two dimes, and four pennies?"

"Tell you what," Simon said, pulling out a wad of money. "I'll pay you an even three thousand up front if you throw in that Afro pick with the red-and-green handles."

"You've got yourself a deal!"

CHAPTER 28

I t was a typical muggy summer night in August. Malcolm was standing outside on his balcony admiring his view of the ocean from twenty stories up. The view was breathtaking. For the first time in years he was beginning to feel at peace. Having Toni in his life was the inspiration he needed to change the direction of his life. It had been almost three weeks since she left for Europe with her dance company and he was really missing her. But he had to put all those romantic thoughts aside. There were still some important appointments he had to keep, and he didn't want to be late. He took one last hit of his drink and slipped into his Armani suit. The clock on his nightstand read 8:50 P.M. and his limo was supposed to meet him downstairs in the lobby at nine.

As he was going out the door, the phone rang. The double ring let him know it was his business line. He was hoping it wasn't one of his horny clients calling for a last-minute appointment.

"Tremell Agency," he answered.

"Hey Cool Breeze!" Melvin yelled. "I called your business number to see if you quit the escort business like you said you would. I can see you're doing business as usual." He sounded disappointed.

"I am out of business after tonight," he said. "I couldn't turn down five thousand bucks just for escorting some rich broad to a dinner party for two hours. It's easy money."

"What do you need with five thousand dollars? I thought you told me you had a record deal in the works?"

"I told you I had an agent. Until I actually sign a contract, I still have bills to pay and the taxes and maintenance on this expensive-ass condo are no joke. Not to mention the insurance on that Lamborghini. Besides, I'm doing it as a favor to Helen. We fell out on bad terms in Atlanta and I wanted to make it up to her."

"Stop making excuses, Cool Breeze. Why don't you just admit that you can't give up the life? You love playing mind games on these women too much. And you love the variety of sex, too," he said. "Face it, you're addicted to women!"

"The only thing I'm addicted to is money."

"Okay, then, I'll give you five thousand dollars to stay in tonight."

"Yeah, right."

"I'm dead serious," Melvin told him.

"So what's the catch?"

"There is no catch. I just wanna keep you from backsliding. One night can turn into two, then three, and so on. Next thing you know, you're caught up in the game again."

"Nice try with the morality speech, old man. But I'm still going through with this last engagement. It wouldn't be professional to cancel on such short notice."

218

"Five thousand dollars is a lot of money to pass up just to stay at home, eat popcorn, and watch pay per view." Melvin joked. "You sure you don't want to think it over?"

"I'm sure, but if you insist on spending your hard-earned money, why don't you make a donation to a worthy charity, like Players Anonymous," Malcolm said, laughing. "The first step to recovery is admission."

Just then, the other line rang on Malcolm's business phone.

"Hold on, Old Man, I have a call coming in."

"Hello?"

"Mr. Tremell, your car is here," the doorman said.

"Thank you. I'll be right down."

When he clicked back over, Melvin was coughing uncontrollably.

"You all right?"

"I'm fine," he said, still hacking. "I just need a drink of water."

"You don't sound fine to me. Have you been taking your medication?"

"I'm fine, I told you! I've been taking care of myself since before you were a twinkle in your daddy's eye. So stop trying to act like my doctor!" he snapped.

"Stop trying to sound hard," Malcolm snapped back. "You don't scare me like you do those employees at the club. I know you're just a grumpy old teddy bear."

Melvin was laughing so hard he nearly choked himself to death. After a few more coughs, he managed to compose himself.

"You always did know what to say to make me smile, Cool Breeze," he said while clearing his throat. "Look, I know you have to get going. But the first chance you get, I want to meet this special lady of yours. Any woman who can make you retire from the gigolo game must be an angel."

"Well, when my angel comes back from touring in Europe,

I'll ask her if she can fly in on her wings to meet you. But only if you promise to start taking better care of yourself," Malcolm scolded him. "I don't want to take any chances of losing you. You're the most important person in the world to me."

Melvin paused.

"That's a promise, Cool Breeze," he said getting choked up. "Now, get your narrow behind outta there and go take care of business. And you'd better keep your dick in your pants tonight, you hear?"

● ● ●

As Malcolm approached the entrance to the Continental downtown near Bayside, he checked himself in the mirror one last time. Big Al lowered the partition to ask for direction.

"What time do you want me to swing by to pick you up, Mr. Tremell?" Big Al asked.

"Why don't you park over in the waiting area and wait for me; this might not take as long as I planned."

"Yes, sir," he said.

Big Al began to raise the partition, but he suddenly lowered it again.

"Was there something else?" Malcolm asked him.

"I hope this is not out of line, but—

"But what, Big Al?"

"In the few months I've been driving you, you seem a lot more relaxed than when I first met you."

"That's what a good woman will do for you, Big Al; they soften the rough edges."

As the stretch black limousine cruised slowly toward the front of the hotel, the valet rushed to open his door.

"Welcome to the Marriott," he said. "Do you need help with

your luggage, sir?"

"No, thank you. I'm here to meet someone."

Big Al helped Malcolm on with his jacket and he headed for the front entrance through the crowd of tuxedos and long formal dresses. The lobby was buzzing with hundreds of people in formal attire chatting among themselves, mostly about business. When Malcolm looked over at the red-and-white banner hanging on the wall, he understood why they were so stiff. It read: WELCOME NATIONAL ASSOCIATION OF FINANCIAL CONSULTANTS. "What a bunch of tight asses," he muttered to himself.

"My sentiments exactly," a woman said from behind him. "Mr. Tremell, I presume?"

"You would presume correctly," he said as he turned to face her. "And you are?"

"Catherine Howard, your date for the evening." She extended her hand. "Nice to meet you."

"The pleasure is all mine."

Catherine looked to be in her late 50s but she was in extraordinary shape. She bore a stark resemblance to a younger Diahann Carroll. Her hair was shoulder length with grey streaks. She wore a fitted royal blue dress, which accentuated her full figure and dark chocolate complexion.

"You look surprised," she said bluntly.

"You don't miss much, do you?" he blushed. "My facial expression must have given me away."

"Yes, it did," she said smiling flirtatiously. "What were you expecting? A troll?"

"To be honest with you, I didn't know what to expect. Sometimes pictures can be deceiving. But I can tell you that the picture of you in the magazine didn't do you justice. You should have that photographer shot."

"Sometimes when you operate in a man's world, the worst

221

thing to do is try to exude sexuality. It's hard enough to be taken seriously as it is."

"I don't see how being taken seriously would be an issue for a woman worth half a billion dollars. Not to mention your company grossed one hundred and twenty million dollars last quarter. And you've got an offer on the table with China to set up a factory in Beijing. You're also widowed, you have two adult children, five grandkids, and a German Shepherd named Bandit."

"I see you've been doing your homework."

"I like to know the details about the people I spend my time with."

"And your bed, too, I would imagine," she said in a sensual tone.

They continued to talk as they strolled toward the restaurant. Along the way, Catherine attracted a great deal of attention. She was waving and shaking hands as if she were a politician.

"Good evening, Ms. Howard," some said.

"I enjoyed your speech, Ms. Howard," others professed.

"Don't forget to e-mail me that report," a woman added.

Catherine just smiled and kept walking as if it were no big deal. Once they made it through the corporate gauntlet to the restaurant, the maître d' sat them at a reserved table in the back. It was obvious by the way Catherine carried herself that she was accustomed to this kind of preferential treatment.

"So do you come here often?" Malcolm asked sarcastically.

"From time to time," she smiled and inconspicuously grazed his ass with her hand. "What about you? I'm sure that there's not too many hotels in town you haven't frequented."

"*Touché!* You don't pull any punches, do you?"

"No, I don't. That's why I'm the presiding officer of this male-dominated organization today. I go for what I want."

"Well, since we're being so direct, what does a beautiful and powerful woman like yourself need with an escort service? It seems to me that you could have any man you wanted."

"Three simple reasons," she said while moving in close so no one could hear her. "One, I need a strong man who knows how to take charge. Highly successful men who earn millions of dollars surround me everyday in the corporate world, but behind closed doors most of them are a bunch of pussies. I need a man who isn't afraid to tell me no. Even a woman of my caliber wants a man with a little street in him."

Malcolm nearly choked on his water.

"Could you please be a little more direct?" he responded while trying to clear his throat.

"Don't act so surprised. If you read the article you should know I'm from the Garden Valley projects in Cleveland. And you know we keep it real on the east side."

They fist bumped as she went on.

"The second reason is most men are very insecure, especially black men. If they can't handle a sistah making fifty thousand, what makes you think they can handle a woman whose net worth is five hundred million?"

She cleverly slid her hand underneath the table and began moving it slowly up his thigh.

"And what's number three?" Malcolm asked while trying to keep a straight face.

"I love attractive young men with big dicks," she said bluntly. "And yours came highly recommended."

Malcolm's dick got as hard as a petrified jawbreaker. And it didn't help that Catherine had unzipped his pants and was massaging his balls. He tried to keep his composure as people began to stare. But Catherine didn't even flinch. She just kept stroking his penis and talking dirty.

"Why don't we stop wasting time and go upstairs to my suite.

I have a bottle of Champagne chilling in a bucket of ice and a Bill Evans CD. I heard you love jazz."

"I see you did your homework, too!"

"That's the first thing they teach you in Business 101: always have a plan."

"I'll tell you what, I'm going to the little boys' room to give you some time to cool down. And when I come back, we're going to have a nice dinner and good conversation. Then I'm outta here." Malcolm stood up from the table and put his hand in his pocket to conceal his erection.

"Can I order you anything to drink while you're gone? A screwdriver, perhaps?"

"Very cute," he said smiling. "But I'll just have Vodka and Cranberry. On second thought, make that a double shot of Tequila, tell them to hold the lime."

On his way to the restroom he saw a familiar face sitting inside the bar area. He moved in closer to make sure his eyes weren't playing tricks on him. But when she turned to the side, he was sure it was psychotic Tina. "What the hell is she doing here," he said to himself. Last he heard, she had settled with her NBA husband for ten million cash and the house. I'm sure he would've paid twice that just to get rid of her crazy ass, Malcolm was thinking. She was having drinks with a gigolo named Dexter. He was an up-and-coming young player who mostly worked in West Palm Beach and Boca Raton. Malcolm quickly turned away and walked back toward the restaurant as fast as he could. He knew Tina would make a big scene if she saw him.

When he made it back to the table, Catherine was sipping on a margarita with a horny look in her eyes. Malcolm didn't want to lead her on by going upstairs to her room, but he couldn't take a chance of running into Tina.

"Boy, that was quick," she said.

"I think I'll take you up on that offer to go upstairs."

"What about dinner?"

"We can eat upstairs," he told her.

"I like the way that sounds," she said with a sly grin. "Just let me pay for these drinks and we can start with dessert."

While she charged the bill to her room, Malcolm was trying to devise a plan to separate himself from Catherine long enough to get past the bar, which was on the way. He wasn't about to take a chance on Tina seeing him and Catherine together. He had to think of something fast.

"All right, let's go," she said.

"Aw, damn! I left my wallet in the limo," He said while patting his pockets. "Why don't you get a head start and I'll meet you upstairs?"

"I don't mind going with you. I wanted to get a breath of fresh air anyway."

"I'd rather do it myself," he told her. "Besides, that will give you time to slip into something more comfortable."

That idea must have appealed to her because she promptly wrote her room number down on a napkin and handed him an extra key.

"Now don't keep me waiting," she said seductively. "I've got a fire that needs to be put out."

"Don't worry, baby, I'll be right behind you with my hose."

She gave him a peck on the cheek and rushed off. Once she was out of sight, Malcolm made his way towards the door feeling relieved. "That was too close for comfort," he sighed. Just then Tina and Dexter came strolling out of the bar headed straight for him. He stooped down and tried to mix in with the crowd, but at six-three he was hard to miss. Before he could make a getaway down the opposite side of the corridor, she spotted him. "Malcolm, is that you?" she hollered. He wanted to walk off, but he knew Tina could get ignorant and draw even more attention to him. So he played it off by waving and giving her a phony smile.

Tina grabbed Dexter by the hand and rushed over. There was no way she was going to let him get away without bragging about how much money she had gotten from her divorce. She also wanted to flaunt Dexter in his face. It was well known that they were competitors and they didn't like each other.

"Well, well, well, if it isn't Malcolm the Lover," she said.

"Hello, Tina. Nice to see you."

"Don't give me that shit. You know I'm the last person on earth you want to see."

"If you knew that, why did you rush your ass over here?"

"Watch your mouth when you're talking to a lady," Dexter said, trying to sound hard.

"Look, young buck, you need to stay out of grown folks' business," Malcolm said, walking closer to him. "Now, I know you think you're hot shit up there in West Palm Beach but you're in south Miami...with the big dogs now. So I suggest that you rest that chivalry role before I toss your young ass over that banister."

Dexter and Malcolm were about the same height but he was thin, at least fifteen pounds lighter. Dexter saw the look in his eyes and quickly backed down. He knew Malcolm had a reputation for knowing how to handle himself and was one second away from dropping him. Men read one another's eyes that way. It's a street thing.

"Baby, could you excuse us for a second?" Tina said to Dexter. "I want to talk to Malcolm alone for a minute."

"Yeah, Dexter, why don't you go kick some rocks like a good little boy. I promise I won't keep her long," Malcolm said conceitedly.

226

Once Dexter was gone, Tina's whole attitude changed. Her tone was more polite and she began rubbing on his chest.

"Malcolm, why haven't you returned my calls? You know I need my monthly fix."

"I've been busy."

"For a whole month?"

"Look, Tina, You're not my wife. I don't owe you an explanation. Besides, I can't deal with your dramatic mood swings."

"I'm much better now that my divorce is final. Didn't you hear about the settlement on ESPN?"

"Yes, I heard, congratulations," he said sarcastically. "Now why don't you get a life and leave me alone?"

"Because I'm in love with you. And I just can't cut my feelings off like a faucet the way you do."

"Yeah, right. You're so in love with me that you've been laying up with a different gigolo every weekend. I heard it through the grapevine that you've been buying dick all over Florida." Malcolm looked her up and down like she was a piece of trash. "What's wrong? Your crazy ass can't get laid without paying for it?"

Smack. She slapped him right in the face. The entire room turned in their direction to see what was going on.

"Fuck you, Malcolm!" she shouted. "Whatever rich bitch you came here with is no better than me. How much did she pay for some dick tonight?"

"This conversation is over," he said as he began to walk away. "Have a good night."

"Don't you walk away from me, you arrogant bastard, I'm not through with you yet!"

People rushed out of the restaurant and the sports bar to watch the circus. Some of them even had the nerve to take pictures. He walked as fast as he could toward the elevator with Tina trailing him screaming obscenities. Luckily, the elevator was waiting when he got there. He frantically pushed the button for the fifteenth floor trying to force the doors shut.

"It's not over between us!" she yelled. "I bought your ass before and I can buy you again. You ain't nothing but a piece of meat who sells to the highest bidder."

As the elevator doors closed, she took off her high-heeled shoe and flung it at him. It grazed him on the right side of the forehead drawing blood.

"Take that, you pretty motherfucker."

When he arrived at Catherine's suite, he went inside the bathroom to find a towel to put on his face. The bleeding wasn't bad, but it did require a bandage. After he patched himself up with the first-aid kit, he walked out into the candlelit room. "My Foolish Heart" by Bill Evans was playing softly in the background. Catherine was lying on the bed face up, wearing a see-through black negligee and sipping on a glass of Alizé. She looked him up and down like a slave on the auctioning block without ever acknowledging the bandage on his head.

"So, how do you like it?" Catherine stood up and modeled.

"That's very nice," he said, trying to sound interested.

"Nice enough to eat?"

"Like I said, you get straight to the point."

He was about to go into a big discussion about how the agreement was not to have sex, but he was feeling so low he figured, what the fuck, and began taking off his clothes.

Catherine was looking good and he needed to let off some steam. While he stripped out of his clothes, he tried to put Toni out of his mind. When that didn't work, he played mind games with himself trying to justify what he was about to do. She's probably screwing some guy in Europe right now, he was thinking. What she doesn't know won't hurt her was another thought. It's not like we're married, was the last worst idea he tried to tell himself while he ate Catherine out. After she climaxed, she jumped on top of him and insisted on returning the favor.

When it was all over, he put on his clothes, collected his five thousand dollars, and headed for the door. No thank-you, and no good-byes, not even eye contact. Catherine just turned over, lit a cigarette, and ordered room service. She got what she wanted and she was through with him.

As he walked down the corridor toward the service elevator, he rubbed the bandage on his head and tried to pretend like it was business as usual. But in the back of his mind he was replaying what Tina had said to him. "You're just a piece of meat who sells out to the highest bidder." He heard her voice say it over and over again. And he knew she was right, but this time he knew he had sold more than his body. He had sold his integrity.

CHAPTER 29

Teddy was naked except for his underwear and one sweat sock. "Come on, seven!" he yelled as he prepared to roll the dice. He and Cheryl were playing strip Monopoly and Teddy's dog game piece was sitting on Pennsylvania Avenue. He needed seven to pass Go and collect two hundred dollars. If he rolled a three or five, he would land on Park Place or Boardwalk, properties that belonged to Cheryl.

Teddy blew on the dice and rolled them gently onto the board. "Come on, lucky seven!" he hollered. The dice seemed to turn in slow motion and finally landed flush: the total was five.

"You landed on Boardwalk, now take off those drawers!" Cheryl screamed as she jumped up and down on the bed.

"Wait a minute, baby. Your braids got in my eyes," Teddy said getting upset. "I get another turn!"

"I hate playing Monopoly with you, Teddy. You're such a sore loser."

"I'll show you who's a sore loser."

231

Teddy grabbed Cheryl by the hair and slammed her down onto the bed. He ripped off her panties and rammed his penis inside of her.

"Ouch, baby, not so rough," she screamed. "I'm still dry."

"Well, you better start thinking wet because I'm not about to stop."

Just as Teddy was getting into a nice groove, he heard a car door shut in the driveway. He quickly hopped off Cheryl and peeped out the window.

"Guess who's coming to dinner?" Teddy said jokingly.

It was Cheryl's husband, David. Cheryl slipped on a pair of shorts and a T-shirt and began straightening up the bed.

"Don't just stand there, Teddy, give me a hand."

"I don't do beds," he said arrogantly.

"Damn you, Teddy. I don't want to lose my family over this."

"You should have thought about that two years ago when you started fucking me in your husband's bed."

She didn't have time to argue. She fixed the bed herself and then sprayed the room with Lysol, all the while giving Teddy a dirty look. By the time she was finished, her husband had walked through the front door.

"Honey, I'm home!"

"I'll be right down, sweetheart!"

Teddy was still standing there in his drawers with one sock on, acting as if nothing was happening.

"Hurry up. Hide in the closet!"

"How do you expect me to get my big ass in that tiny space?"

"Teddy, please!" she begged.

"Who are you talking to, honey?" David asked.

"Nobody, sweetheart."

She could hear David coming up the stairs. She looked Teddy dead in the eyes and begged him again to hide. But he wouldn't budge.

"I'll never forgive you for this," she said as she rushed out into the hallway to intercept her husband. "Hey, baby, you're home early. What happened to your business trip?"

She tried to intercept him at the foot of the stairs with hugs and kisses, hoping to turn him around, but he was carrying a heavy suitcase and was determined to set it down in the bedroom.

"My meeting in Kansas City was canceled, so I decided to come home to my beautiful wife."

"Well, let me take your suitcase and you can recline in your chair in the living room while I make you something to eat."

"I'm not hungry," he said as he made it to the top of the stairs. "I just want to take off my clothes and get into bed."

Cheryl closed her eyes and put her hands over her ears as David walked into the bedroom. But nothing happened. When she nervously peeked into the room, Teddy was gone. The window was wide open, so she thought he had climbed out.

"What was all that screaming about?" David asked while undressing.

"What screaming?"

"I heard you screaming when I pulled into the driveway."

"Oh, I was just doing some crunches. You know I've been trying to stay in shape for you."

"And you look damn good, too, baby," David said, reaching out his arms. "Now come here and give your old man a real hug."

While they were embracing, Cheryl saw a finger come out of the closet. It was Teddy and he was pointing toward the door. That was his signal telling her he wanted to get out.

"Honey, don't you want to shower before you go to bed?"

"I just had a shower before I got on the plane," he said, trying to unzip her shorts. "But what I think I could use is some good loving to help me relax."

That's not what Cheryl had in mind, but she figured any distraction was better than none. She began undressing herself and laid him down on the bed. Suddenly, David sprang up out of the bed and headed toward the closet.

"Wait a minute, let me get my High Karate cologne out of the closet. When we first met, that aroma used to drive you crazy."

"No!" she shouted as he went to open the door. "I mean that was ten years ago, sweetheart. All I want to taste is you."

David took his hand off the knob and went back to bed. Right away Cheryl covered him with the blanket and jumped on top, blocking his view of the closet. Teddy came creeping out with his clothes balled up in his arms. But instead of rushing down the stairs, he stood in the doorway while he got dressed. Cheryl was irate at first but then she became turned on. It was the best sex she had had with her husband in years.

When Teddy had seen enough, he blew Cheryl a kiss and nonchalantly walked down the stairs and out the door. As he walked across the street to his truck wearing a devilish smile, his pager went off. The number on the display read 2911. It was his girlfriend, Karen. As he headed home to deal with the latest crisis, he was his usual arrogant self. "Whatever the problem is, baby, I've got a perfectly good lie to explain it," he said, laughing.

• • •

Teddy was feeling cocky as he pulled into the circular driveway, until he saw the bright yellow Corvette parked behind Karen's Mercedes. It belonged to Karen's younger sister, Lisa. She was also a lawyer. He tried to straighten out his wrinkled clothes as best he could, then he took a hard swallow and went inside.

He could hardly open the door with all the boxes piled up

against it. On the side of each one was marked GARBAGE in bold black marker. Karen and Lisa were carrying the last box down when he walked into the living room.

"What's this supposed to be, spring cleaning?" he joked.

"I'm glad you think this is funny, you two-timing snake, because you'll be laughing on the streets tonight," Karen said as she set the box down.

"Okay, calm down for a minute and tell me what's going on."

"Well, let me see." Karen began to count on her fingers. "First there were the phone numbers in your pocket, then there was the lipstick on your collar. Last month I found a pair of Victoria's Secret panties that mysteriously buried themselves in my drawer. And now I come home from a hard day's work and I hear a message on my machine from one of your tramps."

"What message?" Teddy asked, playing dumb.

"We don't even need to go there, Teddy. Just get your stuff and leave."

"So what is Lisa here for?"

"To make sure you don't try to talk me out of it. I usually don't make a fool of myself when people are around."

Lisa was standing off to the side quietly. It was obvious she didn't want to be there.

"How are you doing, Lisa," Teddy asked.

"I'm fine, Teddy," she said passively.

"How's business at the firm?"

"Business is fine, too."

"All right, that's enough of this family reunion. Get your boxes and get out!" Karen yelled.

"Can't we talk about it, baby? You know I love you."

"You don't love anybody but yourself, you bald-headed bastard. Now get out before I call the police and have you thrown out."

"So it's like that, huh? Okay, then, have it your way. I'm outta here."

Karen stood at the door like a drill sergeant until Teddy loaded the last box into his truck. When he walked out of the door with the last one, she slammed the door shut behind him.

"And stay out!" she yelled.

"Don't you want your house keys back?"

"The locksmith is on his way over to change the locks. You can keep yours as souvenirs," she said to him from the window.

"You're really serious this time, aren't you?"

"Serious as a lawsuit. Speaking of which, I heard about all your kids. I hope they catch up with you one day and put you under the jail, you deadbeat!"

"I'd rather be a deadbeat than a lonely old woman with stretch marks and a worn-out pussy," he said while opening the door to his truck. "And by the way, thanks for the Navigator, the credit cards, the Versace suits, and the Rolex. Thanks to you, I've finally saved enough money to get a place of my own."

Karen ran to the door, while trying to pull the ring he had given her off her finger.

"You go to hell, Theodore, and take this Cracker Jack ring with you!"

When she finally managed to get the ring off, she threw it at him. It ricocheted off the truck and fell onto the driveway.

"Hey, you need to be more careful. This truck cost a lot of money," he laughed. "But I guess I don't need to tell you that, now do I?"

As he was about to drive off, he looked over at Lisa as she walked across the lawn towards her car. She was wearing a yellow halter-top and miniskirt to match her corvette. It was an outfit she had worn for Teddy many times before while Karen was out of town. It was his favorite.

They made eye contact on the down low, then he sped off. As he turned the corner, he laughed out loud knowing he had another place to go home to. That's probably what Lisa wanted all along, he was thinking. Maybe that's why she'd buried her yellow Victoria's Secret panties in her sister's drawer.

CHAPTER 30

I t was early Saturday afternoon. Ariel barely made it inside the door before she collapsed onto the living room floor. She had lifted weights at the gym for an hour and jogged five miles around Stone Mountain. It was the first time she had exercised all summer and it showed. She was so out of shape she had charley horses in both legs. After she caught her breath, she peeled out of her sweaty Howard University T-shirt and went upstairs to run a shower. While she was stripping off the rest of her clothes, she noticed the message light on her answering machine was blinking. Ariel was hoping it was her latest blind date, Raymond.

"Hey, baby, it's me," a man's smooth and masculine voice said. "Just wanted you to know that my plane landed safely. I've got to drop off some presents for my girls and then I'll be headed your way. I should be there by five o'clock. By the way, I brought you a souvenir from Mexico. I hope you like it. See you in a minute. Bye."

239

Ariel smiled. It was the call that she had been waiting for all day. She rushed back into the bathroom and jumped into the shower. It was 3:30 P.M. and she wanted to have everything ready when Raymond got there.

• • •

By 4:45 P.M. Ariel had created a nice romantic atmosphere. The dining room table was set with long white candles and a bottle of white Zinfandel was chilling in a bucket of ice. She even broke out the good china to add a touch of class. But Ariel wanted Raymond to admire more than the place setting. After she checked on the shrimp casserole, she rushed upstairs to get changed. Instead of putting on the conservative sundress she had laid out, she put on a pair of low-cut shorts and a white cotton tube top to show off her pierced belly button. "Girl, you know you got it going on!" she said as she admired herself in the mirror.

While she waited impatiently for Raymond to arrive, she sipped on a glass of wine and masturbated. And the more she drank, the hornier she got. She was contemplating whether or not to break out her vibrator when the phone rang. "Please, God, don't let this be Raymond calling to cancel," she said to herself.

"Hello."

"Hey, sweetheart, just called to see how you were doing. Hope I wasn't interrupting anything."

"As a matter of fact, Mama, you were!"

"Well, excuse me, Ms. Thang. I'll just let you go then." She sounded hurt. "Good-bye!"

"Wait a minute, Mama. I'm sorry for snapping at you," Ariel apologized. "I've got a quick minute to talk."

"I don't know what's going on with you, young lady, but I don't like it."

"I've been under a lot of pressure lately; you know, with the situation with Lawrence and all."

"I thought you told me he stopped calling weeks ago."

"He did, but it's going to take awhile to adjust to my daily routine without looking over my shoulder."

"You managed to adjust well enough to go out with what's his name."

"His name is Raymond, Mama."

"Why haven't you brought him over to meet me?" she asked. "From what you told me about him he sounds like a nice young man. Didn't you say he was a doctor?"

"Yes, he's a doctor and he's very busy. He spends a lot of spare time with his two daughters, and he runs his own practice," she told her. "And for your information, he's not just a regular doctor, he's a heart surgeon."

"Listen to you sounding all proud; I'd like to meet any man who can impress you this much."

"I'm impressed, all right." Ariel was admiring the picture of Raymond hanging over her fireplace.

"It sounds to me like you finally met Mr. Right," her mother said. "I just find it hard to believe that a man with his credentials is still single."

Suddenly, the phone went silent. Ariel cleared her throat a few times then tried to change the subject.

"So have you talked to Joyce or Sheila lately? How are the kids doing?"

"Ariel Michelle Daniels!" Mama interrupted. "I know you're not messing around with no married man. I didn't raise you that way!"

"Calm, down, Mama. I'm not trying to take him away from his wife and kids. I just want to have a little fun, that's all."

"Lord, I know your father is rolling over in his grave," she

241

said. "Why can't you find a nice single man to get involved with, like your friend Chris? What's wrong with him?"

"Chris is okay, but he's not my type. He's short, light skinned, and he's not aggressive enough for me," she explained. "Raymond is tall, dark, and handsome, and I admire what he's doing with his life. That's a combination hard to find in any man, married or single."

"But baby, what about having a family of your own. Don't you want to get married and have kids someday?"

"Mama, that whole fantasy of the all-American family with the four-bedroom house, the mini-van, and the two-point-five kids is the reason why I've been alone for all these years. Ever since I was a little girl I've been sizing up every man up as a potential husband. But what I should've been looking for was someone who makes me happy."

"And you think sleeping with a married man is going to make you happy?"

"Yes, it will, Mama. And it's damn sure better than being alone," Ariel said, getting emotional. "I'll be thirty-five years old next month and I'm going to spend my birthday with someone that I'm interested in, not some boring, watered-down substitute for a man, and I don't give a damn whether he's married or not!"

"Don't you realize there are other people affected by your decision? Have you even stopped to think about his wife and kids? When you're spending time with him, do you ever think about the time he's taking away from them. Do you?"

"When I met Raymond online, he was up front about being married. But he said he was going through some problems. It's not my fault that his wife can't take care of her business."

"Ariel, don't be such a damn fool. All married men lie about having problems. It's all a game."

"To be honest with you, Mama, I don't care if he's lying or not.

All I know is he makes me laugh, we enjoy each other's company, and the sex is good," she said defiantly. "He may not be all mine, but half a man is better than no man."

Ariel heard Raymond's car pull into the driveway. She wiped the tears from her eyes and checked her makeup in the hallway mirror.

"I'm sorry, Mama; I've got to go now. Raymond is here."

"I'll let you go, Ariel, but you better take some time out to read your Bible. Galatians six, verse seven. 'A man reaps what he sows.'"

"Thanks for the sermon, Mama," she said sounding smart. "Good-bye."

CHAPTER 31

S imon was in the kitchen cooking a pot of spaghetti when he realized Cynthia had been gone for more than twenty minutes. She told him she was feeling ill and needed to step outside for some fresh air. He looked for her on the patio and in the backyard, but she was nowhere to be found. He figured she was lying down in bed again. For the past week she had complained about headaches and dizziness.

On his way to the bedroom, he noticed a light coming from the bathroom. He crept over to the door and put his ear next it. He could hear Cynthia talking on the phone, almost in a whisper and then she began coughing violently.

"You all right in there?" Simon pounded on the door.

"I'm fine," she said as she flushed the toilet.

A minute later she opened the door. Her skin was pale and her eyes were swollen and red.

"Cynthia, you look terrible." Simon tried to put his arm around her. "Are you sure you don't need to see a doctor?"

"I told you I was fine!" She backed away from him. "Stop babying me!"

"Whom were you talking to on the phone?"

"You need to stop eavesdropping on me!"

"You're damn right I was eavesdropping. This is my house!"

"For your information, I was talking to my doctor."

"Your doctor, huh? Why in the hell do you have to whisper to talk to your doctor?"

"Because I didn't want you to know I was sick, that's why!" she said angrily. "You always make such a big deal out of everything."

"Most women would appreciate a man who cared about how they were doing!"

"Well, I'm not most women!"

Cynthia stormed into the bedroom and began collecting her belongings. She packed her makeup bag, a toothbrush, and a set of silk pajamas that she always kept at Simon's house.

"What is this, another break up?"

"I love you, Simon, but I need a break!"

"If it's just a break, why are you taking your toothbrush and pajamas?"

Cynthia took a deep breath, then unpacked her things. "Now, are you satisfied," she said as she picked up her bag.

She tried to hurry by him but he grabbed her car keys out of her hand.

"Give me back my keys, Simon."

"Not until you tell me what's really going on."

"Nothing is going on. I'm just feeling a little sick, and want to go home and lie down."

"Why can't you lie down here?"

"Because I want to be in my own bed, that's why. And besides, the smell of that spaghetti is making me throw up."

"If that's what's bothering you, just give me a minute and

I'll get rid of it."

"Damn you, Simon! Stop trying to fix shit all the time!" she screamed. "Just give me my keys and let me go home!"

"Fine!" He tossed the keys at her.

Cynthia grabbed them out of the air with one hand and rushed out the door. Simon paused for a minute then he hurried outside after her. Just as she was about to drive off, he ran over to her car and knocked on the window. She let the window down to hear what he had to say.

"Hold up, Cynthia," he said leaning inside the window. "I'm sorry for trippin'. It's just that we haven't spent any time together lately and I miss you."

"I miss you, too, Simon, but sometimes people need space."

"Can we at least get together for lunch tomorrow and try to work things out?"

"I told you earlier this week that I was doing a live remote from my church tomorrow. After that, I have a meeting with my producers."

"At first I was the one who was busy all the time. Now that I've taken time out from the club to spend more time with you, you're the one who's too busy," he said. "Funny how the script has been flipped, huh?"

"It'll all work out, Simon. Like I told you, I just need some space."

She gave him a dispassionate kiss and drove off. Just as her taillights disappeared over the hill, Simon's phone went off. It was Roundtree, the private detective. As he pushed the button to answer, his hands shook slightly in anticipation of getting bad news.

"Hello, Roundtree? So, what's the verdict?"

"Well, do you want the good news or the bad news?"

"Give me the bad news first."

"Your fiancée is definitely fucking around," he said bluntly. "And when I say fucking, I mean it literally."

"And what's the good news?"

"The good news is now you don't have to marry this tramp, end up in divorce court, and lose half your shit!"

But that was no concession for Simon. The woman that he loved had allowed another man to defile her body. And she did it while sharing his bed and lying to his face. He felt like a fool. The phone went silent as the rage built up inside of him. His throat got dry and his fists were balled.

"Mr. Harris, are you still there?"

"Yeah, man, I'm here," he said while trying to clear his throat.

"So what's your next move?" Roundtree asked him. "You want to get together tomorrow and look over the pictures, or what?"

"To hell with tomorrow! I want to see everything you got on that cheating bitch tonight! I'll be at your place in fifteen minutes."

• • •

Simon burned rubber as he came to an abrupt stop in front of Roundtree's rundown building. He jumped out of his car without bothering to lock it and hurried inside. He was so enraged that he didn't even notice the stench of urine and vomit in the hallway. When he arrived at the second floor, Roundtree was waiting with the door already open.

"Damn, that was fifteen minutes flat!" he said while glancing at his watch.

"Let's get down to business!"

Roundtree pulled out an iPad from his desk drawer and sat it down in front of him. "You wanna get down to business, huh?" He turned on the device and opened a file on the desktop. There were fifty different video files and jpeg photos. "How's that?"

"What is this?"

"It's called technology, my man!"

"Well, open some of these files and let's see what this trick has been up to. Show me this one first," Simon pointed at the file labeled, Deep Throat: 7/21, 11:30 P.M.

"Why don't you start with the PG-13 stuff and work your way up to the triple X?" Roundtree told him. "That one is some pretty raw shit!

"Don't play games with me, man. I'm not in the mood."

"Okay, it's your dime," he said, then clicked on the icon. "But remember, I tried to warn you."

The beginning of the video was blurred. When it came into focus, the camera zoomed in on a man sitting in the passenger seat of Cynthia's Range Rover. It was too dark to see his face through the window, but when they stepped out of the truck and into the moonlight, his features were very distinguished. He stood about six feet tall and was of medium build. His hair was short and wavy, like he had a relaxer in it. And he wore a well-groomed beard.

Cynthia opened the hatch and pulled out a blanket and basket. They walked to the beach and laid a blanket down near the water. While she laid the basket on the sand, the man pulled out a bottle of wine and poured two glasses. They appeared to be very familiar with each other as they cuddled on the blanket and talked with their feet in the water. Cynthia occasionally laughed and gave him pecks on the cheek.

But the romantic scene soon turned erotic. Cynthia pulled up her skirt and sat between his legs. From a distance it looked innocent, but when the camera zoomed in, the expression on her face was a dead giveaway. She was frowning and biting down on her finger to keep from screaming. The man was slapping her on the ass forcefully and you could read his lips asking, "What's my name?"

But the most painful part was the passionate expression on Cynthia's face; she wasn't just screwing this man, they were making love. The camera equipment was state-of-the-art so Simon could see every detail, from the perspiration running down her back to the veins in her neck as she moaned in ecstasy.

"Okay, turn it off. I've seen enough."

"Hold up, here comes the part where he slaps her on the ass with his Bible," Roundtree joked.

"I said that's enough, goddammit!"

Roundtree pressed the stop button and stood by quietly. Simon put his hands over his face and leaned back against the sofa.

"Did you find out who he is?" Simon asked.

"I know everything there is to know," Roundtree boasted. "Where he works, where he lives, his Social Security number, his credit rating, and his shoe size."

"Why don't we just start with where he works."

Roundtree handed Simon a five-by-eight photo of the same man standing in a church pulpit.

"What is this?"

"That's a picture of our man at work. His name is Reverend James Young from the First United Baptist Church."

"He's a goddamned preacher?"

"A part-time preacher and full-time manipulator," Roundtree said. "He runs a bogus counseling service out of an office in Ft. Lauderdale. That's usually where he and your fiancée meet up for sex."

"I knew that heifer was lying when she told me she was going to Bible study."

"Oh, but there's more!" Roundtree told him. "She's not the only woman in the congregation that he's boning."

Roundtree pulled out another set of pictures. They were of the same man with different women. Some of the photos showed them kissing and hugging. And others were more explicit.

"This guy is a true player," Roundtree went on. "And he's very particular about the type of women he sleeps with. Most of them are married and have high-profile jobs such as politicians, lawyers, and TV personalities. In other words, he chooses women who have something to lose if they open their mouths."

"Well, you can call me a player hater because this son-of-a-bitch is going down!" Simon said ruthlessly. "Do you have this backed on a thumb drive?"

"Way ahead of you!" Roundtree handed him the small device. "Whatever you plan to do, count me in," Roundtree said.

"Thanks for the offer, but I don't want to get you involved. What I'm about to do is pretty low-down."

"Low-down is my middle name! Besides, there ain't nothing in the world I hate more than a hypocritical preacher."

Simon paused for a second to reconsider. There was no one else he could trust to go through with such a vengeful deed, not even Malcolm.

"All right, you're in!" He gave Roundtree a high five. "Now go grab a couple of cans of Old E and I'll tell you the plan."

CHAPTER 32

It was early Sunday morning and the parking lot of the First United Baptist Church was filled with expensive cars and a van marked EYEWITNESS NEWS. The church was holding a special service at eleven o'clock honoring a local civil rights leader. Every television station in town was there for the big event, including Cynthia's station, WBBQ. Simon and Roundtree crept around the back disguised as technicians and blended in with the army of television people who were setting up for the live broadcast.

Once they were inside the building, Simon played lookout while Roundtree broke into the media room and hacked into the church Facebook and Twitter accounts. There were over 300,000 friends and fans, some of them in other cities and countries. After they downloaded all the church members' profile addresses, they snuck into the projection room and switched the media card for the video presentation. The church security was so busy trying to get their faces on camera they didn't notice what was going on. Within thirty minutes, the trap was set.

"Now what?" Roundtree asked.

"We go have a seat and wait for the fireworks to begin."

Services began promptly at eleven with the praise team firing up the congregation. The atmosphere was joyful and full of energy.

"Praise the Lord," some shouted.

"Thank you, Jesus!" others prayed.

As Simon watched the enthusiastic crowd, he wondered if he was having second thoughts about what he was doing, especially with so many children present. But his sympathetic feelings quickly faded once Reverend Young was introduced. He strutted onto the stage dressed in a bright yellow suit and toting a Bible. Simon wanted to choke the shit out of him as he charmed the mostly female audience with his self-righteous grin. "Smile while you can, you perpetrator," Simon said to himself. "Vengeance will be mine."

After the pastor led the opening prayer, the choir rose to sing the musical selection "Someone's Knocking on My Door." They looked magnificent in their royal blue robes as they lined up perfectly on the elevated tiers. When the song ended, Reverend Young swaggered up to the microphone in his flashy suit to acknowledge the media and special guests. Meanwhile, the ushers hurried to set up the screen for the video presentation. The ceremony for the honoree was about to begin with the showing of clips from the civil rights documentary *Eyes on the Prize*. Simon's stomach was in knots as he watched and waited.

"On my cue, send out the tweets and Facebook post," he told Roundtree.

"I'm ready like Freddy," Roundtree replied. "Their little performance should be playing worldwide by lunch time!"

Once the screens were set up, Reverend Young gave the signal for the ushers to dim the lights. As the room darkened, Simon caught a glimpse of Cynthia and her girlfriend Debra sitting at the front of the church in the VIP section. "I guess screwing the pastor has its privileges," Simon said to Roundtree.

The opening of the tape was a series of quick snapshots of Reverend Young and the married women, kissing and having sex. Roundtree edited the tape perfectly so that each picture was distinct. There was no mistaking who was doing what. Almost immediately you could hear men screaming out from the darkness.

"Hey, that's my wife!" one man yelled.

"And that's mine!" another hollered.

But the show was only just beginning. The pictures were quickly followed by the video of Reverend Young and Cynthia having sex on the beach. You could hear the hands of parents slapping against their children's faces as they attempted to block their view.

"Turn that garbage off!" Reverend Young yelled out at the projectionist. But the tape continued to play. It was Reverend Young's bad luck that the projectionist was a horny 17-year-old boy who was learning more from watching three minutes of that tape than he had in four years of sex education. Someone else had to charge upstairs to the booth to turn off the tape. But by that time the tape had played up to the part where Reverend Young slapped Cynthia on the ass with the Bible and asked, "What's my name?" You could hear the entire congregation gasp.

"Ok, send the tweets and Facebook post now!"

Suddenly all the cell phones in the congregation began to ring and vibrate simultaneously. To make sure everyone opened the link, Simon had labeled it: YOU JUST WON A MILLION DOLLARS! Everyone was clicking like crazy to see what they won, but what they got was a link to the same video they were watching on the screen.

When the lights came up, Reverend Young was standing at the pulpit sweating like a Klansman at a Black Panther rally. Cynthia was sweating, too, as the camera crews from every television station in Atlanta, including her own, focused on her.

"Calm down, please. This whole thing is a big misunderstanding." Reverend Young pulled the handkerchief from his suit pocket and wiped his brow. "That tape was made many years ago when I was still living in sin."

"You must think I'm a damned fool," one man yelled out as he paused the video on his BlackBerry. "The truck in that video is a 2011 model."

"And how do you explain those pictures with my wife, you crooked bastard," another man yelled, looking at the video on his iPhone.

The situation erupted into a free-for-all as several men charged the stage. Simon wanted a piece of him, too. He fought his way through the impassioned crowd until he reached the stage. But the burly security guards had created an impenetrable wall around the pulpit to protect the pastor.

"Hey, preacher, over here!" Simon yelled until the pastor looked his way. The expression on his face left no doubt that he knew who Simon was.

"What the hell do you want?"

"I just wanted to quote a scripture to you. Exodus, chapter twenty verse seventeen. 'Thou shalt not covet thy neighbor's wife.'"

"I've got a scripture to quote to you, too: Kiss my ass!"

"No thanks, I've seen your ashy black ass on video and it ain't nothing nice to look at," Simon told him.

The security guards quickly ushered the pastor out the side doors away from the cameras. However, Cynthia wasn't so lucky. Reporters were swarming around her and shoving microphones in her face.

"Is it true that you were having an affair with the Pastor?" one reporter asked.

"How can you call yourself a role model when you're having

sex with a man of the cloth?" another reporter added.

Simon could see the look of humiliation in her eyes, the same humiliation he felt watching her play herself. Debra was standing off to the side watching helplessly as her girlfriend was being ripped apart. Simon walked up from behind Debra and tapped her on the shoulder. She was stunned when she saw who it was.

"Simon, what are you doing here?" she asked looking stunned.

"That's not important," he told her. "I just need you to give this to Cynthia." He handed her a plastic bag.

"What is this?"

"It's a going-away present," he said with a smirk. "She'll understand."

Simon walked toward the exit where Roundtree was waiting. Once they were out of sight, Debra ripped opened the sealed package. Inside was a pair of white silk pajamas, a toothbrush, and a blank white card. Being the nosy woman that she was, Debra couldn't resist opening it.

Inside the card was a caricature of a man kicking a woman out of a house, with her luggage flying. Printed underneath it in bold letters was:

Enjoy your space.
Yours truly, Simon

CHAPTER 33

The three-hour flight from Miami to New York had gone by quickly. Malcolm had been working on his musical arrangements since the plane took off, and he hadn't lifted his head up once except to ask for a glass of water. As the plane was getting close to landing, the flight attendant was determined to get his attention.

"Excuse me, sir, can I get you another glass of water, or anything else?" she asked flirtatiously.

"No, I'm fine, thanks," Malcolm replied without looking up at her.

"I don't mean to be forward, but you haven't even looked out of the window since you boarded the plane. That must be some awfully important work when you get there!"

MICHAEL BAISDEN

"As a matter of fact, it is," he said while looking up at her. "I'm a musician and I've got a meeting with some record people about releasing a CD!"

"Really, what kind of music?" she asked while placing her hand on the back of his seat. "I love all kinds of music!"

"I play piano and I do some composing."

"Can I hear some of it?"

"Sure, put these in!"

Malcolm handed her his headphones and turned up the volume on his laptop. The flight attendant snapped her fingers off beat and smiled.

"That sounds great! Is that you?"

"Thank you and yes it is."

"You're very talented, Mr.—!

"Malcolm," he said gently shaking her hand. "Malcolm Tremell."

"Well, Malcolm, is there any way we can get together so I can hear more?"

"Once upon a time I would have jumped at that offer, but I have a beautiful and extremely talented woman in my life. But thanks for the offer, I'm really flattered."

"Well, here's my card just in case you change your mind!" she said, not caring who was watching or listening. "You can never have too many friends or fans, right?"

"No thank you, miss," Malcolm pushed the card back to her. "I've got all the support I need."

The fight attendant walked away looking embarrassed.

"Excuse, me," Malcolm summoned her back. "How long before we land?"

"We should be touching down at LaGuardia Airport in fifteen minutes," she said, with an attitude.

Just then, the other flight attendant came over the intercom to announce their approach to LaGuardia. He pulled up his window shade to check out the awesome view of downtown Manhattan. The skyscrapers seemed more like mountains as they blocked out the setting sun. Even Chicago with the Sears Tower and John Hancock buildings paled in comparison to the immense New York skyline. It was truly Gotham City.

Once the plane landed, Malcolm tried to call Simon again to share the good news, but he hadn't been able to reach him in three days. As his phone rang, he was hoping not to get his answering machine again.

"Hello, this is Simon. Sorry I'm not available to take your call. Please leave a message at the tone and I'll return your call at my earliest convenience. Thank you." Beep.

The message sounded dry and cold. Not at all like Simon. Malcolm didn't bother to leave a message. He was sure he had received his previous ten. He was desperate for answers, so he dialed the only other number where he knew he could be reached, Club Obsession. Normally, he respected Simon's need for privacy, especially after such a traumatic experience. But he had a gut feeling that something was wrong.

As the phone to the club rang, Malcolm was pulling his luggage through the busy crowd on the way to the terminal exit.

"Hello, Club Obsession," a woman's voice answered.

"Is Mr. Harris in?"

"No, he isn't. Would you like to leave a message?"

"Yeah, tell him to call his buddy Malcolm, ASAP."

"Malcolm, thank goodness, it's you!" Her demeanor changed completely. "It's me, Ariel!"

"Ariel, can you tell me what the hell is going on? Simon's not answering my calls!"

"I haven't heard from Simon since that drama at the church," she said, sounding stressed. "And the media has been camped

261

outside the club looking for him. It looks like the O.J. Simpson trial out there."

"Did Simon say where he was going?"

"All he said was he needed to go home to get his head together. But when I drove by his house, his car was gone and all his lights were out."

Malcolm knew exactly where Simon was. He was in Chicago, back in the old neighborhood. That's where he always went to sort things out.

"Try not to worry, Ariel. I think I know where Simon is," he told her. "Just give him a few days and I'm sure he'll call to let you know he's okay."

"Malcolm, I wish you could be here for him. He really needs a friend right now."

"As soon as I meet with my agent in New York, I'll go track Simon down and have a long talk with him."

"Before you go, Simon told me about your record deal. Congratulations!"

"Well, it's not official yet. My agent had his final meeting with the record company today. Hopefully, we'll have something to celebrate when I meet up with him tonight."

"I know Toni is happy for you!" she said excitedly. "Is she in New York, too?"

"Unfortunately, she's on tour in Europe until next week," he told her. "I really wanted her to be here to celebrate with me. Without her, none of this would've been possible. She put me in touch with the right people and it's been smooth sailing ever since."

"Good luck with everything, Malcolm, and thanks for calling. I know it's going to happen for you."

"You sound more confident than me."

"I know a winner when I see one," she said bluntly. "Just don't forget where you came from when you make it to the big time. Some brothas develop a serious case of color blindness after that first million."

"You don't have to worry about me selling out. I prefer my coffee black, no sugar, no cream," he laughed.

When Malcolm reached the curbside, it had just begun to drizzle. He noticed a short, elderly, black man standing next to a stretch limo holding up a sign with his name on it.

"I'm Malcolm Tremell," Malcolm said to him.

"Hello, Mr. Tremell, I'm your driver, Otis. May I take your bag?"

"But I didn't order a stretch."

"Your agent, Jerry Cross, thought it would be a nice surprise!"

"In that case!" Malcolm handed him his heavy garment bag. "Let's roll!"

Otis pulled out a tiny umbrella and held it over Malcolm's head until he stepped inside the car. As soon as the door shut, then someone yelled out, "Surprise!" It was Toni. She was wearing a sexy short black dress and holding two glasses of champagne.

"Surprise is right!" Malcolm said, then leaned over to give her a hug and kiss. "When did you get back from Europe?"

"I flew in late last night. Jerry and I have had this planned for weeks," she replied. "I wanted to be here to celebrate with you just in case the deal went through. I hope you don't mind."

"There's no one else in the world I would rather share this moment with than you."

When they pulled apart from hugging, she noticed the gash on his forehead—the one from Tina's high-heeled shoe.

"Oh, Malcolm, what happened!"

"It's no big deal. A guy scratched me while I was playing ball."

"Are you sure you're okay, baby?" she asked in a motherly tone.

"I'm fine, Toni. So, where is Jerry now?" he was trying to change the subject.

"We're supposed to meet him at ten o'clock at a club in Manhattan called the Ritz. It's a popular hangout for people in the recording industry. In the meantime, let's get our private celebration started."

She handed him a glass of champagne, dimmed the interior lights, and slid in a Lauryn Hill CD. As the song "Nothing Even Matters" played softly in the background, she lifted her glass to make a toast.

"Here's to you, Malcolm. May God bless you with all the success you deserve."

"No, here's to you, because there's no amount of success or money in the world that can replace the value you have in my life."

Her eyes became misty as they clinked glasses and took a sip. But the taste of the champagne and the moment was bittersweet because he had told another lie. Deep in his heart he knew all his lies would come back to haunt him. Lies always do.

CHAPTER 34

I t was raining heavily by the time Malcolm and Toni arrived at the Ritz nightclub in Manhattan. Otis pulled up as close as he could to the club and escorted them to the door while holding an umbrella over their heads.

"I'll be parked across the street," he said. "Just step outside when you're ready to go."

"You can take a long nap, Otis," Toni said. "I'm in a party mood tonight!"

The moment they walked inside the club they could feel the walls vibrating. The song "Just Be Good to Me" by the SOS Band was playing and the dance floor was crowded with professionally dressed men and women getting their groove on.

"This place is off the hook!" Malcolm shouted over the music.

"Yeah, I know. This used to be my regular hangout. Eric and I used to come here once a month for Old School Friday."

"You and Eric, huh?"

"I'm sorry, sweetheart, I didn't mean to bruise your ego," she said playfully. "I know how territorial men can be."

"I'm not one of those insecure men who gets jealous over ex-boyfriends," he told her. "I wouldn't mind running into him tonight to say hello."

"Oh, no. I made sure he was out of town before I made reservations. I didn't want to take any chances of you two bumping heads tonight. Once that testosterone kicks in, it's all over."

"What does your former fiancé do for a living, anyway?"

"He tells rich people how to invest their money. As a matter of fact, he's at a convention in Miami with some of his nerdy accountant friends. I'm surprised you two haven't crossed paths as often as he is in South Beach. I think you would have a lot to talk about considering you have so much in common."

"Like what?"

"Both of you are intelligent and arrogant."

"Who me? Arrogant?"

"Malcolm, you love attention. I saw you flirting with your eyes the minute we walked in the door," she joked. "But it's okay, honey. You don't have to explain. I know it's a horrible disease and you men can't help yourselves. As long as you look and don't touch, I won't have to show the ghetto side of me."

She gave him a peck on the cheek and grabbed him by the hand.

"Now let's go find our table so I can set my purse down and show you how we do it, New York style," she continued. "I'm going to wear your butt out on the dance floor tonight."

The hostess escorted them over to a table that overlooked the huge oval dance floor, right next to the bar. Toni didn't waste any time taking off her shoes and dragging him out into the crowd of gyrating bodies.

266

"I hope you don't think I'm going to let you embarrass me, do you? I used to start the party back in the day," Malcolm boasted.

"And I used to shut them down, baby, so bring it!"

When the deejay mixed in the song "Shame" by Evelyn "Champagne" King, he took her to school.

"Come on, baby, show me what you got!" he said while dancing circles around her.

"All right, Malcolm. Don't make me embarrass your old ass out here in front of all these people."

"I ain't scared of you, Ms. Ballerina. Come on with it."

Toni broke out into a move right out of the movie *Flashdance*. She kicked her leg straight up over her head, did a pirouette, and came down into a split. Malcolm took a hard swallow and looked around to see if anybody saw her. They did!

"You go, girl!" the woman next to them shouted.

"Damn, did you see that?" the man on the other side yelled.

The deejay must have known Toni personally because he got on the microphone and gave her a shout-out.

"Ms. Antoinette Grayson is in the house tonight, ladies and gentlemen. It's show time!"

The deejay mixed in "Bad Girls" by Donna Summer and the dance floor parted like the Red Sea. Before Malcolm knew what happened, he was standing alone in the middle of the floor with a professional dance machine. She was having a ball and making him look bad, spinning and sliding all over the place like she was on Broadway.

"Okay, sweetheart, you made your point," he whispered in her ear. "Can I please get the hell out of here now?"

"Not yet, one more song!" she screamed.

"You know you're wrong for this, don't you?"

"Yeah, I know. But you're secure enough to handle it, right?"

They danced for another song then walked off the floor

to a standing ovation. When they made it back to their table, Malcolm's clothes were soaked.

"Remind me to pay you for that lesson," Malcolm told her while wiping his face with a napkin.

"You can write me a check after you see the private show I have planned for you at the hotel tonight."

"If you have half as much energy in bed as you do on the dance floor, I'm in for a long night."

"My passion for dance is a passion for life, and it will all be transferred to you tonight."

"Right now, I need to make a transfer in the men's room," Malcolm said as he stood up from the table. "And I need to wash some of this sweat off my arrogant face, unless you need to go to the ladies' room first?"

"I'm fine," she said looking cool. "I haven't broken a sweat yet."

"Show off!"

Malcolm walked into the men's room to loud chatter of the uppity men who were standing in the foyer bragging about their cars and how much their homes cost. The most annoying one was a proper-talking jerk that made sure to talk louder than everyone else. He was so annoying to listen to that Malcolm couldn't focus on taking a pee.

"I wonder how the poor black folks are living," he blurted out.

"Yeah, those lazy niggas in the hood are probably drinking forty ounces right now," another man said.

"Well, let's make a toast to the brothas who couldn't be here," the loud one slurred and poured some of his martini into one of the sinks.

Malcolm tried to ignore their snobbish comments, but the guy with the loud mouth wouldn't shut up. And the more he spoke, the more familiar his voice began to sound. Malcolm knew he had heard his voice somewhere before, but he couldn't place him.

After he finished relieving himself, he maneuvered his way over to the sink to wash his hands. When he came face to face with the jerk, he couldn't believe his eyes. It was the same loud-mouth from the Fox Theatre in Atlanta. When their eyes met in the reflection of the mirror, he recognized Malcolm right away. He intentionally stood right next to Malcolm while he brushed the rain off his jacket, purposely hitting him with a few drops.

Malcolm ignored him, determined not to ruin the special night Toni had worked so hard to set up. He gave him an intimidating stare to let him know he was crossing the line. He just smiled back at Malcolm daring him to retaliate.

"I know you from somewhere, don't I?"

"Don't even pretend like you know anything about me!" Malcolm stood erect.

"No, I know you, alright. I just haven't put it together yet, but I will," he said with a sly grin.

On his way out of the bathroom Malcolm bumped into him slightly, "Punk motherfucker," he said loud enough for him to hear.

When he made it back over to the table, Toni was signing autographs for some fans. Malcolm stood back and admired the way she handled the horny men as they tried to flirt with her. She was so smooth and poised they hardly realized they were being rejected. After a couple of minutes passed, he went to break up the party.

"Ahem," he cleared his throat.

"Hey, sweetheart." She sprang up from her seat to give him a kiss.

That was her way of making it clear that she belonged to him. Shortly after, the vultures scattered.

"So, are you having a good time tonight?" she asked while sitting on his lap.

"As long as I'm with you, every night is a good time."

"Well, I promise you it's going to get even better. I have a big surprise for you when we get to the hotel."

"You're not a transsexual, are you?"

"No, silly. I was referring to your career."

"Speaking of my career, I'll be glad when my agent gets here so I can find out what happened at the meeting. I'm getting a little anxious."

"Well, that's the surprise; he just called and—"

She stopped mid-sentence. Malcolm could feel the presence of someone standing behind him. Toni was looking over Malcolm's shoulder, speechless and then she suddenly sprang up from his lap.

"Eric, what are you doing here?" she shouted.

"You know I come here on Friday nights," he said. "The question is what are you doing here?"

"I'm here with Malcolm," she said proudly.

Malcolm played it cool and continued to face in the opposite direction. He recognized Eric's voice as the loudmouth from the bathroom and was trying to stay calm.

"So this is the man you left me for, huh?" Eric said. "He doesn't seem to be the sociable type."

"Hello, and good-bye," Malcolm said in a deep, angry voice.

"Aw, don't be like that, brother," Eric said with his hand on Malcolm's shoulder. "I just want to meet the man who stole my woman."

"First of all, I'm not your brother." Malcolm stood up and got into Eric's face. "Secondly, I can't steal what you never possessed. Now for the last time, I said good-bye!"

"I'll be damned, it's you!"

"You know each other?" Toni asked.

"Oh, I know him all right," Eric said. "I saw him in Atlanta at the Fox Theatre. And I saw him last week at the convention in Miami at the Intercontinental Hotel."

"So what? You saw me out! That doesn't mean you know me; now I'm telling you for the last time to get out of my face, or else."

"Or else what?" Eric said, pushing Malcolm in the chest. "What you gonna do, Mr. Gigolo, sic your little harem on me. Or maybe if I go away, you'll give Toni a discount fuck!"

In one quick motion, Malcolm grabbed Eric's arm, twisted it behind his back, and slammed his face into the table. "Thanks for giving me a reason to fuck you up!" he whispered in his ear. Then he spun Eric around and punched him in the stomach three times with three quick punches. Bam, Bam, Bam! The force of the blows was so intense Toni could hear them over the loud music.

"Malcolm, stop!" Toni yelled.

"How does it feel, Mr. Big Shot? You got something to say to the poor black folks in the ghetto now?"

Eric's nose was broken and blood was dripping from his mouth. Two of his friends rushed over to help him. When they tried to swing at Malcolm, he used Eric as a shield, then drop-kicked one of them and knocked the other out cold with a stiff uppercut. Shortly after, the security guards rushed over to break it up.

"Malcolm, what's gotten into you?" Toni cried out.

"I'll tell you what's gotten into him," Eric said, still coughing up blood. "He's a fucking prostitute!"

"Shut your fuckin' mouth before I shut it for you!" Malcolm said, lunging towards him with the muscular security guards holding him back.

"What are you saying, Eric?"

271

"What I'm trying to tell you is that your man is a professional gigolo. He was at the hotel last Friday fighting with one of his tricks. They made a big scene in front of the entire association. If you don't believe me, log onto YouTube," he said while staring at Malcolm, a smirk on his face. "At least a half dozen people recorded the whole thing, all the way up until she threw a shoe at him on the elevator."

Toni took one look into Malcolm's eyes and knew Eric was telling the truth. She walked over to him and slapped him right in the face.

"How could you lie to me, Malcolm?" she said with tears in her eyes. "I believed in you." She picked up her purse off the floor and went over to help Eric.

"Toni, please wait! I can explain."

"There is no explanation for a lie except with another lie." She wiped her eyes with her hand. "I thought you were something special, but you're nothing more than a high-priced hoe."

"Do you wanna press any charges?" the security guard asked Eric.

"No, he's already paid the ultimate price. Let him suffer."

The security guards waited until Eric and Toni were gone, then they escorted Malcolm out, tossing him onto the wet pavement. Otis saw what was going on and sped over in the limo.

"Mr. Tremell, you all right?" he asked while helping Malcolm up.

Malcolm didn't bother to answer him. He just stood in the pouring rain feeling numb. His expensive suit was soaked but he didn't give a damn.

"Mr. Tremell, please...get in the car!"

Malcolm didn't want to make an even bigger scene so he stepped into the stretch limo and then dropped his face into his hands.

"What the fuck have I done?"

Once Otis was inside, he let down the divider and handed him a towel and a white envelope.

"Ms. Grayson told me to give this to you."

In the upper left-hand corner it read Columbia Records. Malcolm began to open it, then he suddenly stopped.

"Otis, where is my agent, Jerry Cross? And why did he rent this car and not show up tonight?"

"I wasn't supposed to tell you this, but Ms. Grayson rented the car."

Everything was beginning to make sense to him. He opened the envelope and found what he expected. It was a recording contract. Malcolm read the section under agent fees, but there was no name. That's when he realized that there was no such person as Jerry Cross. Toni had negotiated the deal herself. That was her surprise.

As the car sped off down the rainy Manhattan streets, he looked at his reflection in the limo window. Toni had made his lifelong dream come true, and he rewarded her with a broken heart.

"Mr. Tremell, you okay?"

"No, I'm not okay, Otis. I'm pretty fucked up right now," he said, trying to regain his composure.

"So, where do you want to go?"

"Take me back to the airport."

"But there are no flights out to Miami until six o'clock tomorrow morning."

"Good! That should give me plenty of time to figure out how I messed up the best thing that ever happened to me."

Ironically, the Lauryn Hill CD was still playing on the stereo. As they drove off into the dreary night, the lyrics to the song "Ex-Factor" were hitting home.

MICHAEL BAISDEN

It could all be so simple, but you'd rather make it hard.
Loving you is like a battle,
and we both end up with scars.
Tell me who I have to be, to get some reciprocity. . . .

Malcolm knew what reciprocity meant: a mutual and honest exchange, to give and take, to feel for, and to take care of. Something he was unwilling or unable to do. He knew his selfishness had cost him dearly this time. Maybe this whole thing was meant to happen, he was thinking. Maybe it was God's way of telling him he didn't deserve Toni after all.

Part VI

SUBMISSION

CHAPTER 35

THE MAINTENANCE MAN

I t was just after two o'clock when Simon arrived at Club Obsession. Two weeks had passed since the incident at the church and he was ready to get back to work. When he drove around back to open the gates, three trucks were already backed against the dock making deliveries. He was wondering who was signing for the orders because he didn't recognize the Chrysler Sebring convertible parked in the manager's space.

"Take those crab legs to the kitchen!" he heard a woman shout. "And you, don't forget to replace those beer kegs in the upstairs bar."

It was Ariel. She was bossing the deliverymen around, as usual. Simon crept alongside the truck and picked up a large box of shrimp off the dock. He concealed his face with it and carried it inside. When he got close to Ariel, he deliberately stumbled and almost knocked her over.

"Hey, watch where you're going, you idiot!"

"Sorry, about that, boss. This is my first day on the job," he said, trying not to laugh.

"You refer to me as Ms. Daniels, not boss, understand?"

"Okay, boss."

"Oh, I see we've got a smart-ass," Ariel said. "Get back to work before I call your supervisor."

Simon moved the box from his face and burst out laughing.

"It's you!" she shouted as she dropped her clipboard. "I've been worried sick about you!" She threw her arms around his neck and kissed him on the lips.

Simon's hand slid down to her butt and palmed it. Only a few seconds later they came to their senses.

"Ok, that was way out of line." Ariel was fixing her hair and adjusting her clothes.

"Yes, it was. I don't want the help to get the wrong idea!"

"Boss, I am so sorry for kissing you on the lips!"

"And I'm sorry for touching you on the...you know, that was very unprofessional."

Ariel smiled nervously. She picked up the clipboard from the floor and began counting the cases on the dock like nothing had happened.

"So, where have you been?"

"I went home to Chicago. I needed time to meditate and think things over."

"Have you heard from Cynthia?"

"No, but her mother called and left a nasty message on my answering machine," Simon said, laughing. "I've never heard that old church woman use so much profanity."

"I can't say that I blame her after what happened."

"Excuse me!"

"Never mind, Simon," she said, backing off. "This is none

of my business."

"No, speak your mind. I want to hear what you have to say."

"Simon, you embarrassed that woman on live TV. They replayed that video every hour on CNN, MSNB, even the FOX network played it. And it's the number one watched video on YouTube. It created a nationwide controversy about infidelity in the black church. Now, don't get me wrong; it was about time somebody exposed these no-good preachers, but Cynthia was just your girlfriend, not your wife. Infidelity was no excuse for destroying her career. Because of what you did, she'll never work in television again. Never!"

"What the hell did you expect me to do, Ariel?" Simon said, getting upset. "I loved her, I trusted her, and I was hurt!"

"You should've simply let her go," she said calmly as she held his hand. "And counted your blessings that you found out before you married her."

Simon's first impulse was to lash out but the more he listened, the more he realized Ariel had a point.

"You know you're right," he submitted. "I was so caught up in getting revenge I not only ruined Cynthia's career, but I jeopardized my own by abandoning my responsibilities for this club for two weeks. If it weren't for you holding things together, I could have lost it all. Sometimes it's hard for a man to admit when he's wrong. Thanks for telling me what I need to know instead of what I want to hear."

"No problem, boss. Now let me get back to work. It's Ladies' Night tonight and you know how crowded it gets when Teddy performs."

Ariel tried to walk away but Simon grabbed her by the arm.

"Oh, no you don't! It was no coincidence that I came back today." He pulled a card out his suit pocket and handed it to her. "Happy Birthday!"

"You remembered," she screamed. "Thank you, thank you, thank you!"

"Now give me that clipboard and take your butt home. You've got the next two nights off."

"You mean it?"

"Yeah, I think I can run this place without you for a couple of nights."

"Thank you, Simon. You're the most decent man I know," she said as she kissed him softly on the cheek. "One day you'll find a woman who truly deserves you."

Ariel ran to her car screaming like a kid on the last day of school. Simon just shook his head as he watched her from the dock. She threw her purse into the car and rolled down the windows ready to get her groove on.

"Hey, birthday girl!" Simon yelled out. "What happened to the Benz?"

"It's in the shop. Some fool sliced my tires last week," she told him. "I just hope it wasn't that fool Lawrence trippin' again!"

CHAPTER 36

A riel was listening to a song by Ledisi called "Pieces of Me" while she got ready for her date with Raymond. She danced provocatively in the mirror as she combed her short Afro then slipped into her fitted white dress. "Just like wine, you keep getting better with time," she said with conceit. It was her 30th birthday, a landmark in a woman's life, and she wanted it to be memorable. On the way home, she had stopped by Fredrick's of Hollywood to pick up a pair of handcuffs, massage gels, and a white teddy with garter straps for that whorish look. Raymond was staying overnight for the first time and she wanted to try something kinky.

By 6:30 she was dressed to kill. She sprayed her neck, wrists, and crotch with perfume and headed for the door. Before she could turn the knob, the phone rang. She was hoping it wasn't her mother calling to lecture her again about dating a married man. They hadn't spoken in weeks and Ariel wasn't in the mood to argue. "Please God, not on my birthday," she prayed.

MICHAEL BAISDEN

"Hello?"

"Hello, stranger, this is Chris. I just called to wish you a happy birthday."

"That's very sweet of you, Chris. Thanks for remembering." She tried to sound cordial, but she was looking down at her watch anxious to leave.

"Did you get the present I sent you?"

"Yes, I did. I meant to call you to say thanks, but things have been hectic at the club lately. I'm sure you understand."

"No, I don't," he said abruptly.

"Look, Chris, I don't have time to get into this right now. I'm late for a date. Can we talk about this later?"

He paused for a moment, then he stopped beating around the bush.

"Look, Ariel, there's no need for us to talk later. I spent two hours walking around the mall to buy you something special for your birthday, and you didn't even have the common courtesy to call and say thank you," he said to her.

"Now, wait one damned minute!"

"No, you wait!" Chris jumped in, cutting her off. "I may not have a master's degree or a fancy car but I do have a good heart. I know that doesn't mean much in this materialistic-ass world, but that's all I have to offer; that, and my friendship. Now, I'm not going to take up any more of your time, Ms. Daniels. Have a happy birthday. And I hope you find whatever it is that you're looking for." Then he hung up.

Ariel stood there with the dial tone ringing in her ear. It was bad enough that her mother was on her case. Now mild-mannered Chris was telling her off. But she knew she had it coming. She hadn't returned his calls in more than three weeks. Not even to say thank you for the gift. The same gift that was still sitting on her dining room table unopened.

• • •

Houston's restaurant in Aventura was unusually crowded for a Thursday night. Ariel had to wait in line fifteen minutes just to get to the hostess. She was livid when she found out that Raymond had forgotten to call in their reservation. The wait for a table was almost 45 minutes. She went over to the bar and ordered a Mojito to kill time until Raymond arrived. He was supposed to meet her at seven but when she checked the clock on her BlackBerry it read 7:35 P.M. "I did hundreds of sit-ups to fit into this tight-ass dress and he has the nerve not to show up on time," she mumbled to herself while sipping on her drink. "Damn men!"

But her tight dress didn't go unnoticed by the men at the bar. They were gawking at her large breasts and round bottom like she was a piece of meat. It was the kind of attention Ariel didn't find flattering. She was careful not to dress too provocatively unless she was on a date with a secure man. Raymond had abandoned her in a den of wolves and that only made her even more upset. She knew it was only a matter of time before they drank up enough courage to come over to try and strike up a conversation. As usual, the young hip-hop types were the most aggressive.

"Excuse me, sweetheart. Can I buy you a drink?" a young man asked. He was wearing a Miami Heat T shirt and his hair had the letter M cut into it.

"No, thank you. I'm waiting on someone," she said politely.

"Well, if you change your mind, I'll be over there with my posse." He whipped out a business card and handed it to her. "My name is Marcus, but they call me L Boogie."

"Okay, Mr. Boogie," Ariel said, trying not to laugh. "Thanks for the offer."

Ariel put the card in her purse knowing it was going straight in the garbage when she got home. When she was younger, she

MICHAEL BAISDEN

would get into long discussions about why she couldn't accept a man's card. But as she matured, she realized the best thing to do was to take it and get rid of it. Besides, some men could become verbally abusive towards women when they got rejected in front of their boys. She wasn't taking any chances on having any drama, especially not on her birthday.

By eight o'clock Ariel was furious. Raymond still hadn't arrived to rescue her from the knuckleheads who were circling her like vultures. One of her biggest pet peeves was promptness. As far as she was concerned, nothing short of death was excusable. When the hostess called out her reservation, she paid her tab and went over to be seated. She was determined to celebrate her birthday with a nice meal, even if it meant doing it alone.

Just as the hostess was leading her to her table, Raymond came rushing in. He waved his arms to get her attention. He was dressed very dapperly in a sharp dark blue suit and tie. Ariel made eye contact with him then turned her head and kept walking. She knew he would follow her over and she wanted to make his trip as uncomfortable as possible. Once they were alone at the table, Raymond gave her a kiss on the cheek and poured on the old charm.

"Baby, I can't tell you how sorry I am for being late. My wife was supposed to pick the girls up from dance class, but she had to work overtime. I ran every red light on Biscayne trying to get here on time," he said sounding sincere. "Please give me a chance to make it up to you."

Ariel couldn't help blushing whenever she looked into Raymond's light brown eyes. He was a pretty boy: six feet tall, light brown skin, wavy hair, athletic build, the whole nine, not usually her type. She preferred her men dark chocolate. But the dick was good and he had a deep, sexy voice. Not soft and squeaky like so many corporate black men she dated when she lived in D.C.

284

Raymond could make her wet just by calling to say hello. But wet panties and all, she was still disappointed. It was the fifth time in the last month he was either late for a date or had to cancel.

"I'm getting sick and tired of you showing up late for our dates, Raymond" she said angrily. "If it's not the kids, it's one of your patients. It's always something!"

"Look, Ariel, I told you up front that my career and family came first," he said sternly. "I'm still a married man and a father; that means I have responsibilities. Now if you can't handle that, maybe we need to stop seeing each other."

Ariel wanted to tell him to go to hell. She wasn't accustomed to playing the role of the other woman. But she swallowed her pride because it was her birthday and she was horny as hell. Raymond hadn't given her any sex in almost two weeks and she needed some maintenance.

"Okay, I forgive you, this time," she said. "So are you still spending the night?"

"I can stay for a while, but I've got to get up early in the morning."

"For what?"

"I rushed out of the house and forgot to bring an extra set of clothes for work."

"I don't appreciate all these last-minute changes, Raymond. I may be Jump off chic but I need some kind of consistency."

Raymond was facing the front of the restaurant. Ariel noticed he kept looking over her shoulder toward the door. She didn't pay it much attention until he did it a second and third time.

"Are you expecting somebody?"

"No, I thought I saw someone I knew," he said unconvincingly. Then he tried to change the subject. "Look, why don't we skip dinner and go straight to your place. That way we can spend more time together."

285

"But I'm starving! And I spent a lot of time getting myself together to come out tonight. Which reminds me, you haven't even complimented me on my dress."

"You look great, Ariel," he said while looking toward the door again. "When we get to your place, you can model it for me."

Suddenly there was a commotion outside. Ariel heard what sounded like a glass being smashed. Not long after, a woman came barging into the front door dragging two little girls along with her. Judging by the expression on Raymond's face, Ariel knew who it was.

"Just stay calm and let me handle this," Raymond said nervously.

The woman spotted Ariel and Raymond sitting at the corner table and stormed toward them, knocking over a waiter who was carrying a tray of food. When she got up to the table, she walked right up to Raymond and smacked the shit out of him.

"How dare you!" she yelled.

"Calm down, sweetheart. I can explain."

"You can't explain a goddamn thing, you two-timing bastard. I know who this bitch is!"

Ariel held her tongue to avoid escalating the situation.

"I slave around that house all day raising your kids and washing your dirty drawers. I'll be damned if you're going to disrespect me by bringing one of your hoes out in public."

"Who you calling a hoe, you fat heifer?"

Raymond's wife was a big woman and a strong one. She grabbed a bowl of peach cobbler à la mode off the table next to them and smashed it into Ariel's face. When Ariel tried to retaliate, she gave her a right cross and sent Ariel flying over the table.

"Take that, you slut!" she yelled. "Maybe next time you'll think twice before you fuck with another married man."

The women in the restaurant just stared—not even the female staff made an effort to help Ariel to her feet. It was as if they had vented their own frustrations for all the conniving other women in Miami.

As Raymond's wife stormed out of the door with her girls in tow, there was muffled applause. No one called the police or even tried to stop her.

"I'm sorry about all this, Ariel," Raymond said as he picked her up.

"Just get away from me, Raymond. Go home to your wife."

With peach cobbler running down her face and onto her brand new dress, Ariel calmly put two hundred dollars on the table and walked out. When she got out to her car, the windshield was shattered on the driver's side and the headlights were smashed. The words *Home Wrecker* were spray-painted on the hood and the doors on both sides in bold red letters.

Ariel didn't even react, not outwardly anyway. She got inside the car and drove off as most of the patrons in the parking lot looked on.

She held up pretty well until she made it to I-95. Then she broke down. When she looked at her face in the rearview mirror, she cried even harder. She had a deep cut below her left eye, and her top lip was busted. "That's what you get, stupid!" she said to herself.

After she wiped off her face, she pulled out her cell phone to call her best friend. She needed someone to talk to.

"Hello, Mama, it's me," Ariel said crying.

"Baby, what's wrong?"

"Mama, I'm sorry. You were right. You were right about everything!"

"We don't need to talk about that right now, Sweetheart. Are you all right?"

"I'll be fine. Nothing that a dry cleaner and a bandage won't fix," she said, laughing painfully.

"Why don't you come over and I'll pour us a glass of wine. We can stay up all night and talk like we used to. Remember?"

"Yeah, I remember, Mama, but there's something I have to do. Can I take a rain check for tomorrow night?"

"Sure you can, Sweetheart," she said in that motherly tone. "But what are you about to do, if you don't mind me being nosy."

"I'm going to stop by Best Buy, pick up some microwave popcorn, and go visit Chris," she said to her. "I realized the hard way that what I'm missing in my life is not a husband, or a sex partner, or even a man making six figures. I need a man who is truly a friend."

CHAPTER 37

I t was 9:00 P.M. Ladies' Night at Club Obsession was going strong. Teddy and his dance group, Hot Chocolate, were putting on their best show ever. The room was wall to wall with enthusiastic women buying alcohol like it was going out of style. The restaurant was crowded, too. The kitchen sold out of Buffalo wings and fried shrimp before the show even started. It was the most successful night since the grand opening.

But Simon was not celebrating. He locked himself in his office with a bottle of cognac trying to think through his issues. Usually he would call Malcolm but since the incident in New York, they hadn't spoken. Malcolm was still recovering from losing Toni. And although he tried to act as if it was no big deal, Simon knew he was devastated. It was the most withdrawn he had been since his father died.

The conversation with Ariel was also weighing on his mind. He never considered how his actions at the church would affect Cynthia's career. He only wanted revenge, not to destroy her livelihood. "What the hell have I done?" he asked himself as he stared at the 8x10 picture of Cynthia he still had hanging on the wall behind his desk. After all the trouble he went through to get even, he was still in love with her.

As he took another sip of cognac to quiet his conscience, there was a knock at the door.

"Who is it?" Simon yelled.

"Mr. Harris, come quick!" a waitress said frantically. "The police are arresting Teddy!"

Simon could hear the commotion as he made his way toward the front of the club. Women were booing and tossing paper plates at the two sheriff's deputies who were making the arrest. Simon hurried over to see what the deal was.

"Excuse me, officers, I'm the owner, Simon Harris. What seems to be the problem?"

"There's no problem," one of the deputies said. "Mr. Teddy Bear here is under arrest."

"This is bullshit, Mr. Harris. I'm innocent!" Teddy yelled.

Teddy was naked except for the leopard print G-string he was wearing.

"Do you mind telling me what the charge is?"

"Contempt of court. He failed to appear in court after refusing to pay child support."

A group of nosy women standing nearby overheard their conversation and quickly spread the word. It wasn't long before all the booing turned to cheers!

"Don't just stand there, Mr. Harris, say something," Teddy said as the policemen led him away.

"You're fired!" Simon yelled.

The police escorted Teddy out of the club as fast as they could for his own protection. Women were cursing him out and spitting in his face as he walked by.

"I hope they put your trifling ass under the jail, you dead-beat," a woman hollered.

Teddy was finished as a stripper in Miami. By Monday morning, Simon knew Teddy's business would be all over the radio airwaves, Hot 105, WEDR. Even the gospel station would be talking about it.

Simon took advantage of the situation and closed the club for the night. He refunded everyone's money and sent the employees home. It didn't matter to him that the club was a mess. He just wanted to be alone. Within an hour, the club was deserted.

After he locked the doors, Simon put on his Mike James CD and mixed himself a stiff rum and Coke. While he listened to the smooth instrumental of "Imagine This," he leaned back in a chair and propped his feet up onto the bar. "Ah, that's more like it," he said and then took a long sip. "Now that's real music!"

Just as he was getting his relaxation on, there was a loud knock at the door. "Now what?" he said in disgust. As he went to answer the door, he was hoping it was Ariel. Although he wanted to be alone, he could finally finish giving her lessons on how to step, Chicago style. But when he peeked out the side window, he didn't see Ariel's car. Instead there was a black Range Rover parked out front. It was Cynthia.

He pulled the shades back on the doors and there she was in a pair of dingy blue jeans, a T-shirt, and a Miami Dolphins cap. Her eyes were red and puffy and she looked like she had gained weight. She looked pitiful. Simon thought about not answering, but he still loved and her and he needed closure. As he unlocked the door, he took a deep breath and exhaled.

"What do you want?" Simon asked.

"Don't worry, I'm not going to stay long. I just wanted to tell you to your face how sorry I am for what happened."

"Apology accepted. Now, good-bye!" Simon said, sounding cold.

"How can you talk to me like that, Simon, after all we've been through?"

"It's easy; all I have to do is think about you screwing that phony preacher. By the way, where is your spiritual maintenance man?"

"For your information, I haven't seen him since that Sunday."

"Now why does that not surprise me?" Simon said sarcastically. "I thought you two would be in a big house in the suburbs with a white picket fence living happily ever after."

"Fuck you, Simon!"

"No, fuck you!" Simon yelled. "I trusted you and you went behind my back and laid down with another man. Not once, not twice, but several times. And you expect me to be sympathetic. Hell no!"

"What about you, Mr. Big-Shot Club Owner. When did you ever pay any attention to me?" she yelled back. "You've been cheating on me for three years with your damned job! Everything revolved around work. And when you finally came home, you were tired. I needed someone who was there for me, Simon. To hold me, tell me I was beautiful, and make passionate love to me," she said as tears rolled down her cheeks. "I'm not superwoman, goddammit. I need attention!"

Simon wanted to run over to her and hold her in his arms. He was in just as much pain as she was, but his pride wouldn't allow him to show it.

"Is that all you have to say?" he asked callously. "I've got work to do."

"Fine, Simon. If that's the way you want it. Here, take it!"

She pulled the engagement ring off her finger and threw it at him. "But before I go, I want you to know that I never loved James. He was just a substitute for the man that I love."

Cynthia wiped the tears from her eyes with her hand, then turned toward the door. But before she walked out, Simon yelled, "So, when is the baby due?"

Cynthia stopped dead in her tracks.

"How did you know?" she asked while still facing the door.

"I have two sisters and I've employed women for years who have kids. Did you think I wouldn't recognize when you had morning sickness?"

"The baby is due in April," she said softly.

"Do you know whose it is?"

Cynthia took a deep breath as she turned to face him.

"To be honest with you, Simon, I don't know. But it doesn't matter. I'm putting it up for adoption after it's born. I'm not going to shame my family or myself any further. Now if you're through breaking me down, I'm going to leave. Good-bye!" she said, crying.

"Wait, Cynthia!"

Before she could get inside her car, Simon chased her down and brought her back inside the club. Without saying a word, he cleared the chairs off the dance floor and he switched on his Heatwave CD and forwarded to the song "Always and Forever" and led Cynthia out onto the floor.

"Simon, what are you doing?"

"What I should've done a long time ago," he whispered in her ear. "Giving you the love and attention that you need."

CHAPTER 38

THE MAINTENANCE MAN

I t was just after ten o'clock in the morning when Ms. Ruby rushed into Malcolm's bedroom nearly hysterical.

"Malcolm, wake up!" she yelled as she shook him intensely.

"What's wrong?"

"It's Melvin. He's had a heart attack!"

Malcolm sprang out of his bed and began searching through his closet for something quick to slip into. He pulled out a wrinkled pair of blue jeans and a Chicago Bulls T-shirt.

"When did this happen? Is he okay?"

"About eight this morning. Scottie found him lying on the bathroom floor at his house. The ambulance had just arrived when he called."

"Why didn't you wake me sooner?" he asked angrily.

"I turned off the ringer when I came in this morning," she said as tears began to pour down her brown cheeks. "I was trying not to disturb you, I'm sorry!"

"I'm sorry for snapping at you, Ms. Ruby," he told her while hugging her. "I know you love him as much as I do. Did Scottie mention which hospital they were taking him to?"

"Mercy Hospital at 3663 South Miami Avenue."

"Was Melvin still breathing?"

"He didn't say."

"Was he still alive?"

"I don't know, Malcolm, ok, I don't know!"

"Ok, I want you to try to calm down," he said as he gave her a kiss on the forehead. "I'll call you from the hospital as soon as I know something."

Malcolm grabbed his car keys and cell phone off the kitchen counter and hurried down the stairwell that led to the parking garage. He was not about to wait for the valet to bring him his car. As he ran down the stairs, his heart was racing one hundred miles an hour. The thought of losing the most important man in his life was unbearable.

Once he made it to his car, he sped off and frantically began dialing Scottie's number. "Pick up, goddammit!" he yelled into the phone. But there was no answer. "I can't lose him," he said out loud as he weaved through traffic. "I can't lose him, too!"

● ● ●

The emergency room at Mercy was a madhouse. Doctors and nurses scrambled to stabilize four gunshot victims, all young children no older than ten years old.

"Another drive by," Malcolm heard one nurse say. "And it's not even sundown yet. It's going to be a busy weekend."

The sweltering Miami heat had a way of increasing the body count in the black community. Although it was mid-September, it was more than 90 degrees. After the commotion died down,

Malcolm approached the nurse at the receptionist's desk. She was an elderly Latina woman wearing wire-framed glasses, and she was chatting it up on the phone.

"Excuse me, nurse. I'm looking for a patient who was brought in earlier this morning. His name is Melvin Butler."

She held up her index finger, indicating that she wanted him to wait until she had finished gossiping on the phone.

"Excuse me!" he said much louder. "Would you please get your ass off the phone and give me some assistance?"

He must have scared her to death because she slammed the phone down and gave him her undivided attention.

"When was he admitted?" she asked looking up at him timidly through her wire-framed glasses.

"This morning about nine o'clock."

"Here he is," she pointed out to him on the computer screen. "He's in intensive care."

"Which way is it?"

"Just go down that corridor and turn left."

When Malcolm made it to the end of the corridor, he saw Scottie standing in the waiting room talking with the doctor. When he approached him, he turned and gave Malcolm a hug.

"How is he, Doc?"

"Not good. He had a hemorrhagic stroke, which means he has internal bleeding in the heart," he explained. "I'm sorry; there's nothing we can do."

"I need to see him," Malcolm said.

"No one is allowed to see him except his immediate family."

"I am the immediate family, goddammit! Now take me to him!"

Scottie waited in the hall while the doctor escorted Malcolm into Melvin's room. It was hard for him to see Melvin lying there helpless with all the tubes and electrodes attached to his body.

"Can you please give me a moment alone?"

"No problem, I'll be right outside," the doctor said.

Malcolm stood over the bed and held Melvin's hand. His face was pale and his breathing was weak. He fought back the tears hoping Melvin would open his wrinkled old eyes and tell him one of his dirty jokes. He had been the closest thing Malcolm had to a father and he was losing him. He felt helpless watching him lie there fading away.

Suddenly Melvin's grip tightened around his hand. He cleared his throat and tried to speak.

"Did you open the present I gave you?" he whispered.

"Not yet, old man, but I will as soon as I get you back home." Malcolm was trying to be cheerful. "Did you get my message about my deal with Columbia Records."

"Yeah, I got it. Congratulations. I knew you would be a big star someday."

"Hey, slow down with all the hype. I haven't signed the contract yet."

"It's going to happen for you, Cool Breeze, because it's your time. Just like it was time for you to meet that young lady," he said, sounding sure of himself. "I could tell by the way you talked about her that she was the one. You do love her, don't you?"

"Yes, I do," he told him. "She's everything I've ever wanted."

"I'm just glad I lived long enough to see you happy," he said as the tears welled up in his eyes. "Make sure you take good care of her. I don't want you to end up old and alone like me."

"You're not alone; I'm right here," Malcolm said as he watched Melvin fade away. "Don't leave me, old man. I still need you!"

"Just remember, I'm proud of you, Malcolm. I've always loved you like my own son."

"And I've loved you as a father," Malcolm cried.

He held Melvin in his arms as his eyes slowly shut. He took one last breath and then he was gone.

CHAPTER 39

The day of the funeral was dark and dreary, much like the day Malcolm's father died. A light drizzle fell as the mile-long procession slowly made its way down Dixie Highway to South Memorial Park. The mayor himself would've been envious of the thousands of people who came out to pay their respects. Melvin was practically an institution in the black community and he was going to be dearly missed. The reading of the eulogy took place underneath a small canvas tent. Only fifty people were able to stand out of the rain while the minister spoke words over Melvin's casket. Malcolm held hands with Scottie and the staff from the club and they tried to comfort one another. Aside from a distant cousin, they were the only family Melvin had.

After the eulogy, they joined hands and sang "Amazing Grace." That was the toughest part of the service to get through. Everyone broke down crying, including the minister. But Malcolm held back his tears and saved them for later, just like he did with his father. There were thoughts he wanted to share with Melvin that were personal.

As Melvin was being lowered into the ground, they threw flowers on top of his ivory and gold-plated casket. It was their way of saying good-bye to a man who had been a father and a mentor to all of them. Once it was rested against the cold, dark ground, Malcolm threw in the first symbolic shovel of dirt. With every shovelful of dirt that fell, a part of his soul was being buried, too. "Rest in peace, old man," he said.

When the service was over, those who were outside the tent in the pouring rain still waited in line to pay their last respects. Malcolm waited next to the grave while hundreds of people laid flowers and said their peace. As the procession came to its end, Malcolm saw a familiar face. At first he thought his eyes were playing tricks on him, but after he looked through the bouquet of roses that was obscuring his face, he realized it was Simon. Malcolm had fought to hold back the tears up until that point. But the moment they embraced, he let it all out.

"Déjà vu, huh, partner?" Simon said as they hugged.

"Yeah, déjà vu," he replied. "How did you know I was here?"

"Ms. Ruby told me. I flew out of Atlanta this morning."

"I know I should've called you myself. But I didn't want to burden you. I know you have enough drama to deal with."

"If we weren't in a cemetery, I would slap the hell out of you. You're my brother, Malcolm."

"You're right. I don't know why I'm trippin'; my head hasn't been right for a while."

"Yeah, mine either!"

Simon waited while Malcolm greeted the last of the people in line.

Once they were all gone, he grabbed his umbrella and they took a walk together. It was a painfully ironic reunion. Simon had been by his side to bury both his fathers. Having him there helped alleviate some of the pain, just as it had many years before.

"So how are you holding up?" Simon asked.

"I'm hanging," he told him. "Even though I've been through this before, it doesn't get any easier. Pain always feels brand new, no matter how much experience you've had with it."

"Amen to that, brother!" Simon said. "I've had all the pain I can handle for the next twenty years."

"Speaking of pain, do you mind if I ask you a personal question?"

"Shoot!"

"Whatever happened to Cynthia?"

"I was hoping you wouldn't go there."

"Look, partner, we don't have to talk about it. I was just wondering how things worked out."

"I may as well tell you and get it over with. Cynthia's pregnant and we're getting married in Vegas next month," he said. "Now before you say anything—"

"Congratulations," Malcolm cut him off.

"Excuse me?"

"I said congratulations. I wish you both all the best."

"I'm surprised you didn't try to talk me out of it, or ask whose baby it is."

"Who am I to judge you or anybody else? My life is a disaster. I can't even go out on an appointment to get paid without my conscience kicking my ass," he said. "Can you believe I've been celibate for almost four weeks? That's the longest I've gone without sex since high school."

"Did Toni get that close to you?"

"Toni who? What are you talking about?"

"Don't try to run your game on me, Malcolm. I know you too well," he said. "And any blind man can see that you miss that woman. I'm sure Melvin saw it, too."

"Yeah, I miss her. But that page in my life has been turned."

MICHAEL BAISDEN

"Listen to you trying to sound all hard. You ain't foolin' nobody but yourself. Stop acting like you don't have a heart and go after that woman. She loves you, you arrogant bastard!"

Malcolm dropped the umbrella he was holding and grabbed Simon by the collar of his trench coat.

"Shut the fuck up! Shut up!" he yelled. "You have no idea what I'm going through! There isn't a day that goes by that I don't think about her. I can't even lie down with another woman without seeing her face. So don't run that psychology bullshit on me. I've got a heart, goddammit!"

"Well, stop being so afraid and use it!" Simon said, pushing his hands away. "A good woman like Toni is not going to respond to your manipulative games. But let me tell you this, if you can't be consistent, if you can't allow yourself to be vulnerable, if you can't stand the pain of loving someone, then don't waste your time or hers. It's time for you to stop giving part-time maintenance man and start offering full-time love and commitment. Otherwise, you're going to end up alone, alone or dead!"

Simon pulled a laminated piece of paper out of his coat pocket and handed it to him. It was an article from the *Atlanta Journal Constitution.* The headline read LOCAL STRIPPER SHOT AND KILLED BY JEALOUS HUSBAND. Malcolm only had to read the first few lines to get the point. The man killed was listed as Theodore Simmons, a.k.a. Teddy Bear. The story went on to read: SIMMONS WAS SHOT IN THE HEAD WHEN THE HUSBAND OF A WOMAN HE WAS HAVNG AN AFFAIR WITH CAME HOME EARLY AND CAUGHT HIM IN BED WITH HIS WIFE. Ironically, it was the same story of what happened to Malcolm's father.

"There are no coincidences in life, Malcolm. Everything happens for a reason," Simon said. "You have to take advantage of all the hurt and pain in life and grow from it. I learned that lesson the hard way. And if your father or Melvin were alive, they would tell you the exact same thing."

They stood in the heavy rain staring at one another. They didn't care that the umbrella had blown across the cemetery and they were getting soaked.

"I'll be damned!" Malcolm said, laughing nervously. Then he walked over and sat down on one of the nearby graves.

"What's so funny?" Simon asked, as he went and sat down beside him.

"The student has finally become the teacher," he said. "I was trying to teach you the game and here I am breaking the cardinal rule in the *Player's Handbook.*"

"What's that?"

"Never fall in love."

They hugged in that brotherly way that men do to say they're sorry. Shortly afterwards, Simon left to catch his flight back to Atlanta. Malcolm stayed at the cemetery to say his good-byes to Melvin. He wanted to tell him that he was going to be okay and that he would do everything in his power to get Toni back.

• • •

That night Malcolm took a long walk near the ocean to reflect on the meaning of life, the universe, and all that other philosophical shit you think about when you're trying to get your head together. He was in a creative mood, so he brought along a spiral notebook, and downloaded John Coltrane's *Ballad* CD on his iPod. He found a secluded spot away from the crowds and laid his blanket down near the water. As he watched the full moon gleaming off the still ocean, he thought about the night that he and Toni spent on the lakefront in Chicago. He reminisced on how they watched the sun come up together talking about their hopes and dreams.

That night seemed like such a distant memory. Since the incident in New York with Eric, he hadn't heard from her. When he tried calling to apologize, her home and cell number had been disconnected. The thought crossed his mind to show up on her doorstep unannounced, but he quickly dismissed that idea. It was too inappropriate and he didn't want to get his feelings hurt. Her e-mail address was blocked, so that wasn't an option either.

He knew there was only one chance at getting Toni back and that was to take a page from her playbook. She had reached out to him with a letter in the mail. Why couldn't he do the same, he was thinking. God had blessed him with the gift of writing music. All he had to do was transfer that same passion into words.

Dear Toni,

It's hard to know where to begin when you've lost a woman's trust. The words I'm sorry seem so inadequate, so empty. I would have preferred to express my feeling for you in song on the piano. But I doubt even a melody could express the degree of pain I feel for letting you down. Lately, I've been praying at night to rid myself of the guilt from that moment. You know how religious black folks can get when things get tough. I got down on my knees and prayed for another chance to hold you again, and to show you that I am the man you need me to be: caring, affectionate, and most of all, honest. Toni, I am all those things, and much more. It just took someone like you to come along to bring out that part of me, that part that wants to love and be loved, unconditionally.

I know starting over would be hard. It always is when the trust is lost. But I'm willing to do whatever it takes to rebuild that trust and make you happy. I miss holding you, and talking on the phone with you until 2:00 in the morning. And I miss watching you dance. I'll never forget the first time I saw you. You looked

306

like an angel. In a very short period of time, you have become a necessary part of my life, and a part I need to feel at peace and to feel whole.

Love always,
Malcolm

P.S. Whatever happens, please don't ever stop believing in me. That means more to me than anything else in the world, even more than your love.

EPILOGUE

I t was a typical Thursday night. Melvin's Jazz Club was stand-ing-room only. Hundreds of people turned out for the special memorial party Malcolm was throwing for Melvin. His mother even flew in from Chicago and she hated airplanes. Simon and Cynthia were there, too. They had just returned from Vegas and were sporting their diamond wedding bands. They never looked happier.

While the staff and guests were preparing for the celebration, Malcolm and Scottie were going through the files in Melvin's office trying get his business in order.

"I can't believe he didn't leave a will," Scottie said while stacking another box. "There is no way in hell I'm working for his crooked-ass cousin."

"You won't have to worry about working here if the courts make him the executor of Melvin's estate. That fool will sell out to a condo developer so fast it'll make your head spin!"

"Over my dead body!" Scottie asserted. "My whole life is here in the club, and so is most of the staff."

"Calm down, nothing is final yet; my lawyers are doing everything in their power."

"I know, Malcolm, but we're running out of arguments!"

Malcolm tried to put those thoughts aside as he relaxed in Melvin's office. It was a quarter to nine, fifteen minutes before show time. He wanted to stay focused on his music. To take his mind off the situation, he pulled out some of Melvin's old photo albums and began thumbing through. As he turned the dingy pages, he was in awe of the artists who had performed at the club over the years: Ray Charles, Thelonious Monk, Sarah Vaughan, and countless others.

"Come here, Scottie, look at this old fool!" Malcolm said, spreading the album out on the desk.

Melvin was his usual flamboyant self, all decked out in his pin-striped suits with his hair slicked back. As always he was chewing on his trademark Cuban cigar. Malcolm smiled as he reflected on how smooth he must have been back in the day.

"Knock 'em dead in heaven, you old player." Malcolm said.

The sudden roar of the crowd let them know it was almost show time. The band had taken the stage and was warming up.

"That was his cue!" Scottie said. "You need anything before I leave?"

"No, just buy me another ten minutes, I want to open that present Melvin left me."

"You mean the one he gave you for your birthday back in June?"

"I know, I know," Malcolm said, getting defensive. "I promised myself to open it after the funeral; I just haven't gotten around to it. It's still wrapped with the red bow on top."

"You wanna know what I think?"

"No, I don't want to know what you think, Scottie. But since when did that stop you from telling me anyway?" Malcolm joked.

"I think you're afraid of the responsibility attached to whatever is inside that box. You were the closest person to Melvin. You should have opened that box when he asked you to a long time ago." Then he walked out the door, slamming it shut.

Malcolm twirled the box around in his hands and then shook it several times with his ear pressed up against it. He sat the box on the desk and began putting on his suit jacket. "This can wait until after the party," he said. "It's waited this long; what's the big deal?"

He grabbed the knob for the door while staring back at the box, and then turned and walked back to the desk. "Aw, what the hell!" he said, ripping the paper off. The more he unwrapped it, the more his hands shook. Once he got all the wrapping paper off, he searched inside the desk drawer for something sharp to remove the thick tape. But before he could find a pair of scissors, someone pounded on the door.

"Malcolm, let's go! It's show time!" Scottie yelled.

"Give me a couple of minutes," he said, trying to bite the tape off the box.

"You don't have a couple of minutes. Everybody is waiting!"

"You're not getting away today," he said to the box. "I'll be back!"

As he made his way toward the stage, it finally dawned on him that this could be the last time he walked down these historic halls. Forty years of blood, sweat, and tears down the drain, he was thinking. As he was being introduced, he bowed his head in silent prayer. "Lord, if this is my last gig at Melvin's, help me give the performance of my life!" He kissed his hand and raised it in the air. "This one's for you, old man!"

When he walked onto the stage, the crowd erupted in

applause. The media was everywhere, mostly because of all the celebrities and politicians who were there. Also, there was an enormous amount of media attention on Malcolm's legal battle to keep the club open. The *Miami Herald* had dedicated an entire page to the story.

"Thank you very much," Malcolm said as he took a bow. "Please have a seat!"

When he sat down at the piano, he immediately noticed something was different. The house piano had been switched. In its place was his Steinway, the one his father had given him on his eighteenth birthday. Malcolm ran his fingers across the engraved initials M.T. to make sure he wasn't dreaming. As he scanned the room through the bright stage lamps, he saw Simon sitting in the front row with a grin on his face.

Malcolm rushed off the stage and wrapped his arms around Simon. The audience applauded as they embraced. It was an emotional moment seeing two men showing love for each other out in the open.

"Now, show them who you really are," Simon said aloud. "Turn this mother out!"

"I love you, man," Malcolm said to him.

He walked back toward his piano with a look of confidence and determination. He had intended to play a song by Cole Porter, but he closed the book of music that was open in front of him and closed his eyes. As the stage lights dimmed, he began to play.

"This song is dedicated to the two men who taught me everything I know about music and life. My father, Joseph Tremell, and Melvin." He paused and played a few notes. "I also want to thank the woman who, without knowing it, taught me the meaning of love. The name of the song is 'When Players Pray.'"

It was the song he had written for his father before he died years ago. Ironically, he wrote the lyrics on the same night he wrote Toni the letter. He wasn't much of a singer, but he gave it his best shot. The melody of the song was similar to "Fortunate" by Maxwell.

> *I played the game for selfish reasons,*
> *The love you gave so freely was for but one season.*
> *My heart was so very cold and locked away,*
> *Never to feel the warmth of a holy wedding day.*

After that first verse, the audience was swaying back and forth to the rhythm and holding up their cigarette lighters. The atmosphere was electric! He went on.

> *Never love more than she, that's the rule*
> *A man who masters his sensitivities*
> *will seldom play the fool.*
> *But the game is not eternal,*
> *there's always a spiritual price to pay,*
> *Heavenly Father, is it too late to repent?*
> *Is it too late for a player to pray?*

After that second verse, there wasn't a dry eye in the house. Malcolm continued to play, even though he was overwhelmed with grief. All the repressed feelings he had toward his father, Melvin, and Toni came pouring out onto the keys. It was his most intense performance ever. At the end of the song the audience gave him a standing ovation. "Encore! Encore!" the crowd screamed. He inconspicuously wiped the tears from his eyes and he stood up to take a bow. His mother, who was sitting at the table with Simon, was wiping the tears from her eyes, too. More than anyone else, she understood how significant that moment was for him.

As he exited the stage, full of emotions, he went rushing back towards Melvin's office. Before he could get inside, Scottie rushed behind him, carrying flowers."

"Malcolm, hold up!"

"I need to be alone right now, Scottie!"

"I understand, but I really think you need to take a look at this!"

Scottie handed him a bouquet of red roses; there were twelve stems but only eleven rose petals.

"What the heck is this?"

"Just read the card!"

Attached to the bouquet was a small card that read: I STILL BELIEVE IN YOU!

"Where did you get these?" he asked, sounding anxious.

"That woman over there," he pointed in the direction of the bar but no one was there. "At least that's where she was standing a minute ago."

"What did she look like?"

"She was a classy-looking lady about five-eight, medium-length hair, and brown skinned," she said.

He knew it had to be Toni. The card could have come from anyone, but the eleven roses were a dead giveaway. Malcolm had given her eleven roses when they met the first time at the Fox Theatre in Atlanta. He rushed through the thick crowd after her. The audience was still applauding as he made his way towards the front door. Judging by the sly expression on Simon's face as he passed by him, Malcolm suspected he was responsible for her being there.

Once he made it outside, he noticed a woman in a short black dress stepping into a taxi across the street. At first it was hard for him to tell if it was her, but just as she dipped her head to get inside, their eyes met and he knew it was her. "Toni, wait!" he yelled, running across the busy intersection, almost getting run over.

When he bent down to peek inside the taxi, she was staring at him with those beautiful brown eyes.

"Hello, stranger," she smiled nervously.

"Hello to you," he replied. "Leaving so soon?"

"I—I have another stop to make," she stuttered.

"I guess you were just in the neighborhood, huh?"

"Actually, I wanted to stop by and pay my respects to Melvin. I know how much he meant to you."

"How did you find out what happened?"

"I went by Club Obsession to say hello to Simon and he told me what happened."

"Look, I don't mean to break up this romantic reunion but I've got a job to do," the taxi driver said. "Are you going or not, Miss?"

"Yes," Toni said.

"No!" Malcolm quickly replied.

"Which one is it going to be?" the driver asked, getting frustrated.

"Toni, don't go like this," he begged. "I know you didn't come all the way to Miami just to give me flowers. Can I talk to you for just a minute, please?"

Toni sat there for a moment to contemplate. Then she gave the driver ten dollars for his inconvenience and stepped out of the taxi.

"Malcolm, before you get started, I want you to know I can't stay long. Eric is waiting for me at the hotel. We're engaged again."

"Eric?" he said in disgust. "No, Toni, that can't be. Anybody but him! He's not right for you!"

"He may not be perfect but he's there for me and he respects me enough to be honest with me!"

315

Malcolm stood there in silence and stared at her. Then he grabbed her by the hand and kissed it.

"You're right, how can I ever expect you to trust me? I guess there isn't much for me to say after all. Sometimes you have to love someone enough to let go, right?"

Malcolm gestured to Big Al who was parked in front of the club.

"I'll have my car take you back to your hotel."

As he escorted her back across the street, he couldn't even look her in he face. Knowing she was back with Eric was too painful an image. Just as Toni was about to step inside the limo, she grabbed Malcolm by the hand and pulled him towards her.

"Malcolm, why won't you look at me?"

"How could you go back to him?"

"Because I can trust him, that's why!"

"Is that all you need to be happy?"

"No, but it's the most important thing in a relationship!" she fired back. "But I guess you wouldn't know anything about trust and honesty, now would you?"

"Why are you saying these things to me when you know how sorry I am. Didn't you get my letter?"

"Those are just words, Malcolm!"

"Words are all I have since you won't let me close enough to tell you how I feel!"

"Well, here I am!"

Toni was trembling as she stared back into his eyes. Her strong and agile dancer's legs seemed limp as she tried to take a stance. Malcolm was tense, too. This was his final chance at redemption. He set aside his insecurities and ego and spoke from the heart.

"You are the most important person in my world. I didn't know how incomplete I was until you came along and filled that void. You taught me to believe in myself and to never give up on my dreams," he paused. "What I'm trying to say is, I love you. And I need you in my life!"

"I'm scared, Malcolm," she said crying. "I don't want to end up hurt and alone."

"I'm scared, too. I've never been in love before. But I'm ready to take that chance in order to be happy. What about you?"

Tears rolled down her cheeks as she looked deep into his eyes. She leaned in closer; he moved in closer, too, their lips almost touching.

"I'm ready, Malcolm," she said. "I don't want to live without you, either!"

They embraced and kissed with unapologetic passion right in front of the eleven o'clock news cameras and the hundreds of people standing outside in line. People were driving by blowing horns and whistling.

"Malcolm, everybody's watching," Toni said, pushing away.

"Woman, it's taken me thirty-seven years to find my soul mate. I wanted the whole world to know you're mine!" Malcolm said. "But I do have a question, what are you going to do about Eric?"

"Eric who?" she said bluntly.

Malcolm laughed and picked her up into the air.

"Oh shit, I almost forgot!" Malcolm blurted out.

"Almost forgot what?"

"Look, I need you to wait right here," he told her. "I'll be right back."

"Where are you going?"

"I'm going to get something out of the office, then we're outta here!"

"Malcolm, this is an important night. You can't just leave."

"Watch me!"

Malcolm ran back inside the club to get his birthday present from Melvin's office. On the way out, he congratulated Simon and Cynthia on their marriage. It was the first time he had ever kissed Cynthia. He felt good finally putting their issues to rest. Then he gave his mother a kiss on the cheek and told her he loved her. She just looked at him and smiled. On the way out the door, he shook hands with the staff and then stopped to kiss the ground in front of Melvin's. He felt strange walking out of those historic old doors knowing it was for the last time. When Malcolm made it back to the limo, Toni was already inside with two champagne glasses in her hand.

"So, where to now, Mr. Tremell?" Big Al asked.

"Just drive towards the ocean and stop when you get there."

"Aren't you going to open your gift before we leave?"

"I already have everything I need right here. It's time for me to get on with my life as a recording artist and as a man in a committed relationship. And what better way to start than to watch the sunrise with the special lady in my life?"

"I've got a better idea. Let's start the new chapter of our life by closing an old one. Open the box, Malcolm!" Toni said looking concerned. "It's time!"

With Toni by his side he finally had the courage to open his birthday present. He cut the tape off with Toni's nail file and pulled back the flaps. Inside the box was an old King James Bible and a white envelope. On the envelope were the words *To My Son* in cursive writing on the back. Inside the envelope was a copy of Melvin's last will and testament.

"Oh, my God, Malcolm; he left it all to you." Toni said while reading the document along with him.

Malcolm couldn't make out all the legal language, but one thing was clear; he was the beneficiary of Melvin's Jazz Club.

"Aren't you going to go back inside and tell everyone the

318

good news?"

"No, baby, I just want to celebrate with you." Malcolm said. "Big Al, let's go!"

He should have been elated by his newfound wealth, but he wasn't. All he had on his mind was how much he missed his father and Melvin, and beginning a new life with Toni. While they drove down 195 headed towards Miami Beach, Malcolm pulled the old King James Bible out of the box. It was the same one Melvin's father had given him before he died. There was a marker inside the Book of Proverbs with the inscription, 18:22. He turned to the chapter and read the verse out loud.

"Whoso findeth a wife findeth a good thing."

"What a coincidence," Toni said.

"You know a good friend told me there are no such things as coincidences. Everything happens for a reason," Malcolm said. "I've finally come to understand what he meant. In life, and especially in love, everything happens in God's time."

MICHAEL BAISDEN

MAINTENANCE MAN II

Money Can't Buy Everything!

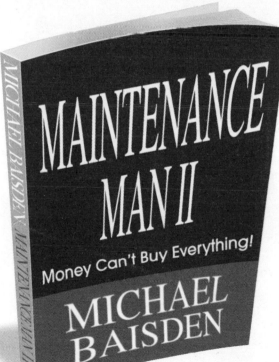

MONEY CAN'T BUY LOVE

MONEY CAN'T BUY LOYALTY

AND MONEY CAN'T PROTECT YOU FROM A MAN SET ON REVENGE.

Turn the page to read an excerpt. ➡

WOMEN HAVE
NEEDS TOO

MAINTENANCE MAN II

Malcolm woke up the next morning just before sunrise. He could see Alex through the window lying on the balcony naked smoking a joint. He grabbed his cell phone and poured a tall glass of wine and stepped out onto the balcony naked and joined her.

"I see you found my stash."

"It wasn't hard to find, you still keep it in the same place you did when we were at the music academy together," she replied while passing the joint to him.

"Old habits die hard!"

"Ain't that the truth?"

323

Alex took a long sip of wine and laid her head down in Malcolm's lap. They took turns taking pulls off the joint until it was gone then Malcolm thumped it over the balcony into the sand twenty-stories below.

"This is what I missed most," he said while stroking her hair, "waking up to nothing but the sound of the ocean!"

"You know what I miss?"

"What's that?"

"I miss waking up happy," she said to him. "Ever since Derrick raped me in college, I've been searching for love in all the wrong places. I was always attracted to powerful men because I thought they would protect me, but instead they ended up trying to control me. And I put up with it all these years because I was afraid they would either hurt me or leave me, but I'm not afraid anymore" she went on. "I envy you Malcolm, you've always had the courage to do what you wanted to do. Me, I've spent my entire life trying to fit into other people boxes."

"It doesn't work, does it?" Malcolm replied. He was thinking back on his relationship with Toni.

"No, it doesn't," she laughed sarcastically and took another sip of wine. "It's taken me all these years to finally figure it out, we should fall in love with our friends and just date the men we think we love. That way you don't waste time and no one gets hurt!"

Alex sat up and turned towards Malcolm. They were face to face. She sat the wine glass down and kissed him.

"What was that for?"

"That was for all the years of being my knight in shining armor, for forcing me to come on stage, and most of all for last night," she said. "Thanks for making me feel beautiful and desired. Whatever you're charging for your services, it's worth ever dime!"

"Is that an endorsement?" he smiled.

"No, silly, it's a compliment," she took his hand and placed it on her breast. "How much would tonight have cost me if I were a customer?"

"Trust me, you couldn't afford me, especially not on your fiancée' salary," Malcolm laughed.

"Gary has a ton of money and it's definitely not coming from his government salary as a state Senator. He drives a Bentley and a Porsche. I use to ask him where all the money was coming from but after listening to all the ridiculous explanations I just stop asking and went along for the ride!"

"He's dirty just like the rest of them. There's so much money being passed under the table it's ridiculous. Some of them have the balls to pay for strip clubs and prostitution services on their government credit cards."

"Are you serious?"

"I have the receipts, photos, and videos to prove it!"

"Ooh, can I see?" She said jumping up and down like a little kid. "Please, Malcolm, please!"

"Hell no, woman, are you crazy," Malcolm laughed while trying to hold her down. "I **am** a professional. What happens with a Maintenance Man stays with a Maintenance Man."

"Is that your motto?"

"No, I just made it up, but come to think of it, it would look good on a bumper sticker."

"Do you have any video of Gary?"

"No, but there have been rumors!" Malcolm said. "All of these rich perverts have secrets and if any of them try to strong arm me or my crew, I'll put on a show they'll never forget! All it takes is one click of a button and photos and videos of threesomes, bondage, and boy on boy sex will be all over the Internet!" he went on. "I've been in this game a long time, I know all their dirty little secrets."

325

"You make it sound so exciting!" Alex said while sitting on Malcolm's lap. "Can I be your assistant? It can be just like our music academy days. Remember how I use to set you up with my rich girlfriends back in school?"

"Ok, I think you've had enough to drink," Malcolm took the glass out of her hand. "This wine is starting to go to your head."

"Come on Malcolm! I'm bored to death! I know dozens of wives at the country club and they are just as lonely and horny as I am—and their husbands are loaded!"

Malcolm knew he needed new clients. His new crew was going to expect to start making money right away. Alex was just what he needed, someone with affluent contacts, someone he could trust, and someone who knew the drill.

"Okay, I'll let you help under one condition."

"And what's that?"

"Never use my name, never use the word sex and money in the same sentence, and never give them a phone number," Malcolm said with his finger in her face. "Just tell them about the escort service and I'll take it from there."

"Yes, sir," Alex said while guiding his finger into her mouth. "Looks like Bonnie and Clyde ride again!"

"Speaking of riding, your break time is over."

Malcolm lifted her up and carried her back into the hotel room then laid her down gently on the bed.

"There is one more condition I didn't mention!" He said while spreading her legs and then slowly licking her between her thighs.

"And what's that?"

"I want dinner... and desert at least once a week."

She held him by the head and guided him down to her clit.

"Well, bon appetite!" she moaned and threw her head back. "ahhhh!"

DIRTY POLITICS

The sounds of fists being smashed against flesh echoed through the abandoned warehouse in downtown Miami. Vincent, who was wearing a ski mask, stopped beaten the Cuban man who was handcuffed to a chair. He sat down calmly in front of him and lit a cigarette.

"Have one?" he jokingly asked.

The man lifted his bloodied head and nodded no.

"I don't blame you, these things will kill you!" he laughed.

He smoked half of the cigarette and then put it out on the man's forehead.

"Urrrgh!" he screamed out!

"That's for trying to register those fucking niggers and boat rowers to vote!"

Suddenly, the phone rang! Vincent looked down at the number; it was Senator Nelson.

"You mind if I take this?" he asked sarcastically.

He pressed the answer button and walked into an adjoining room, closed the door, and peeled off his mask.

"Yes, sir!"

"How's it going?"

"Everything is going like clockwork. Mr. Gomez and I were just discussing illegal immigration and conservative values."

"Well, I'm sure you'll make him see the light!" he laughed. "When you get done there's some business we need to handle over in Miami Gardens."

"What's the problem?"

"Some black preacher is getting his flock all fired up about voter suppression and civil rights."

"You want me to eliminate him or just scare him?"

"We don't need any martyrs this close to the election. Just send him a message—are we clear?"

"Crystal, sir."

"There's only a month before the special election. We've got to turn this blue district red in a hurry. The only way we can lose is if the black and Latino areas have a high voters' turnout. Now that we have a law requiring voters to show a state ID, that should reduce the votes by fifteen or twenty percent. And I've got friends who can knock a few thousand democrats out of the database, but that will not be enough if these voter registration drives continue to grow. My career, and yours, depends on a victory! The U.S. Senate today, the Presidency tomorrow!"

"Don't worry about it, Senator. I've got it all under control,"

Vincent said while pulling his nine millimeter pistol out of the holster.

"And don't forget, we have a meeting with the Kross Brothers in D.C. next week, so let's make sure our poll numbers look good. In other words, get rid of all the trouble makers, starting with this goddamned preacher!"

"I'll be done here shortly and I'll be on my way."

"Do me a favor since you're coming back north, stop by Tom Jenkin's and pick up an order of barbecue."

"You want coleslaw with that?"

"No, just make sure you get plenty of hot sauce!"

"Hot sauce it is, sir!" he replied, then hung up.

Vincent walked back into the empty warehouse with his gun by his side and the trigger cocked. When the Cuban man saw he wasn't wearing his mask, he panicked, pulling and jerking on the handcuffs as hard he could, trying to break loose of the metal chair.

"Looks like play time is over!" Vincent said without emotion while staring at his watch. "Tick tock, tick tock!"

"No, please no!" he screamed. "I have a wife and kids!"

"You should've thought about that when I warned you the first time," Vincent said, pointing the gun at the man's head. "You people just don't get it, do you? Democracy is an illusion; those who have the money have the power!" Then he pulled the trigger.

ABOUT
MICHAEL BAISDEN

Michael Baisden is undeniably one of the most influential and engaging personalities in radio history. His meteoric rise to #1 is redefining radio with the numbers to back it up. The show is syndicated by Cumulus Media and is heard in over 78 markets nationwide with over 8 million loyal listeners daily. His career began when he took a leap of faith to leave his job driving trains in Chicago to self-publish his book, and began touring the country selling books out of the trunk of his car. Through the power of his sheer determination, Michael carved a unique niche as a speaker, radio personality, and social activist. He is always in the lead when it comes to helping those who don't have a voice. "I'm not one for just talking; either do something or get out of the way!"

Baisden, who now has four best selling books to his credit, has hosted two national television shows, and has recently produced three feature films.

Nationally Syndicated
Radio Personality

Baisden Communications: His radio career began in 2003 when 98.7 KISS FM in New York City offered him a position as the afternoon drive-time host. Because of budget constraints the station was unable to offer him a salary. Michael's response was, "Just give me the mic!" And sure enough, within six months, their afternoon drive ratings went from number 9 to number 1.

After eight months of consistently high ratings, Michael suggested taking his show national, but management was apprehensive, suggesting that New York wasn't ready. A few months later, Michael threatened to quit if management did not pursue a syndication deal. "There was no doubt in my mind that I could have one of the hottest shows on radio! I knew the impact it would have on people all across the country and I wasn't taking no, for an answer," Michael rebutted.

Since his radio show debuted nationally in 2005, Michael has captured the hearts and minds of millions of Americans with his provocative mix of relationship talk, hot topics, politics and the best of old school with today's R&B. When it comes to entertaining, enlightening and educating, no one in talk radio compares. His high energy and love for interacting with his listeners are just two reasons for the popularity and success of "The Michael Baisden Show." Michael ignites heated discussions with explosive episodic themes like: Infidelity In The Church, Deadbeat Parents, Talking To Your Children About Sex, and Do Women Know What They Want?

BEST SELLING AUTHOR

Baisden Publishing: According to Simon & Schuster, Michael Baisden is "probably the most successful self-published African-American male author out there today." With nearly 2 million books in print, both hardcover and softcover, his books blend the perfect combination of entertainment, humor, provocation and sexuality. Michael's vibrant personality on and off the air has made him a people magnet.

He began attracting attention with primarily female followers as author and publisher of the highly successful best selling books: *Never Satisfied: How and Why Men Cheat, Men Cry in the Dark, The Maintenance Man, God's Gift to Women* and, most recently, a hot new book, *Never Satisfied: Do Men Know What They Want?* Two of his titles ultimately were adapted into stage plays playing to sold-out crowds across the U.S.

TELEVISION SHOW HOST

The author and relationship expert previously hosted a nationally syndicated talk show, "Talk or Walk," which was a compelling and fast-paced reality series that combined the emotion of talk, the conflict of court shows and the fascination of a relationship series.

Another dream was to host a Late Night Talk show. He got that chance in the fall of 2007, when he partnered with TV One to host and co-executive produce *Baisden After Dark*, featuring comedian George Willborn and band leader Morris Day. The show was a smash hit, breaking records for viewers on the network. The show currently airs weekdays.

PRODUCER / FILM MAKER

Baisden Film Works: Michael has two successful national stage plays (based on his novels), which toured the U.S. playing to sold-out crowds; an award-winning feature-length film presentation documentary titled *Love, Lust & Lies* that deals with relationships and sexuality based on the perspective of people of color; and two seminar tapes, *Relationship Seminar* and *Men Have Issues Too.*

His television career kicked off in 2001 with "Talk or Walk" distributed by Tribune Broadcasting, which was a nationally syndicated Daytime TV Talk show he hosted that dealt with relationships. In 2006 he created, hosted and executive-produced a Late Night TV Talk show with co-host comedian, George Willborn, and band leader, Morris Day, which still airs on TV One titled "Baisden After Dark". In 2011 Michael produced a TV Special titled "Do Women Know What They Want?" that is currently airing on Centric of the BET Network and is based on his upcoming film. In 2011 Michael struck up a distribution deal for 3 feature films with TimeLife: *Do Women Know What They Want?*, *Love, Lust & Lies*, his two relationship films, and a comedy show titled *Turn Around* featuring his radio show co-host George Willborn.

In 2011, Michael continued to expand his media reach when he produced, wrote, and directed a groundbreaking relationship film titled, *Do Women Know What They Want?* The reviews have been amazing! "It was time for something new and exciting, and no one else was doing it, not like this!" Michael said. Get ready! It looks like the baddest man on radio and late night TV will be in theaters near you soon!

Michael continues to entertain, enlighten and educate as he pursues one of his first dreams, to have his novels adapted to major motion pictures.

MOTIVATIONAL SPEAKER

Baisden Entertainment: The Love, Lust & Lies Relationship Seminar Series attracts thousands of standing-room only, sold-out crowds nationwide as he tours the country. As a motivational speaker he has been an inspiration to hundreds of thousands attending his seminars and events. As well as numerous national Baisden Live Tours, he has also produced international Island Jam events in Jamaica and has an exclusive upcoming trip to South Africa.

PHILANTHROPIST

The Michael Baisden Foundation: A non-profit organization was formed with a goal to eliminate illiteracy as well as promote technology and is dedicated to education, support and advancement in our communities. Michael's own passionate testimony as to how books changed his life gives hope to those who have been enslaved by the shackles of illiteracy.

In December 2009 Michael called for a National Mentor Training Day and announced his plans for a 2010 nationwide campaign. He pledged up to $350,000 of his own money to be donated in over 72 markets he would visit on a bus tour. The outreach was named "One Million Mentors National Campaign To Save Our Kids." Michael challenged his listeners to match or beat his donations and get involved.

In October 2010 President Barack Obama publicly congratulated Michael on his efforts. He founded the Michael Baisden Foundation focusing on education, literacy and mentoring.

Michael believes "books change lives" and he is living proof!

SOCIAL ACTIVIST & COMMUNITY LEADER

Baisden's proudest moment came on September 20, 2007, when he passionately and skillfully spearheaded the famous Jena 6 March in Jena, Louisiana. This historic and momentous occasion garnered tens of thousands of citizens of all races to peacefully march in support of six young men who have been unfairly treated by the justice system. In addition, he urged millions of listeners to wear black on September 20 in protest of unequal justice. The news traveled throughout the country. Everyone from college students of all races to corporate executives wore black in support of the Jena 6.

Another historic year was 2008. In late January Michael endorsed Sen. Barack Obama in the Democratic Primary. He celebrated President Obama's victory with over 4,000 fans at a watch party in Miami on election night. The Obama camp along with millions of listeners credited Michael with being one of the major forces behind this historic victory to elect the first African-American to the Presidency of the United States.

In 2009 he again stepped up and answered the call of the National Association of Free Clinics. With Michael's help they were able to get more volunteers than they needed and get the word out to the countless thousands that needed the free health services.

One Million Mentors National Campaign to Save Our Kids Tour went to over 72 cities nationwide in 2010 with him donating over $350,000 of his own money while recruiting mentors and working with organizations. While impactful only 15 percent of the nationwide mentoring network's male mentors are Black, with African American boys disproportionately represented on waiting lists. In 2012 Baisden partnered with Big Brothers Big Sisters of America and its national African American fraternity partners [Alpha Phi Alpha, Kappa Alpha Psi and Omega Psi Phi] for *Mentoring Brothers in Action*, an initiative to recruit volunteers and raise funds to provide mentors for African American boys. Baisden has contributed $10,000 to the initiative, making $105,000 his total donation to BBBS. "If you can't become a mentor, invest and support mentoring programs with your dollars. These children need our help," Baisden says. Go to www.MentoringBrothers.org for more information.

Stay tuned—it's just the beginning of the Baisden legacy.

Follow Michael on Facebook, Twitter
or YouTube @ BaisdenLive.
www.MichaelBaisden.com
www.BaisdenLive.com
www.MingleCity.com

Congratulations Michael Baisden
The *MOST* Influential Man In Radio

THE MICHAEL BAISDEN SHOW
Informative, Engaging...Funny!

The show is syndicated in nearly  80 markets nationwide making it easy for you to get connected and stay connected with Michael no matter where you are! Keep up with all of the latest and get first notification of exclusive online events, contests, activities and tours. The show airs weekdays from 3-7 p.m. EST. Listen live online or via app, download podcasts and check out the daily show features.

For more information, go to the office show website at: **www.BaisdenLive.com**

SOCIAL NETWORKING:

www.MingleCity.com is the online community for drama-free adults. It is a place for singles, couples, groups and friends to interact with other  like-minded members in their area, across the country and the world. Create your own personal webpage, invite your friends, start or join groups, find events, chat, blog, post your favorite photos and videos.

SOCIAL MEDIA @ BAISDENLIVE:

**Follow Michael @ Twitter:
BAISDENLIVE**

**Be A Facebook Fan @
BAISDENLIVE**

**Tune In on YouTube @
BAISDENLIVE**

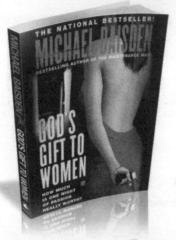

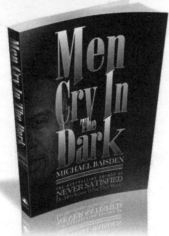
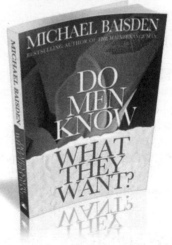

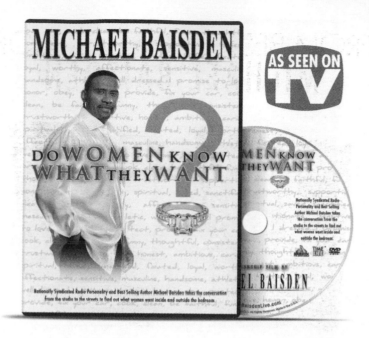

DO WOMEN KNOW WHAT THEY WANT?

What started out as a cordial conversation with one simple question "Do Women Know What They Want?" exploded into a battle of the sexes that will have you laughing hysterically one minute and shouting at the screen the next!

No longer anonymous voices on the radio, can men be honest about their multiple relationships, interracial dating, and why they choose to date but not marry some women? And can women admit to having afairs with married men, take responsibility for their bad choices, and explain why they fake it?

Suggested Retail Price: $16.95
Available in Cut and a *Too Hot for TV,* UN-CUT version!

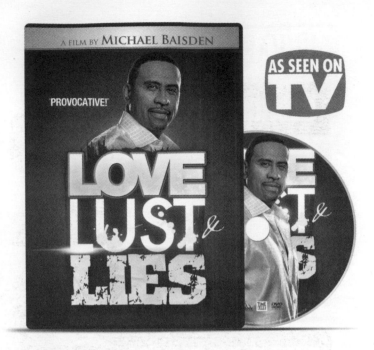

LOVE, LUST & LIES

We've all seen documentaries that deal with relationships and sexuality, such as "Real Sex" on HBO. But if you're like me, you've thought about how exciting it would be to experience a program that deals with these issues from the perspective of people of color. Well the wait is over.

"It's amazing to me how many people are afraid to be open about what they want inside and outside the bedroom," Michael says. "Hopefully, after watching these interviews they'll be more willing to explore their sexuality and to discuss issues such as infidelity, adult toys, and the swinging lifestyle."

Suggested Retail Price: $16.95

Available in Cut and a *Too Hot for TV,* UN-CUT version!

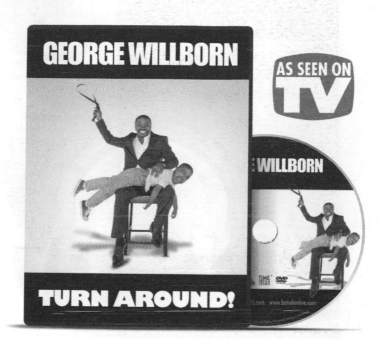

TURN AROUND!

"Turn Around!" Comedy Show featuring George Willborn aka The "Stress Reliever" and Co-Host of the Nationally Syndicated Michael Baisden Radio show takes the stage to deliver his unique brand of cruelly honest comedy with Special Guest comedians including Vanessa Fraction, Damon Williams, Alex Ortiz, Tyler Craig and Deon Cole.

Suggested Retail Price: $16.95

MI
BO
Fil
wo
uni
inte
of

On
Su